Teach Yourself VISUALLY™

Illustrator® 10

by Mike Wooldridge and Michael Toot

Visual

From
maranGraphics®

&

Hungry Minds™

Best-Selling Books • Digital Downloads • e-books • Answer Networks
e-Newsletters • Branded Web Sites • e-learning

New York, NY • Cleveland, OH • Indianapolis, IN

Teach Yourself VISUALLY™ Illustrator® 10

Published by
Hungry Minds, Inc.
909 Third Avenue
New York, NY 10022
www.hungryminds.com

maranGraphics, Inc.
5755 Coopers Avenue
Mississauga, Ontario, Canada
L4Z 1R9

Library of Congress Control Number: 2001099317

ISBN: 0-7645-3654-0

Printed in the United States of America
10 9 8 7 6 5 4 3 2

IK/SQ/QS/QS/IN

Distributed in the United States by Hungry Minds, Inc.

Distributed by CDG Books Canada Inc. for Canada; by Transworld Publishers Limited in the United Kingdom; by IDG Norge Books for Norway; by IDG Sweden Books for Sweden; by IDG Books Australia Publishing Corporation Pty. Ltd. for Australia and New Zealand; by TransQuest Publishers Pte Ltd. for Singapore, Malaysia, Thailand, Indonesia, and Hong Kong; by Gotop Information Inc. for Taiwan; by ICG Muse, Inc. for Japan; by Intersoft for South Africa; by Eyrolles for France; by International Thomson Publishing for Germany, Austria and Switzerland; by Distribuidora Cuspide for Argentina; by LR International for Brazil; by Galileo Libros for Chile; by Ediciones ZETA S.C.R. Ltda. for Peru; by WS Computer Publishing Corporation, Inc., for the Philippines; by Contemporanea de Ediciones for Venezuela; by Express Computer Distributors for the Caribbean and West Indies; by Micronesia Media Distributor, Inc. for Micronesia; by Chips Computadoras S.A. de C.V. for Mexico; by Editorial Norma de Panama S.A. for Panama; by American Bookshops for Finland.

For corporate orders, please call maranGraphics at 800-469-6616 or fax 905-890-9434.

For general information on Hungry Minds' products and services please contact our Customer Care Department within the U.S. at 800-762-2974, outside the U.S. at 317-572-3993 or fax 317-572-4002.

For sales inquiries and reseller information, including discounts, premium and bulk quantity sales, and foreign-language translations, please contact our Customer Care Department at 800-434-3422, fax 317-572-4002, or write to Hungry Minds, Inc., Attn: Customer Care Department, 10475 Crosspoint Boulevard, Indianapolis, IN 46256.

For information on licensing foreign or domestic rights, please contact our Sub-Rights Customer Care Department at 212-884-5000.

For information on using Hungry Minds' products and services in the classroom or for ordering examination copies, please contact our Educational Sales Department at 800-434-2086 or fax 317-572-4005.

For press review copies, author interviews, or other publicity information, please contact our Public Relations department at 317-572-3168 or fax 317-572-4168.

For authorization to photocopy items for corporate, personal, or educational use, please contact Copyright Clearance Center, 222 Rosewood Drive, Danvers, MA 01923, or fax 978-750-4470.

Screen shots displayed in this book are based on pre-released software and are subject to change.

Trademark Acknowledgments

Permissions

Hungry Minds™ is a trademark of Hungry Minds, Inc.

U.S. Corporate Sales	U.S. Trade Sales
Contact maranGraphics at (800) 469-6616 or Fax (905) 890-9434.	Contact Hungry Minds at (800) 434-3422 or fax (317) 572-4002.

Some comments from our readers...

"I have to praise you and your company on the fine products you turn out. I have twelve of the *Teach Yourself VISUALLY* and *Simplified* books in my house. They were instrumental in helping me pass a difficult computer course. Thank you for creating books that are easy to follow."

–Gordon Justin (Brielle, NJ)

"I commend your efforts and your success. I teach in an outreach program for the Dr. Eugene Clark Library in Lockhart, TX. Your *Teach Yourself VISUALLY* books are incredible and I use them in my computer classes. All my students love them!"

–Michele Schalin (Lockhart, TX)

"Thank you so much for helping people like me learn about computers. The Maran family is just what the doctor ordered. Thank you, thank you, thank you."

–Carol Moten (New Kensington, PA)

"I would like to take this time to compliment maranGraphics on creating such great books. Thank you for making it clear. Keep up the good work."

–Kirk Santoro (Burbank, CA)

"I write to extend my thanks and appreciation for your books. They are clear, easy to follow, and straight to the point. Keep up the good work!

–Seward Kollie (Dakar, Senegal)

"What fantastic teaching books you have produced! Congratulations to you and your staff. You deserve the Nobel prize in Education in the Software category. Thanks for helping me to understand computers."

–Bruno Tonon (Melbourne, Australia)

"Over time, I have bought a number of your 'Read Less–Learn More' books. For me, they are THE way to learn anything easily."

–José A. Mazón (Cuba, NY)

"I was introduced to maranGraphics about four years ago and YOU ARE THE GREATEST THING THAT EVER HAPPENED TO INTRODUCTORY COMPUTER BOOKS!"

–Glenn Nettleton (Huntsville, AL)

"Compliments To The Chef!! Your books are extraordinary! Or, simply put, Extra-Ordinary, meaning way above the rest! THANK YOU THANK YOU THANK YOU! for creating these.

–Christine J. Manfrin (Castle Rock, CO)

"I'm a grandma who was pushed by an 11-year-old grandson to join the computer age. I found myself hopelessly confused and frustrated until I discovered the Visual series. I'm no expert by any means now, but I'm a lot further along than I would have been otherwise. Thank you!"

–Carol Louthain (Logansport, IN)

"Thank you, thank you, thank you....for making it so easy for me to break into this high-tech world. I now own four of your books. I recommend them to anyone who is a beginner like myself. Now....if you could just do one for programming VCRs, it would make my day!"

–Gay O'Donnell (Calgary, Alberta, Canada)

"You're marvelous! I am greatly in your debt."

–Patrick Baird (Lacey, WA)

maranGraphics is a family-run business
located near Toronto, Canada.

At **maranGraphics**, we believe in producing great computer books — one book at a time.

maranGraphics has been producing high-technology products for over 25 years, which enables us to offer the computer book community a unique communication process.

Our computer books use an integrated communication process, which is very different from the approach used in other computer books. Each spread is, in essence, a flow chart — the text and screen shots are totally incorporated into the layout of the spread.

Introductory text and helpful tips complete the learning experience.

maranGraphics' approach encourages the left and right sides of the brain to work together — resulting in faster orientation and greater memory retention.

Above all, we are very proud of the handcrafted nature of our books. Our carefully-chosen writers are experts in their fields, and spend countless hours researching and organizing the content for each topic. Our artists rebuild every screen shot to provide the best clarity possible, making our

screen shots the most precise and easiest to read in the industry. We strive for perfection, and believe that the time spent handcrafting each element results in the best computer books money can buy.

Thank you for purchasing this book. We hope you enjoy it!

Sincerely,

Robert Maran
President
maranGraphics
Rob@maran.com
www.maran.com
www.hungryminds.com/visual

CREDITS

Acquisitions, Editorial, and Media Development
Project Editor
Maureen Spears
Acquisitions Editor
Jen Dorsey
Product Development Supervisor
Lindsay Sandman
Copy Editor
Jill Mazurczyk
Technical Editor
Jennifer Alspach
Editorial Manager
Rev Mengle
Permissions Editor
Laura Moss
Editorial Assistant
Amanda Foxworth

Production
Book Design
maranGraphics®
Production Coordinator
Nancee Reeves
Layout
Melanie DesJardins, LeAndra Johnson,
Adam Mancilla, Kristin McMullan, Jill Piscitelli
Screen Artists
Mark Harris, Jill A. Proll
Illustrators
Ronda David-Burroughs, David E. Gregory,
Sean Johannesen, Greg Maxson, Russ Marini,
Steven Schaerer, Anthony Stuart
Proofreaders
Laura L. Bowman
Quality Control
John Bitter
Indexer:
Sharon Hilgenberg
Special Help
Tim Borek, Shelley Lea, Shelley Norris, Judy Maran

ACKNOWLEDGMENTS

General and Administrative

Hungry Minds Technology Publishing Group: Richard Swadley, Vice President and Executive Group Publisher; Bob Ipsen, Vice President and Executive Publisher; Mary Bednarek, Editorial Director, Networking; Joseph Wikert, Vice President and Publisher, Web Development Group; Mary C. Corder, Editorial Director, Dummies Technology; Andy Cummings, Editorial Director, Dummies Technology; Barry Pruett, Vice President and Publisher, Visual/Graphic Design

Hungry Minds Manufacturing: Ivor Parker, Vice President, Manufacturing

Hungry Minds Marketing: John Helmus, Assistant Vice President, Director of Marketing

Hungry Minds Production for Branded Press: Debbie Stailey, Production Director

Hungry Minds Sales: Michael Violano, Vice President, Sales Sub Rights

ABOUT THE AUTHORS

Mike Wooldridge is a technology writer, Web designer, and educator in the San Francisco Bay Area. He is also the author of several other VISUAL books, including *Teach Yourself VISUALLY Dreamweaver 4*, *Teach Yourself VISUALLY Photoshop 6*, and *Master VISUALLY Dreamweaver 4 and Flash 5*.

Michael Toot is a Seattle-based consultant and author, writing on both desktop Web applications and middleware technology. Prior to consulting he was a senior program manager and senior product manager at Attachmate Corporation and Digital Equipment Corporation, developing enterprise middleware solutions for Fortune 2000 customers. Before working full-time in the computer industry he was a litigation defense attorney. When not writing books he can be found reading, renovating a 94-year-old home with his wife and two cats, or sailing on Puget Sound.

AUTHORS' ACKNOWLEDGMENTS

Mike Wooldridge

Thanks to Maureen Spears, Jen Dorsey, Jill Mazurczyk, and the rest of the editorial crew at Hungry Minds. It was great working with everyone again. Also, thanks to Mark Harris, Jill A. Proll, Ronda David-Burroughs, David E. Gregory, Sean Johannesen, Greg Maxson, Russ Marini, Steven Schaerer, and Anthony Stuart for their hard work on the art for this book. And thanks to my co-author Mike Toot for being so easy to work with.

Michael Toot

Everlasting thanks for help on this book go to: Jen Dorsey, my acquisitions editor, who was always upbeat and cheerful despite all the curve balls I threw at her; Maureen Spears, hard-working and ever-helpful project editor, who masterfully balanced everything so the book came out right; Tim Borek, project editor, and Jill Mazurczyk, copy editor, who gently unmangled every tortured sentence that somehow snuck into my drafts without my knowledge; Jennifer Alspach, technical editor, who pointed out better and simpler ways to do things instead of my complex and difficult ones; Lindsay Sandman, who kept production of the graphics rolling smoothly; Barry Pruett and Darlene Pitts in the front office, who managed the business side while us creative types thrashed around; the unsung heroes who created the concept art, reworked the screen shots, and polished the layout — you guys are underpaid, let me tell you; and last but not least, my co-author, Mike Wooldridge, who was easygoing and pleasant to work with, especially when the pressure was on. This was a team effort, and all the credit goes to the team for a job well done.

TABLE OF CONTENTS

Chapter 1

INTRODUCING ILLUSTRATOR

Work with Images 4
Understanding Illustrator 6
Navigate the Illustrator Work Area 8
Start Illustrator on a Macintosh or a PC 10
Create a New Document 12
Save a Document 14
Open a Saved Document 16
Close a Document 17
Get Help 18

Chapter 2

UNDERSTANDING ILLUSTRATOR BASICS

Change Document Settings 22
Change Preferences .24
Switch Between Views 26
View Rulers and Grids 28
View a Palette 30
Dock a Palette 31
Change Palette Options 32
Using the Zoom Tool 34
Using the Selection Tool 36
Using the Direct Selection Tool 38
Copy and Paste an Object 40
Undo or Redo a Command 42

Chapter 3

WORKING WITH PATHS

Understanding Paths 46
Draw Straight Lines with the Line Tool 48
Draw Freehand Lines with the Pencil Tool 50
Draw Curves with the Arc Tool 52
Draw Straight Lines with the Pen Tool 54

Draw Curves with the Pen Tool 56
Reshape a Curve 58
Reshape a Line with the Reshape Tool 60
Close an Open Path 62
Open a Closed Path 64
Delete Paths 66
Erase Parts of a Path 68
Smooth a Path 70

Chapter 4

USING ADVANCED PATH TECHNIQUES

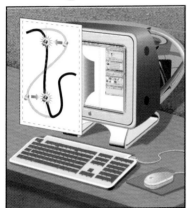

Add or Remove Anchor Points 74
Convert Anchor Point Type 76
Remove Excess Anchor Points 82
Clean Up Stray Anchor Points 84
Average Points 86
Join Points 88
Using Add and Subtract Commands 90
Using the Intersect Command 92
Using the Exclude Command 93
Create a Compound Path 94

Chapter 5

WORKING WITH OBJECTS

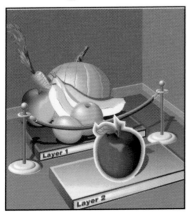

Draw a Rectangle or Rounded Rectangle 98
Draw an Ellipse or Circle 100
Draw Regular Polygons 102
Draw Stars 103
Create a Spiral 104
Create a Rectangular Grid 106
Create a Polar Grid 108
Rotate an Object .110
Reflect an Object .111
Scale an Object 112

TABLE OF CONTENTS

Apply Shear to an Object 114
Align Objects 116
Move Objects Forward and Back 118
Group and Ungroup Objects 120
Cut Objects with the Knife Tool 122

Chapter 6

ADVANCED OBJECT EFFECTS AND SYMBOLS

Understanding Object Effects and Symbols 126
Warp Objects 128
Using the Free Transform Tool 130
Apply the Envelope Distort Tool 132
Using the Liquify Tools 134
Create a Flare 136
Create a Symbol 138
Insert and Delete Symbols 140
Edit and Update Symbols 142
Apply Symbol Effects 144

Chapter 7

APPLYING COLOR

An Introduction to Color 148
Create and Save a CMYK Color 150
Create and Save an RGB Color 152
Fill an Object with Color 154
Stroke an Object 156
Paint with a Calligraphic Brush 158
Customize a Calligraphic Brush 160
Apply and Customize a Scatter Brush 162
Paint with an Art Brush 164
Fill an Object with a Gradient 166
Create a Multicolor Gradient 168
Fill an Object with a Pattern 170

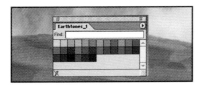

Save Colors with the Eyedropper 172

Apply Colors with the Paint Bucket 173

Adjust Opacity of an Object 174

Adjust Blending of an Object 175

Chapter 8 — WORKING WITH TYPE

Understanding Type in Illustrator 178

Insert Point Type 180

Insert Area Type 181

Type Text Along a Path 182

Change Font and Font Size 184

Change Paragraph Alignment 186

Change Type Case 188

Using Smart Punctuation 189

Check Spelling .190

Link Type Blocks 192

Wrap Type Around an Object 194

Convert Type to Outlines 196

Chapter 9 — EFFECTS, FILTERS, AND STYLES

An Introduction to Effects, Filters, and Styles 200

Apply the Roughen Effect 202

Apply the Feather Effect 204

Edit an Effect 206

Apply the Hatch Effects Filter 208

Apply the Pointillize Filter 210

Using the Appearance Palette 212

Apply a Style 214

Create a New Style 216

Using the Blend Tool 218

Using the Mesh Tool 220

TABLE OF CONTENTS

Chapter 10

CREATING GRAPHS

An Introduction to Graphs 224
Create a Column Graph 226
Create a Line Graph 228
Create a Pie Graph 230
Edit Graph Data .232
Change a Graph Type 233
Add Color to a Graph 234
Import Data for a Graph 236

Chapter 11

WORKING WITH LAYERS

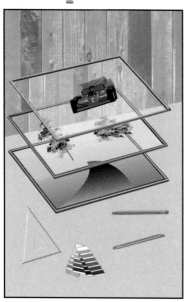

An Introduction to Layers 240
Create a New Layer 241
Delete a Layer 242
Hide a Layer 243
Lock a Layer 244
Rearrange Layers 245
Create a Sublayer 246
Move Objects Between Layers 248
Edit Layer Properties 250
Create a Template Layer 252
Merge Layers 254
Flatten Artwork 255
Release Objects to Layers 256
Create a Clipping Mask with a Layer 258

Chapter 12

WORKING WITH BITMAP IMAGES

Understanding Images 262
Place an Image 264
Transform an Image 265

Trace an Image 266

Rasterize an Object 268

Copy an Image from Photoshop 270

Chapter 13

PREPARING FILES FOR PRINTING

Understanding Printing 274

Understanding Printing Separations 275

Using Process Color 276

Using Spot Color .278

Trap Colors 280

Using Knockouts .282

Create Crop Marks 284

Change Color Modes 285

Print Artwork on a PC 286

Print Artwork on a Mac 288

Chapter 14

CREATING ART FOR THE WEB

Understanding Web Art 292

Select a Web-Safe Color 294

Work in Pixel Preview Mode 295

Save a GIF Image for the Web 296

Save a JPEG Image for the Web 298

Make a Button 300

Slice Artwork 302

Export Sliced Artwork 304

Export a Flash Animation 306

Appendix

SHORTCUT KEY QUICK REFERENCE

Shortcut Key Quick Reference

HOW TO USE THIS BOOK

Teach Yourself VISUALLY Illustrator 10 contains straightforward sections, which you can use to learn the basics of Illustrator. This book is designed to help a reader receive quick access to any area of question. You can simply look up a subject within the Table of Contents or Index and go immediately to the section of concern. A *section* is a set of self-contained units that walks you through a computer operation step-by-step. That is, with rare exceptions, all the information you need regarding an area of interest is contained within a section.

The Organization Of Each Chapter

Each task contains an introduction, a set of screen shots, and, if the task goes beyond 1 page, a set of tips. The introduction tells why you want to perform the task, the advantages and disadvantages of performing the task, and references to other related tasks in the book. The screens, located on the bottom half of each page, show a series of steps that you must complete to perform a given action. The tip portion of the section gives you an opportunity to further understand the task at hand, to learn about other related tasks in other areas of the book, or to apply alternative methods.

A chapter may also contain an illustrated group of pages that gives you background information that you need to understand the sections in a chapter.

The General Organization Of This Book

Teach Yourself VISUALLY Illustrator 10 has 14 chapters and an appendix. Chapters 1 and 2 show you all you need to know to get started in Illustrator. Chapters 3 and 4 show how to work with paths. Chapters 5 and 6 cover how to create and manipulate objects to achieve the effect you want. Chapter 7 shows you how to apply colors to objects, while Chapter 8 illustrates how to insert type. Chapter 9 discusses some of the basic Effects, Filters, and Styles you can apply to your artwork. In Chapter 10, you learn to create graphs. In Chapters 11 and 12, you learn how to work with layers and bitmap images. If you intend to create your artwork for personal or profession publications or Web sites, you may find Chapters 13 and 14 useful.

Who This Book Is For

This book is highly recommended for the visual learner who wants to learn the basics of Illustrator, and who may or may not have prior experience with a computer.

What You Need To Use This Book

To perform the tasks in this book, you need a computer installed with Illustrator 10. In addition, you need to meet the following requirements:

Mac Requirements

- PowerPC® processor: G3, G4, or G4 dual
- Mac OS system software version 9.1, 9.2, or Mac OS X version 10.1

Windows Requirements

- Intel® Pentium® II, III, or 4 processor Microsoft® Windows® 98, Windows 98 Special Edition, Windows Millennium Edition, Windows 2000 with Service Pack 2, or Windows XP (recommended upgrade procedure)
- 128 MB of RAM
- 180 MB of available hard-disk space
- For Adobe® PostScript® printers: Adobe PostScript Level 2 or Adobe PostScript 3™

Conventions When Using The Mouse

This book uses the following conventions to describe the actions you perform when using the mouse:

Click

Press and release the left mouse button. You use a click to select an item on the screen.

Double-click

Quickly press and release the left mouse button twice. You double-click to open a document or start a program.

Right-click

Press and release the right mouse button. You use a right-click to display a shortcut menu, a list of commands specifically related to the selected item.

Click and Drag, and Release the Mouse

Position the mouse pointer over an item on the screen and then press and hold down the left mouse button. Still holding down the button, move the mouse to where you want to place the item and then release the button. Dragging and dropping makes it easy to move an item to a new location.

The Conventions In This Book

A number of typographic and layout styles have been used throughout *Teach Yourself VISUALLY Illustrator 10* to distinguish different types of information.

Bold

Indicates what you must click in a menu or dialog box.

Italics

Indicates a new term being introduced.

Numbered Steps

Indicate that you must perform these steps in order to successfully perform the task.

Bulleted Steps

Give you alternative methods, explain various options, or present what a program will do in response to the numbered steps.

Notes

Give you additional information to help you complete a task. The purpose of a note is three-fold: It can explain special conditions that may occur during the course of the task, warn you of potentially dangerous situations, or refer you to tasks in the same, or a different chapter. References to tasks within the chapter are indicated by the phrase "See the section..." followed by the name of the task. References to other chapters are indicated by "See Chapter..." followed by the chapter number.

Icons

Indicate a button that you must click to perform a section.

Conventions That Are Assumed With This Book

Mac and Window Conventions

Although this book shows you how to perform steps using a Mac, you can also perform them with a PC. When there is a difference between the platforms' keyboard or menu conventions, this book lists the Mac convention first, followed by the PC convention. For example:

1 Press `option` + `Shift` + `↓` or `Alt` + `Shift` + `↓`.

Menus versus Shortcut Keys

Because shortcut keys are essential to learning Illustrator, it is highly recommended that the reader become familiar with, and use them whenever possible. This book presents menu commands followed immediately by the corresponding shortcut keys in a bullet. For example:

1 Click **File**.
2 Click **Close**.
■ Alternately, you can use the keyboard shortcut by pressing `⌘` + `W` or `Ctrl` + `W` to quickly close files.

After the introduction of both methods, only the shortcut key is presented. For a full listing of shortcut keys, see the Appendix.

Operating Differences between OS Versions

This book assumes that you have OS 9 installed on your computer.

If you have a different OS version installed, your computer screen may appear differently than the screens presented in this book.

CHAPTER 1

Introducing Illustrator

Do you want to know what Illustrator 10 can do for you? In this chapter, you learn how to start Illustrator, as well as create and save documents.

Work with Images 4

Understanding Illustrator 6

Navigate the Illustrator Work Area 8

Start Illustrator on a Macintosh
   or a PC...10

Create a New Document....................12

Save a Document 14

Open a Saved Document 16

Close a Document 17

Get Help 18

WORK WITH IMAGES

Illustrator lets you create, modify, combine, and publish drawings and images from your computer.

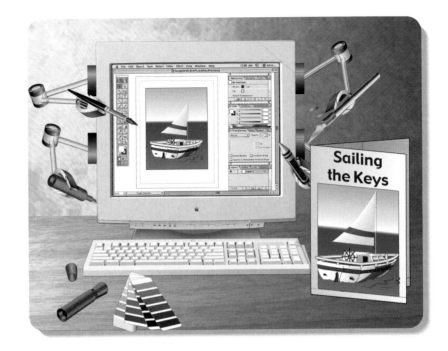

Draw New Images

You can use Illustrator to quickly create new illustrations or images. It is easy to apply colors, patterns, recurring shapes, or effects to create stylized images. Advanced tools make creating complex images nearly effortless.

Edit Existing Images

You can open and edit existing images in Illustrator to make necessary changes. You can make your changes as subtle as a new color shade for a corporate logo or as elaborate as text effects for a Web page. In addition, you can use Illustrator's type tools to create and integrate stylized letters and words into images. To work with color, see Chapter 7. To work with text, see Chapter 8.

Create Composite Images

You can combine different image elements in Illustrator. Your compositions can include pictures, drawings, scanned art, text, and almost anything else you can save on your computer. By placing elements on separate layers in Illustrator, you can move, transform, and customize them independently of one another. To work with layers, see Chapter 11.

Organize Your Images

Illustrator offers powerful ways to keep your images organized after you create or edit them. You can work with collaboration programs such as an image database or a WebDAV server (Digital Authoring and Versioning) to check images in and out automatically. This makes it easy to keep track of changes and undo them if necessary.

Put Your Images to Work

After you create your images, you can use them in a variety of ways. Illustrator lets you print your images, save them in a format suitable for use on a Web page, or prepare them for use in layout programs such as Adobe PageMaker. This makes it easy to switch formats should your images need changes. To print your images, see Chapter 13. To create images for the Web, see Chapter 14.

UNDERSTANDING ILLUSTRATOR

Illustrator's tools let you create and optimize illustrations for nearly any purpose, from Web pages to print media and back again.

Create Vector Graphics and Bitmap Images

You can save computer images in either vector or bitmap form with vector form usually being smaller, and bitmap form larger, in size. Because of their different sizes, bitmap images tend to download slower over the Internet than vector graphics. Illustrator can work with either format and save your files as either type. Vector graphics also display more clearly and look much better than bitmap graphics, especially when zooming in. See Chapter 2 for more information on saving in different file formats.

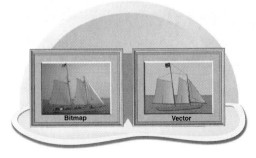

Work with Color

Illustrator lets you apply color to your images by using the Brush, Eyedropper, and Fill tools. These tools fill in your selection with solid or semitransparent colors. You can also add colored textures and patterns using these tools. You can find out more about color in Chapter 7.

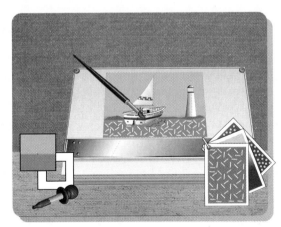

Work with Text

Illustrator's text tools enable you to easily apply text and labels to your images. You can combine these tools with special effects to create warped, 3-D, or wildly colored type. To learn more about text, see Chapter 8.

Create Special Effects

You can add special effects and apply filters like drop shadows, 3-D shading, and other styles to your images. You can also perform complex color manipulations or distortions by using Illustrator's filters. Filters can make your images look warped, underwater, blurred, or altered in other ways. See Chapter 9 for information on filters.

Produce Web- and Print-Ready Images

Illustrator comes ready to create images in both Web-friendly and printing-press-friendly formats. Web images have different format requirements from printing-press formats; these specialized requirements are available to you no matter which format you need. Learn more about Web and press file support in Chapters 13 and 14.

Integrate with Other Adobe Programs

Thanks to Illustrator's support for the most popular formats, you can share images, illustrations, and text among nearly any other illustration or editing program. If you have Adobe PageMaker, Photoshop, GoLive, or LiveMotion, you can freely import and export files between them, saving all your layer information and image customizations.

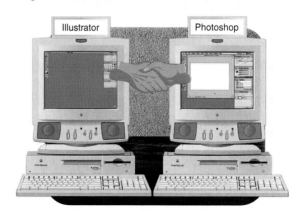

NAVIGATE THE ILLUSTRATOR WORK AREA

Illustrator has several components for working with images, illustrations, and text. Take some time to familiarize yourself with the on-screen components.

Menu Bar

Displays Illustrator menus that, when clicked, show menu commands.

Title Bar

Displays the name of the current document.

Document Window

Includes the artboard and the page, and is where you do most of your work.

Appearance Palette

Lists an object's appearance attributes such as fills, strokes, transparencies, and effects.

Color Palette

Enables you to apply color to an object's fill and stroke, and also to edit and mix colors.

Main Toolbox

Contains shortcut buttons for common commands and tools, such as the Selection tool or the Type tool.

Status Bar

Displays the current tool in use, the amount of available memory, or other information you may find useful.

Page

The actual printing area of your artwork, shown by dotted lines. Depending on your printer, your page may be smaller than the actual physical page dimension.

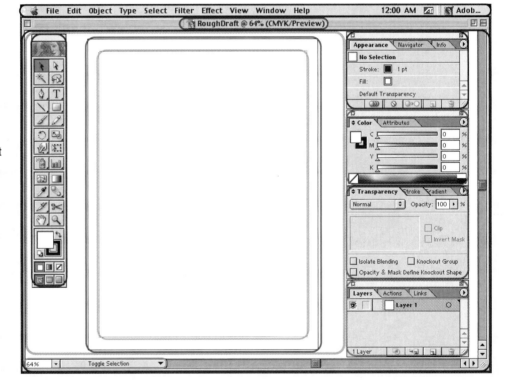

Artboard

The area that includes your document and its printable area. The artboard's boundaries, indicated by the solid dark lines, are usually the same physical size as the printed page.

Pasteboard

The pasteboard is like a giant desktop that can hold many artboards and pages. You can scroll around the pasteboard using the scroll bars in the document window.

Layers Palette

Lists all the layers in a document, starting with the frontmost layer.

Styles Palette

Lets you create, name, save, and apply sets of appearance attributes.

Navigate with the Mouse

Use the mouse to move around the Illustrator work area, select tools, and activate menu commands. To activate a tool or menu, move the mouse pointer ⇖ over the item and click it.

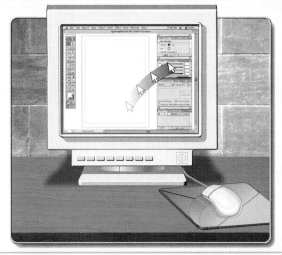

Navigate with the Keyboard

You can also use the keyboard to select commands. For example, Windows users can display the Text menu by pressing and holding the Alt key (Alt) and then pressing the letter T (T). To activate a menu command, press the corresponding underlined character. You can find keyboard shortcut commands scattered throughout the menus and in Illustrator's Help files. See the Appendix for a quick reference of the most commonly-used Illustrator shortcut commands.

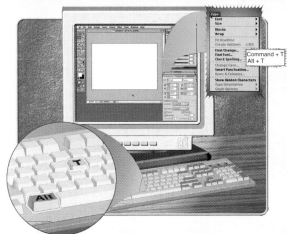

Navigate Palettes

Many of the Illustrator features open into separate on-screen mini-windows called palettes. To close an open palette on the Macintosh, click the palette's Close button (⊠). Windows users can click the Close button (⊠).

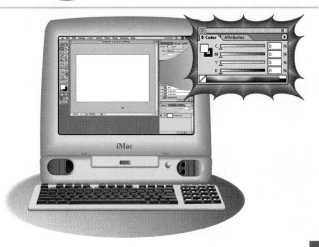

START ILLUSTRATOR ON A MACINTOSH OR A PC

You can start Illustrator on a Macintosh or on a PC.

START ILLUSTRATOR ON A MACINTOSH

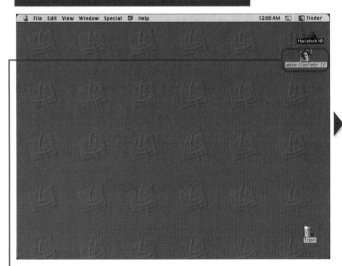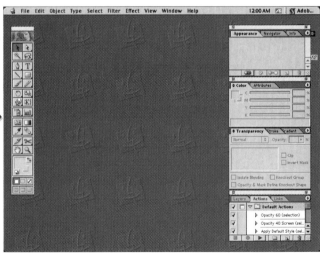

1 Double-click the Illustrator icon (📷).

Note: If you do not see 📷 on your Desktop, open the Illustrator folder on the Macintosh hard drive and drag the folder to your Desktop.

■ Illustrator opens.

Are there other ways to start Illustrator?

You can double-click a previously created Illustrator document. Doing so starts Illustrator and automatically loads the document for you.

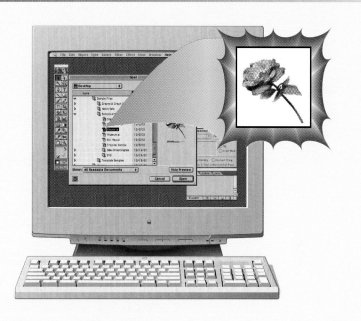

START ILLUSTRATOR ON A PC

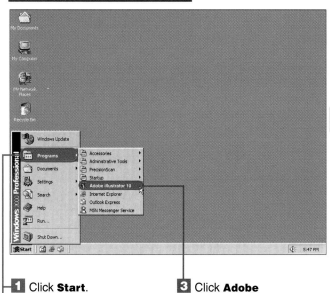

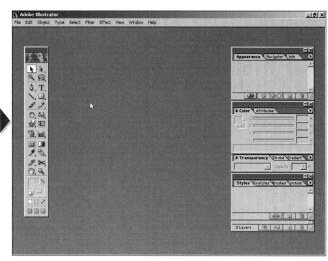

1 Click **Start**.

2 Click **Programs**.

3 Click **Adobe Illustrator 10**.

■ Illustrator opens.

CREATE A NEW DOCUMENT

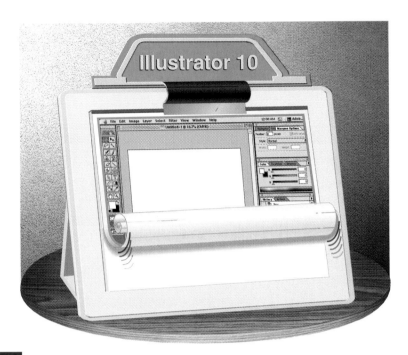

You start an Illustrator project by creating a new document.

CREATE A NEW DOCUMENT

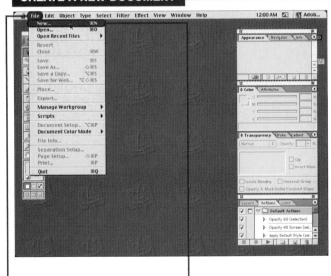

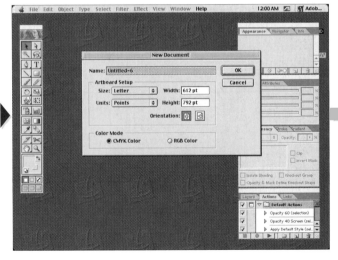

1 Click **File**.

2 Click **New**.

■ The New Document dialog box appears.

What are the other options for in the New Document dialog box?

You can set up several options when you create a new document, including size, measuring units, and color selection. These options are covered in more detail in Chapter 2.

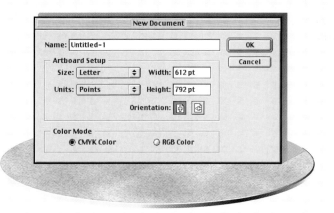

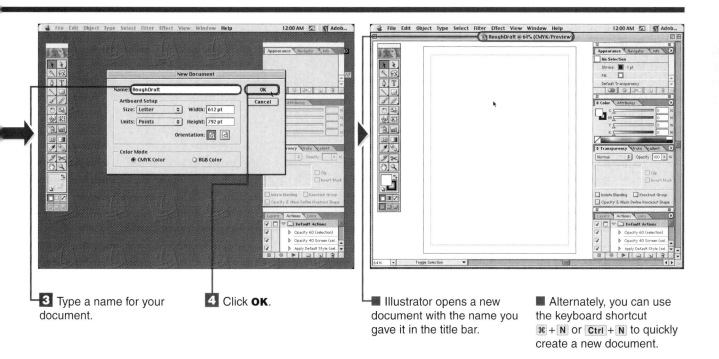

3 Type a name for your document.

4 Click **OK**.

■ Illustrator opens a new document with the name you gave it in the title bar.

■ Alternately, you can use the keyboard shortcut ⌘ + **N** or **Ctrl** + **N** to quickly create a new document.

SAVE A DOCUMENT

As you create new documents, you need to save them in order to work on them again.

Adobe Illustrator (AI) is the default format for your artwork, but you can save your files as Encapsulated PostScript (EPS) or Portable Document Format (PDF) files.

SAVE A DOCUMENT

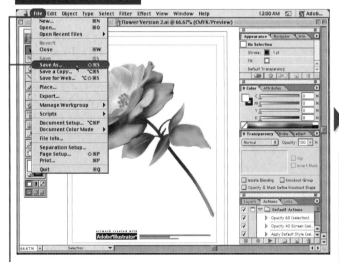

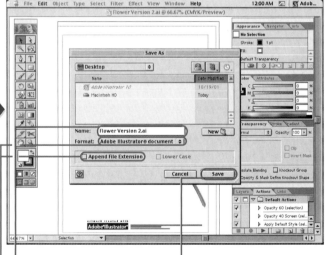

SAVE AS AN ADOBE ILLUSTRATOR (AI) FILE

1 Click **File**.

2 Click **Save As**.

■ The Save As dialog box appears.

3 Type a filename.

4 Click ▲ or ▼ in the Format box and click **Adobe Illustrator document**.

■ To automatically assign the .AI extension, you can click **Append File Extension** (□ changes to ☑).

5 Click **Save**.

*Note: If your filename already exists, Illustrator asks if you want to overwrite it. If not, click **Cancel**, then resave by typing a different name in step 3.*

■ Illustrator saves your file in AI format.

Why would I want to save my files in different formats?

Illustrator offers support for several illustration formats depending on how you use your artwork.

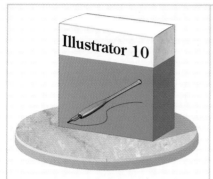

AI is best for performing your day-to-day work in Illustrator.

EPS is best in cases where you open your illustrations in other applications like Adobe Photoshop.

PDF is best for creating illustrations that you want to view in Adobe Acrobat.

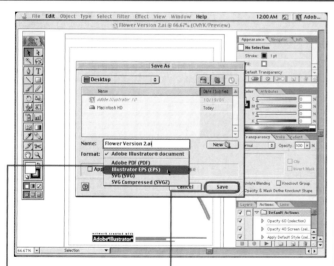

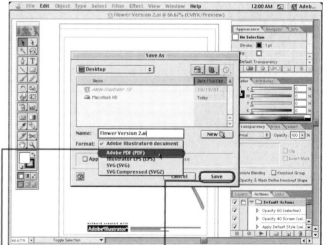

SAVE AS A POSTSCRIPT FILE (EPS)

1 Repeat steps **1** through **3** on the previous page.

2 Click ▲ or ▼ in the Format box.

3 Click **Illustrator EPS (EPS)**.

■ To automatically assign the .EPS extension, you can click **Append File Extension** (☐ changes to ☑).

4 Click **Save**.

■ Illustrator saves your file in EPS format.

SAVE AS A PORTABLE DOCUMENT FILE (PDF)

1 Repeat steps **1** through **3** on the previous page.

2 Click ▲ or ▼ in the Format box.

3 Click **Adobe PDF (PDF)**.

■ To automatically assign the .PDF extension, you can click **Append File Extension** (☐ changes to ☑).

4 Click **Save**.

■ Illustrator saves your file in PDF format.

When you save a
document, you can open
it and work on it again.

OPEN A SAVED DOCUMENT

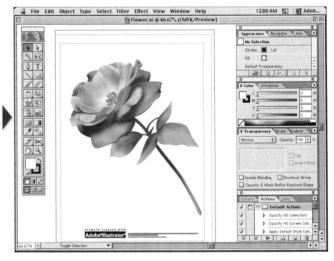

1 Click **File**.

2 Click **Open**.

■ Alternately, you can click
Open Recent Files and
select a file from the list.

■ The Open dialog box
appears.

3 Click the filename.

*Note: A preview of your artwork
appears in the preview area.*

4 Click **Open**.

■ The file opens in the
Illustrator work area.

■ Alternately, you can use
the keyboard shortcut by
pressing ⌘ + **O** or **Ctrl** + **O**
to quickly open files.

CLOSE A DOCUMENT

You can close
your document
once you are
finished working
on it.

You should save
and close
documents you are
no longer working
on to free up
memory on your
computer.

CLOSE A DOCUMENT

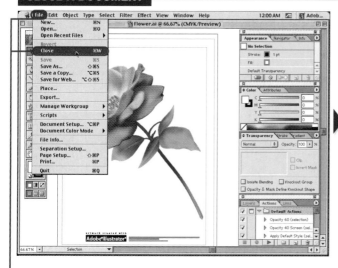
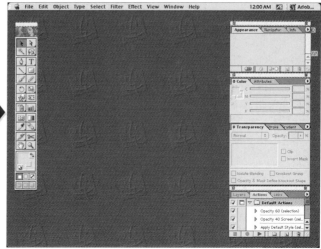

1 Click **File**.

2 Click **Close**.

■ Alternately, you can use
the keyboard shortcut by
pressing ⌘ + **W** or **Ctrl** + **W**
to quickly close files.

*Note: If you have not saved your
changes, Illustrator prompts you to
do so.*

■ The document closes, but
Illustrator remains open.

*Note: Clicking the Close Window
button ( ) closes Illustrator
entirely and may result in lost
changes or files.*

GET HELP

Illustrator comes with extensive documentation that you can access on your computer in case you ever need help.

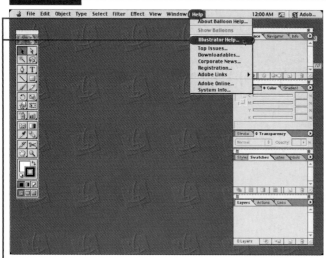

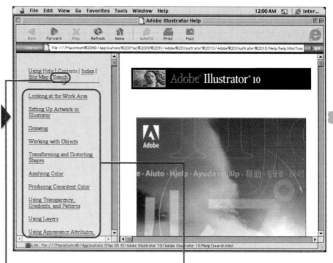

1 Click **Help**.

2 Click **Illustrator Help**.

■ You can use the keyboard shortcut **F1** to quickly open up the Help files.

■ Illustrator opens a Web browser and displays the Help interface.

3 Click the **Search** link.

■ Alternately, you can click a specific topic.

How can I receive additional tips and news about Illustrator?

Click **Help** and then **Adobe Online** to access information about product support, software upgrades, and third-party add-ons for Illustrator. You need an Internet connection to receive information via Adobe Online. Click **Refresh** to make sure you have the latest software to use for this feature.

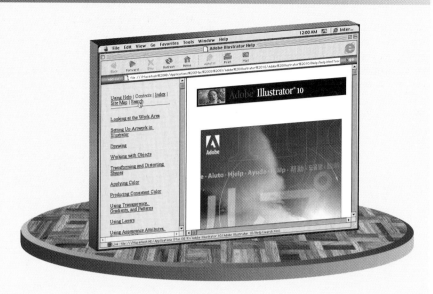

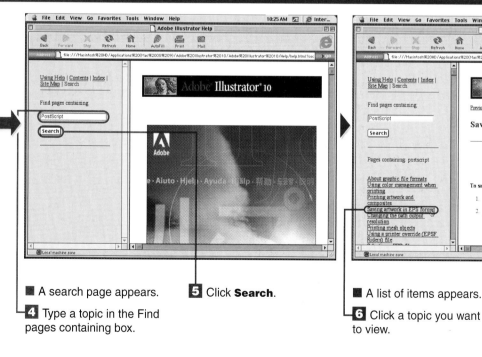

■ A search page appears.

4 Type a topic in the Find pages containing box.

5 Click **Search**.

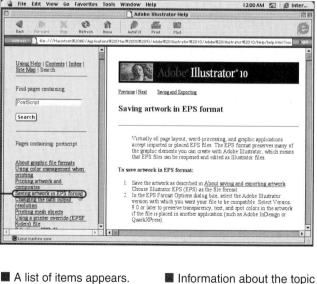

■ A list of items appears.

6 Click a topic you want to view.

■ Information about the topic appears in the right frame.

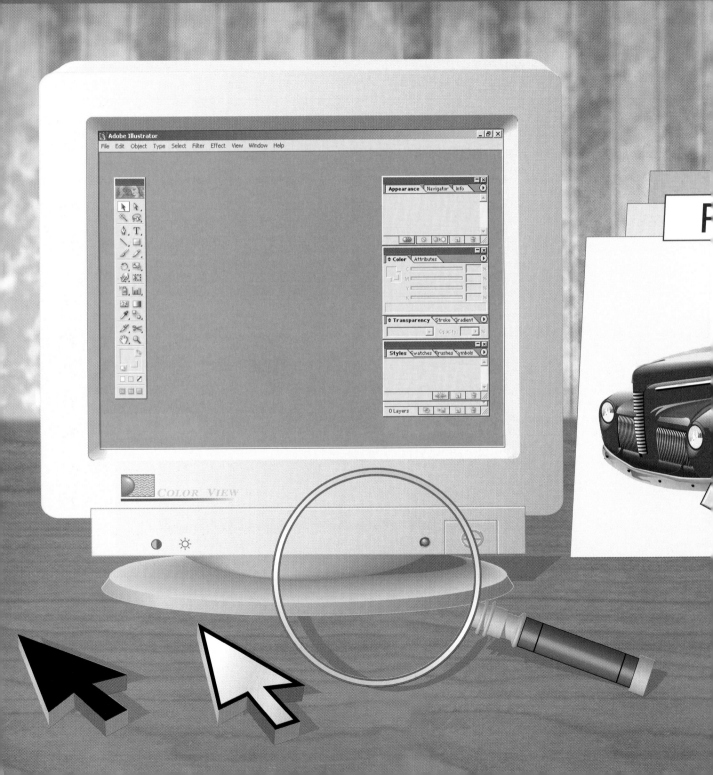

CHAPTER 2

Understanding Illustrator Basics

Are you ready to learn the basic tasks that help you operate efficiently in Illustrator? You can use this chapter to set options, work with palettes, use tools, and more.

Change Document Settings 22

Change Preferences 24

Switch Between Views 26

View Rulers and Grids 28

View a Palette 30

Dock a Palette 31

Change Palette Options 32

Using the Zoom Tool.........................34

Using the Selection Tool 36

Using the Direct Selection Tool 38

Copy and Paste an Object 40

Undo or Redo a Command 42

Palettes

CHANGE DOCUMENT SETTINGS

You can change your document settings at any time. These changes affect the size and orientation of your artwork, and Illustrator applies them immediately.

CHANGE DOCUMENT SETTINGS

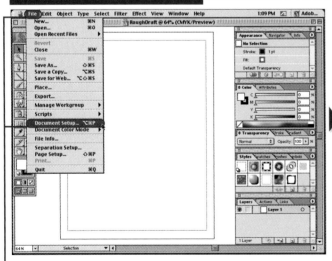

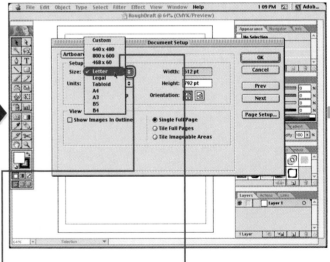

1 Click **File**.

2 Click **Document Setup**.

■ Alternately, you can press option + ⌘ + P or Ctrl + Alt + P.

■ The Document Setup dialog box appears.

3 Click 🖢 or 🖢 on the **Size** list.

4 Click an option to change the page size.

■ You can select common sizes such as Letter, or create a custom size for your page dimensions.

When I create a new document, can I set other properties, such as printing and export?

No. When you create a new document, you can only set the artboard dimensions, color mode, and page orientation through the New Document dialog box. You can change the other settings through the Document Setup dialog box after you open your newly created document in Illustrator. You can open the Document Setup dialog box by clicking **File**, and then **Setup**. To open a saved Illustrator document, see Chapter 1.

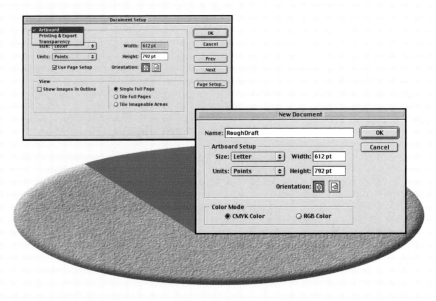

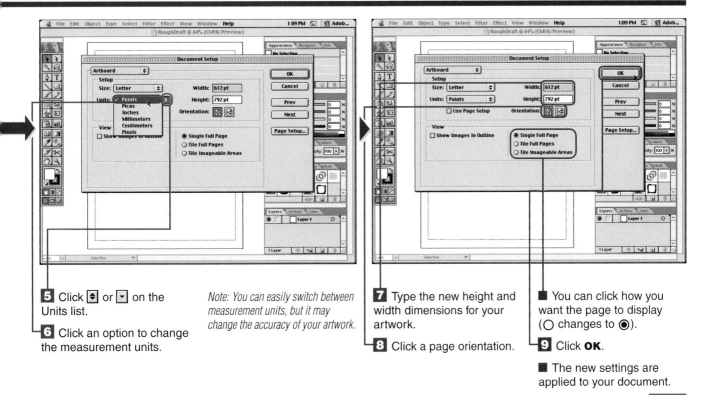

5 Click ⬆ or ⬇ on the Units list.

6 Click an option to change the measurement units.

Note: You can easily switch between measurement units, but it may change the accuracy of your artwork.

7 Type the new height and width dimensions for your artwork.

8 Click a page orientation.

■ You can click how you want the page to display (○ changes to ●).

9 Click **OK**.

■ The new settings are applied to your document.

CHANGE PREFERENCES

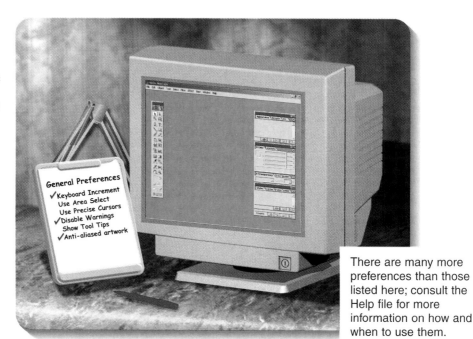

You can customize Illustrator to match the way you work. This makes it more efficient for you to create artwork.

General Preferences
✓ Keyboard Increment
  Use Area Select
  Use Precise Cursors
✓ Disable Warnings
  Show Tool Tips
✓ Anti-aliased artwork

There are many more preferences than those listed here; consult the Help file for more information on how and when to use them.

CHANGE PREFERENCES

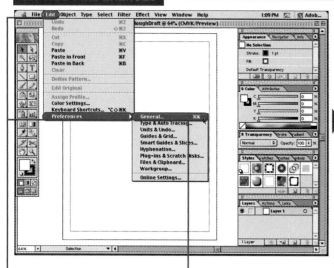

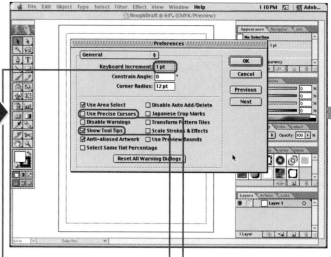

CHANGE GENERAL PREFERENCES

1 Click **Edit**.

2 Click **Preferences**.

3 Click **General**.

■ Alternately, you can press ⌘ + **K** or **Ctrl** + **K** to quickly bring up the Preferences dialog box.

■ The Preferences dialog box appears.

■ This option sets how far an object moves when you select it and press the arrow keys (←, →, ↑, ↓).

■ This option switches between regular cursors and precise cursors.

■ This option displays a popup window when you hover over a tool, showing you the tool name and keyboard shortcuts.

**Why does Illustrator look
different every time I start it?**

Illustrator saves your
preferences and changes
each time you quit, including
window and palette
positions. This is a
convenient way of restoring
your workspace so you do
not spend time readjusting
your settings. Illustrator
stores these changes in the
files Adobe Illustrator
Startup_CMYK.ai or Adobe
Illustrator Startup_RGB.ai,
depending on whether you
use CMYK or RGB color
schemes. To restore
Illustrator to its defaults,
simply delete these files and
new ones will be created.

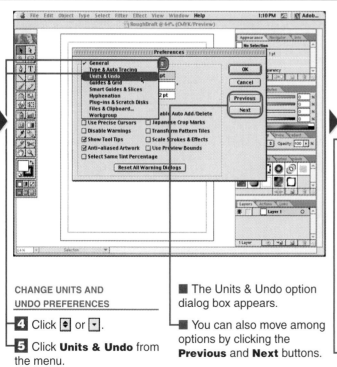

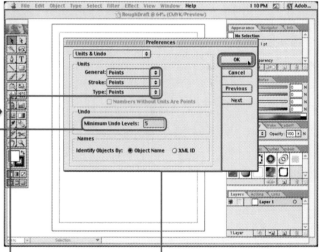

**CHANGE UNITS AND
UNDO PREFERENCES**

4 Click ◆ or ▾.

5 Click **Units & Undo** from
the menu.

■ The Units & Undo option
dialog box appears.

■ You can also move among
options by clicking the
Previous and **Next** buttons.

■ You can set the General,
Stroke, or Type units by
clicking ◆ or ▾ and then
an option.

■ You can set the minimum
number of undo levels in the
text box by typing a number.

*Note: The more undo levels you
set, the more memory you use,
especially with complex artwork.*

6 Click **OK**.

■ Illustrator changes your
preferences.

SWITCH BETWEEN VIEWS

Illustrator can switch
between Preview,
Outline, and Pixel
Preview modes so you
can work in the most
convenient mode, or so
you can see how your
artwork looks before you
save it.

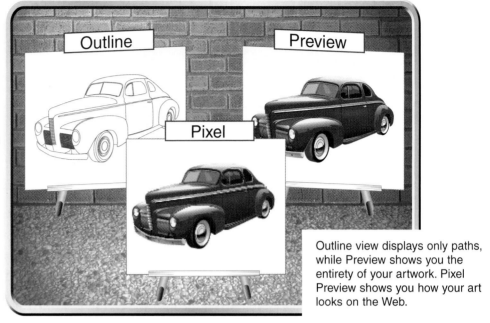

Outline view displays only paths,
while Preview shows you the
entirety of your artwork. Pixel
Preview shows you how your art
looks on the Web.

SWITCH BETWEEN VIEWS

SWITCH TO OUTLINE VIEW

1 Click **View**.

2 Click **Outline**.

■ The document switches to
Outline view.

■ You can also press ⌘ + Y
or Ctrl + Y to switch views.

■ To switch back to Preview
mode, repeat steps **1** and **2**.

Should I work in Outline Mode or Preview Mode?

After you have some practice working with paths, Outline mode is much faster on your computer, especially with complex artwork. Preview mode displays your art complete with fills and color, and helps you see what your final artwork looks like.

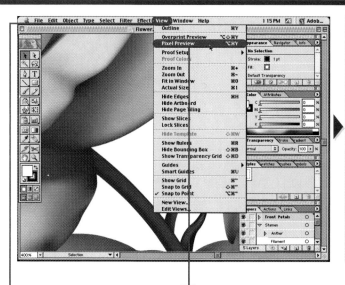

<u>SWITCH TO PIXEL VIEW</u>

1 Click **View**.

2 Click **Pixel Preview**.

■ You can also press ⌘ + option + Y or Ctrl + Alt + Y to switch to Pixel Preview.

■ The document switches to Pixel Preview.

Note: You can see more pixel detail at higher magnification by reviewing the section "Using the Zoom Tool" later in this chapter.

■ To switch back to Preview mode, repeat steps **1** and **2**.

VIEW RULERS AND GRIDS

You can view rulers and grids to help you position elements in your artwork. This gives you increased precision, which is very helpful when accuracy matters.

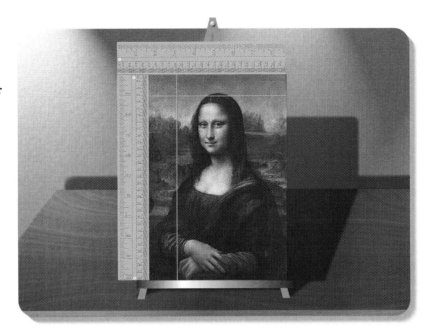

VIEW RULERS AND GRIDS

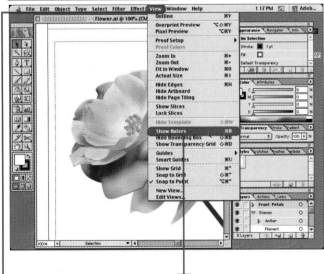

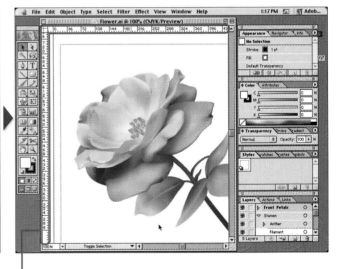

VIEW RULERS

1 Click **View**.

2 Click **Show Rulers**.

■ You can also press ⌘ + **R** or **Ctrl** + **R** to show rulers.

■ Rulers appear in your document window.

■ To remove the rulers, repeat step **1** but click **Hide Rulers** in step **2**.

Note: The measurement units are those set in the "Change Document Settings" section earlier in this chapter.

**Is there an easy way to change
the grid measurements?**

You can quickly change the
default grid lines, subdivisions,
and even color. Click **Edit**,
Preferences, and then
Guides & Grid. Edit your
options in the Preferences dialog
box, then click **OK**. Your changes
take place immediately.

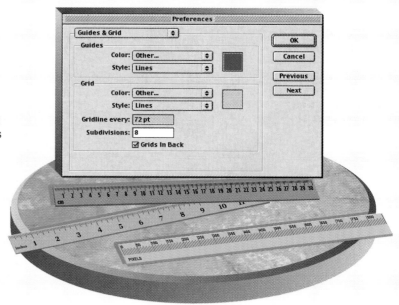

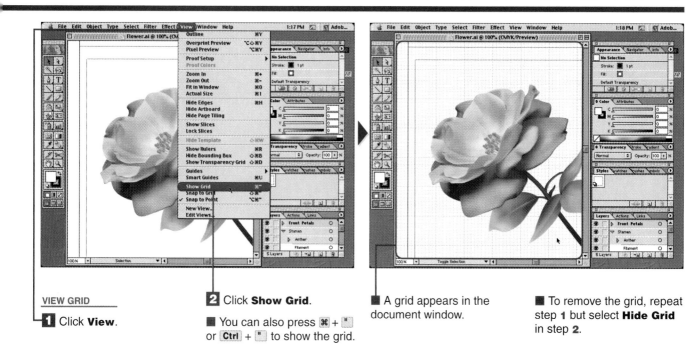

VIEG GRID

1 Click **View**.

2 Click **Show Grid**.

■ You can also press ⌘ + "
or **Ctrl** + " to show the grid.

■ A grid appears in the
document window.

■ To remove the grid, repeat
step **1** but select **Hide Grid**
in step **2**.

VIEW A PALETTE

Palettes are small windows that you can quickly view or hide in Illustrator. You use palettes to change or set options for the many tools selected from the Toolbox, or view artwork or object properties.

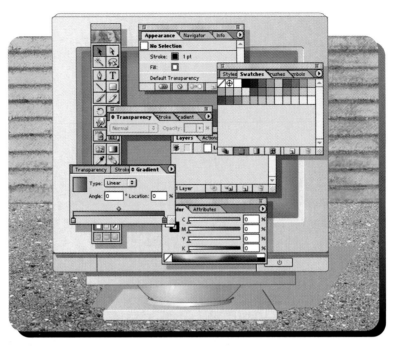

If you have enough screen space, you can have all the palettes open at once.

VIEW A PALETTE

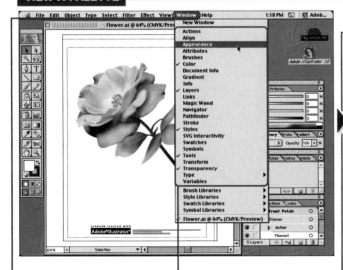

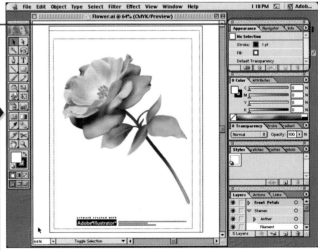

1 Click **Window**.

■ A check mark (✔) appears next to the palettes that are currently visible.

2 Click a palette name.

■ The palette appears.

■ You can also press the keyboard shortcut listed for each palette to make it visible.

*Note: For a list of Mac and Window menu shortcuts, you can click **Edit** and then **Keyboard**. For a listing of the keyboard shortcuts used in this book, see the Appendix.*

■ To hide a palette, repeat steps **1** and **2**.

DOCK A PALETTE

You can move palettes between the palette windows, which is called docking a palette. You can create the most useful combination of palettes for your artwork this way.

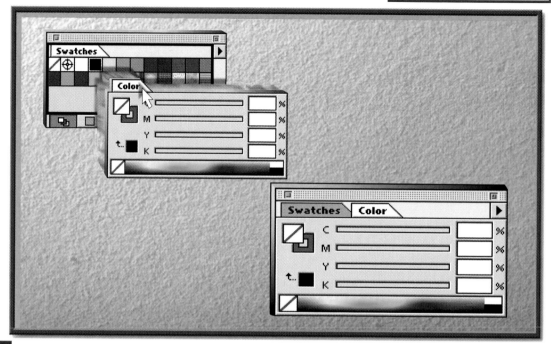

DOCK A PALETTE

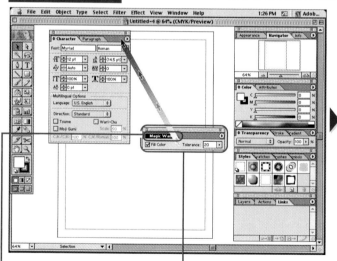

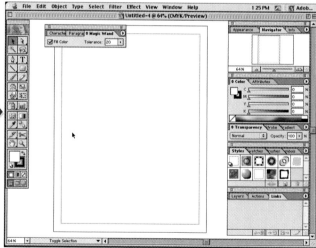

1 Click and hold the mouse cursor (↖) over one tab in a palette.

2 Drag ↖ into another palette.

■ The palette outline shows you where it will appear.

3 Release the mouse button.

■ The tab appears docked in the new palette.

CHANGE PALETTE OPTIONS

You can change the palette viewing area and the commonly used palette options without hunting through menus. This helps keep screen area available for artwork but the tools still ready for use.

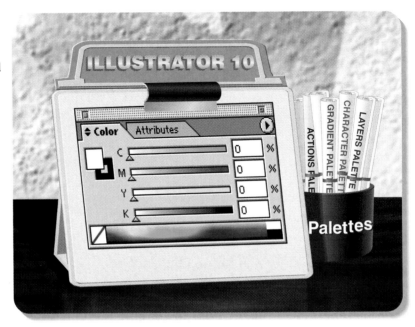

CHANGE PALETTE OPTIONS

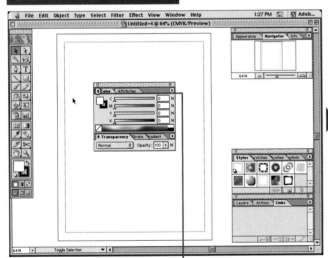

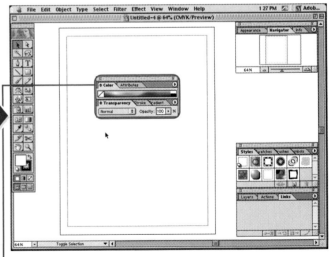

CHANGE PALETTE VIEWING AREA

1 Open a palette that has several tabs in it.

Note: To open a palette, see the section "View a Palette."

2 Click the double arrowhead (⬍) to change the Color palette's viewing area.

■ If there is not a double arrowhead, then the palette does not have other viewing modes.

■ The palette's viewing area reduces.

3 Repeat step **2** to scroll through the viewing modes for a palette.

The double arrowhead (⬍) is not on every tab. Why not?

The double arrowhead (⬍) appears only on the active tab, which is the one at the "front" of the stack. You need to click on each tab to see if it has the double arrowhead on it.

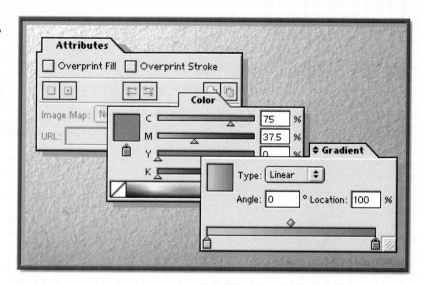

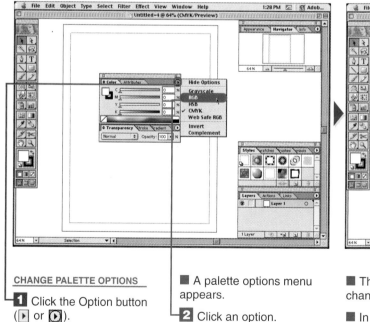

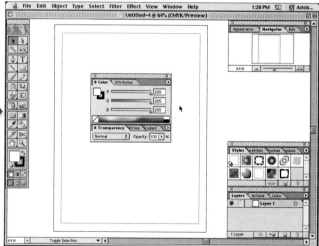

CHANGE PALETTE OPTIONS

1 Click the Option button (▶ or ◉).

■ A palette options menu appears.

2 Click an option.

■ The palette options change.

■ In this example, the Color palette switches to an RGB palette.

Note: The options change depending on which tab is at the front of the palette window.

USING THE ZOOM TOOL

The Zoom tool lets you magnify your artwork for working on fine detail, or to step back from close-up work to see how the overall illustration looks.

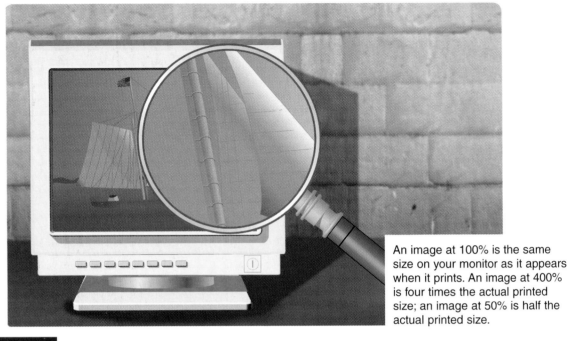

An image at 100% is the same size on your monitor as it appears when it prints. An image at 400% is four times the actual printed size; an image at 50% is half the actual printed size.

USING THE ZOOM TOOL

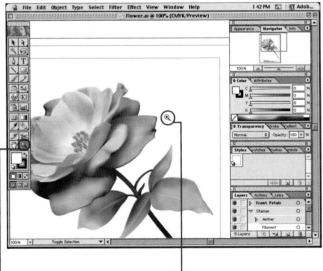

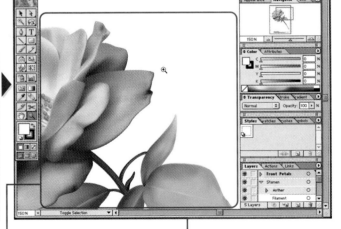

ZOOM IN

1 Click the Zoom tool (🔍) in the Toolbox.

■ Your ➤ changes to a magnifying glass with a plus sign (⊕).

2 Position ⊕ to an area you want to magnify.

3 Click the mouse button.

■ The artwork is magnified, centered on the point where you clicked.

■ The zoom percentage changes in the status bar.

34

Is there a faster way to zoom in or out on my artwork?

The zoom percentage in the status bar is a list box. You can select a zoom percentage directly using the list. You can also type an exact percentage to hundredths of a percent in the box.

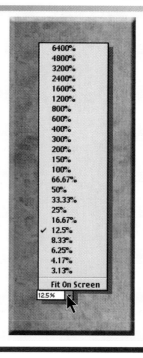

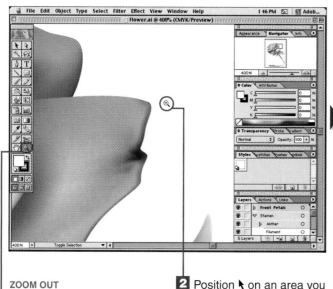

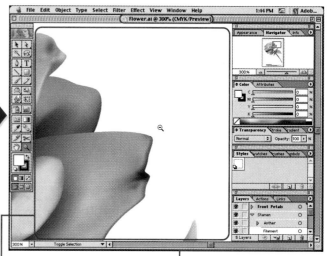

ZOOM OUT

1 Click 🔍 in the Toolbox.

■ The ⬚ changes to a magnifying glass with a plus sign (⊕).

2 Position ⬚ on an area you want to zoom out.

3 Press **Alt**.

■ The ⬚ changes to a magnifying glass with a minus sign (⊖).

4 Click the mouse button.

■ The artwork zooms out, centered on the point where you clicked.

■ The zoom percentage changes in the status bar.

USING THE SELECTION TOOL

You use the Selection tool to select an object or an entire group of paths at one time. You can select objects by clicking them, or by dragging a *marquee box* — which Illustrator represents as a dotted line — around them.

After you select an object, you can move it or resize it on the page. See Chapter 6 to learn how to reshape objects.

USING THE SELECTION TOOL

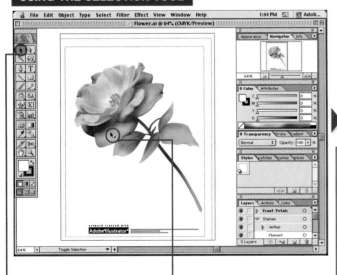

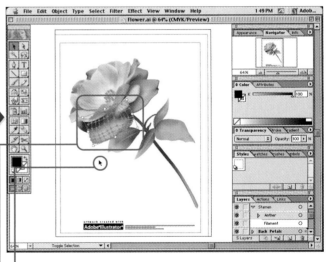

SELECT BY CLICKING AN OBJECT

■1 Click the Selection tool (▶) in the Toolbox.

■ You can quickly choose ▶ by pressing the letter **V**.

■2 Position ▶ over an object.

■ ▶ changes to a black arrow with a square (▶.).

■3 Click anywhere on the object.

■ A bounding box appears around the object, indicating the object is selected.

Note: See Chapter 6 for more information on bounding boxes.

How do I select multiple objects?

If you are using the Selection tool, you select multiple objects by pressing and holding down **Shift**, then clicking ↖ on the object you want to add. You can also deselect objects from a group the same way.

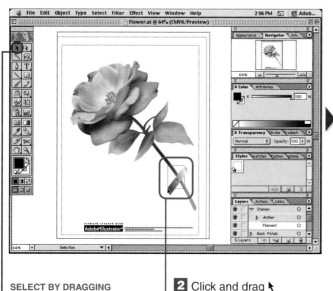

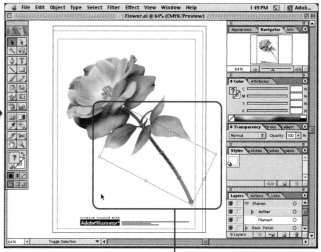

SELECT BY DRAGGING AROUND AN OBJECT

1 Click ↖ in the Toolbox.

2 Click and drag ↖ diagonally to the opposite side of the object.

■ A marquee box appears.

3 Release the mouse button.

■ A bounding box appears around the selected object.

USING THE DIRECT SELECTION TOOL

You use the Direct Selection tool to choose only parts of an object or a path. This helps you perform detail-oriented tasks on your artwork.

USING THE DIRECT SELECTION TOOL

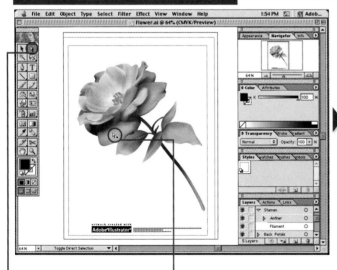

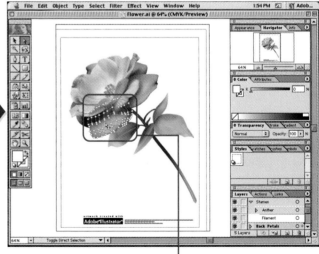

SELECT BY CLICKING AN OBJECT

1 Click the Direct Selection tool ( ) in the Toolbox.

■ You can quickly choose by pressing the letter **A**.

2 Position the ↖ over an object.

■ The ↖ changes to a light arrow with a dark square ( ).

3 Click anywhere on the object.

■ All the paths on the object are selected.

When I use the Direct Selection tool, I do not see a bounding box. Should there be one?

The Direct Selection tool selects only single paths, points, or parts of objects, rather than entire objects or grouped objects like the Selection tool. If you need to create a bounding box so you can resize an entire object, use the Selection tool instead.

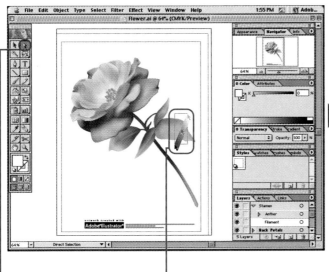

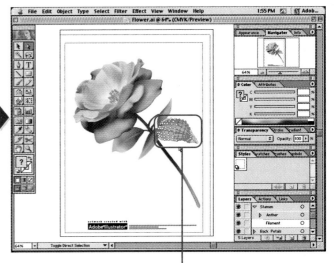

SELECT BY DRAGGING AROUND AN OBJECT

1 Click ![icon] in the Toolbox.

2 Click and drag ▸ diagonally to cover part of the object.

■ A marquee box appears.

3 Release the mouse button.

■ All the paths in the object are selected.

COPY AND PASTE AN OBJECT

Many times you need a repeating object or motif in your artwork. Illustrator lets you quickly duplicate objects using copy and paste, either with the menus or the mouse.

COPY AND PASTE AN OBJECT

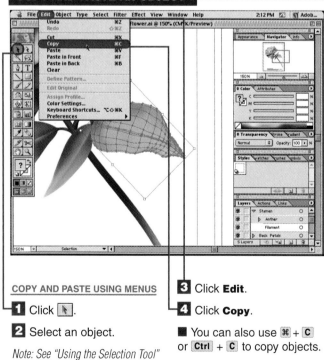

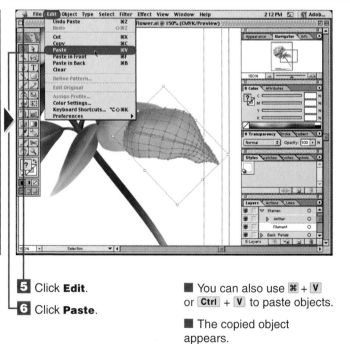

COPY AND PASTE USING MENUS

1 Click ▶.

2 Select an object.

Note: See "Using the Selection Tool" earlier in the chapter to select an object.

3 Click **Edit**.

4 Click **Copy**.

■ You can also use ⌘ + C or Ctrl + C to copy objects.

5 Click **Edit**.

6 Click **Paste**.

■ You can also use ⌘ + V or Ctrl + V to paste objects.

■ The copied object appears.

**Does copy and paste work for
only one object?**

You are not limited to copying
objects one at a time; you can
use copy and paste with a single
object or with multiple objects you
have selected.

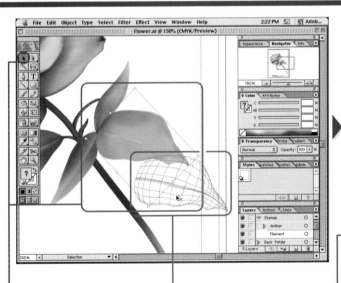

**COPY AND PASTE
USING THE MOUSE**

1 Click ![selection tool].

2 Select an object.

*Note: See "Using the Selection Tool"
earlier in the chapter to select an
object.*

3 Press and hold option
or Alt .

4 Click and drag the ▶ to
another area on the page.

5 Release the mouse
button.

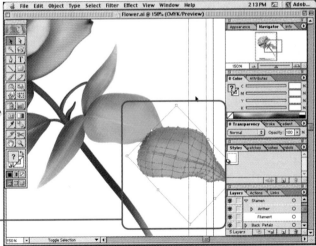

■ The copied object
appears.

UNDO OR REDO A COMMAND

If you make a mistake, Illustrator lets you undo your last command. You can also repeat your last command in order to save time.

UNDO OR REDO A COMMAND

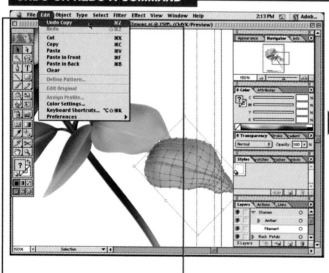

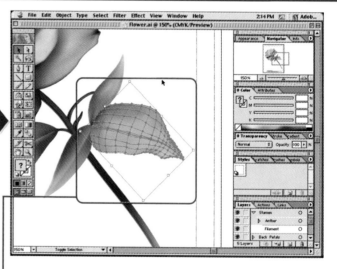

UNDO A COMMAND

1 Click **Edit**.

■ Your last command is listed on the menu.

2 Click **Undo**.

■ You can also press ⌘ + Z or Ctrl + Z to undo a command.

■ Your artwork returns to its previous state.

**How many commands can I
undo?**

See the section "Change
Preferences," earlier in this
chapter, to set the number of
undo commands in Illustrator. The
default is 5; the more undo
commands you set, the more
memory you use.

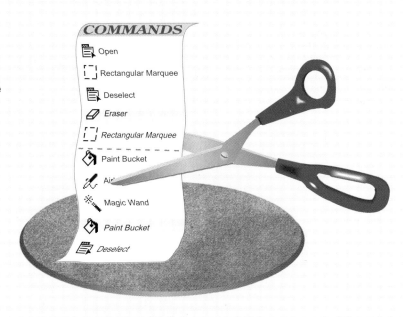

COMMANDS

- Open
- Rectangular Marquee
- Deselect
- Eraser
- Rectangular Marquee
- Paint Bucket
- Air...
- Magic Wand
- Paint Bucket
- Deselect

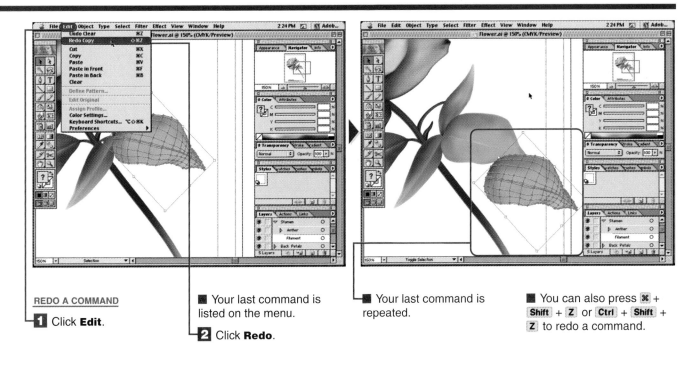

REDO A COMMAND

1 Click **Edit**.

■ Your last command is
listed on the menu.

2 Click **Redo**.

■ Your last command is
repeated.

■ You can also press ⌘ +
Shift + **Z** or **Ctrl** + **Shift** +
Z to redo a command.

CHAPTER 3

Working with Paths

Are you ready to begin drawing in Illustrator? In Illustrator, you draw by creating "paths." Read this chapter to learn about the paths that you can create with Illustrator's various tools.

Understanding Paths 46

Draw Straight Lines
   with the Line Tool 48

Draw Freehand Lines
   with the Pencil Tool.........................50

Draw Curves with the Arc Tool............52

Draw Straight Lines with the Pen Tool 54

Draw Curves with the Pen Tool............56

Reshape a Curve 58

Reshape a Line with the
   Reshape Tool 60

Close an Open Path 62

Open a Closed Path 64

Delete Paths.....................................66

Erase Parts of a Path.........................68

Smooth a Path 70

UNDERSTANDING PATHS

Unlike other illustration programs with which you may have worked, Illustrator uses the concept of "paths" for nearly all its drawing functions. If you want to work effectively with Illustrator, you must understand paths and how they function.

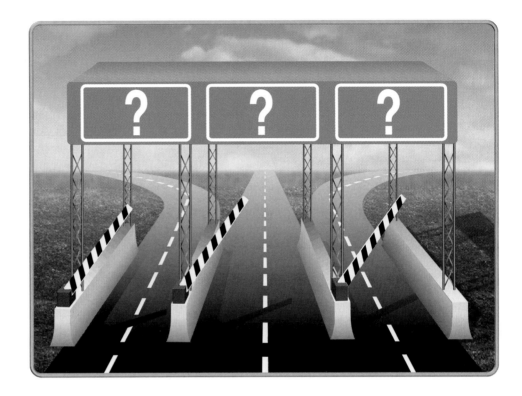

Paths and Bézier Curves

Illustrator's paths are based on *Bézier curves*, which are mathematical formulas that describe lines. This means that when you draw a line, you actually "write down" a mathematical formula on the page. Illustrator hides the math from you; all you see are the lines.

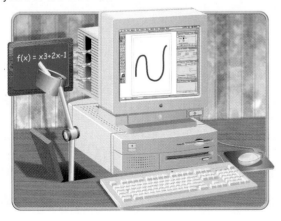

Types of Paths

Paths consist of segments with anchor points at both ends of the segment. Paths come in three types: *open* paths that have two distinct end points, like a straight line; *closed* paths that are continuous with no start or end points, like a circle; and *compound* paths, which consist of both types and which overlap or create closed areas, such as the letter "g." See this chapter and Chapter 4 for information on creating open, closed, and compound paths.

Visible and Invisible Paths

When working with complex projects, you may find it easier and faster to work in outline mode, viewing only the paths. In Outline mode, all paths are visible; in Preview mode, you can only see paths with applied fills and strokes. You use Outline mode when your illustration has a lot of detail or when you work at high magnifications, and Preview mode for doing shading, fills, and print previews. You can make paths visible in Preview mode by selecting an object.

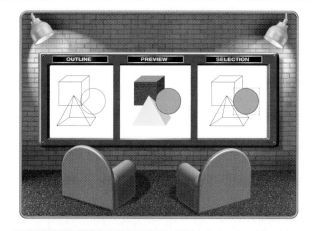

Paths and Anchor Points

Paths have *anchor points*, which start and end every path, even closed ones; you can also have anchor points anywhere along a path. You can have smooth anchor points, which means a path goes through them; corner points, where the path changes direction suddenly; or a combination, which consist of straight and curved points.

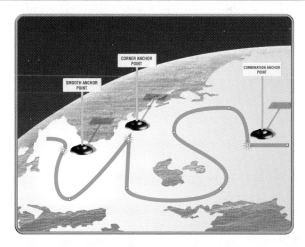

Anchor Points and Control Handles

Anchor points and control handles appear together, but in different combinations, depending on the type of anchor point. Control handles extend from anchor points and you use them to change a curve's direction. Smooth corner points or curved corner points have two handles; combination corner points have only one. Straight corner points do not have control handles. See the sections in this chapter for information on working with anchor points and control handles on the different corner points.

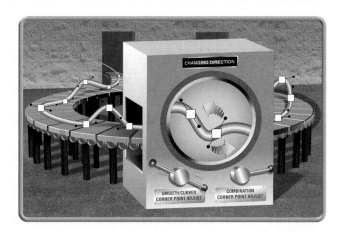

DRAW STRAIGHT LINES WITH THE LINE TOOL

The Line tool draws perfectly straight lines in your artwork.

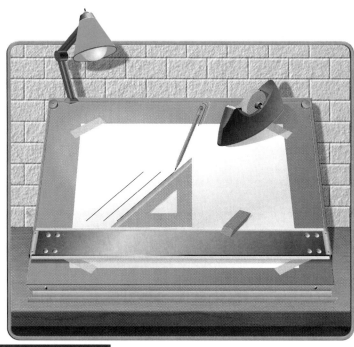

DRAW STRAIGHT LINES WITH THE LINE TOOL

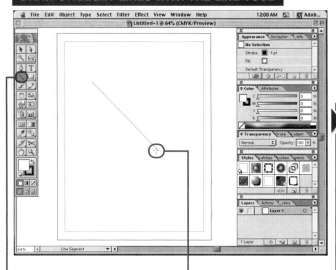

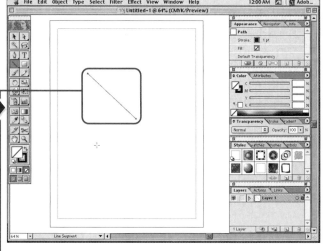

DRAW LINE SEGMENTS

1 Click the Line Segment tool in the toolbox ().

2 Position the mouse (-¦-) over your artwork.

3 Click and drag the mouse to another point on the artboard.

4 Release the mouse.

■ A straight line appears in your artwork.

■ You can press the backslash key (\) to quickly switch to the Line tool.

How do I draw lines at 45° angles?

Press and hold the Shift key (**Shift**) as you draw. Your angles are constrained to increments of 45°.

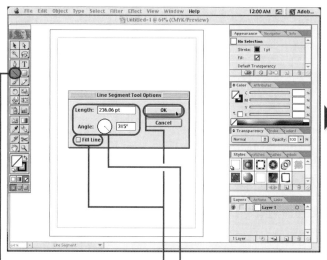

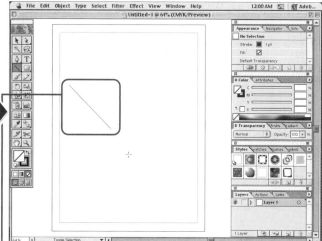

SPECIFY EXACT LINE SEGMENTS

1 Click ▨.

2 Click your artwork.

■ The Line Segment Tool Options dialog box appears.

3 Type values for length or angle.

■ Click this option to use the last line fill (☐ changes to ☑).

Note: See Chapter 7 for more on line fills.

4 Click **OK**.

■ The straight line appears in your artwork.

Note: The dialog box displays the last straight line dimensions you used.

DRAW FREEHAND LINES WITH THE PENCIL TOOL

The Pencil tool lets you draw freehand lines in your artwork. The tool adds anchor points for you automatically as you draw; you can change them after you stop drawing. To learn more about Anchor points, see the section "Understanding Paths."

DRAW FREEHAND LINES WITH THE PENCIL TOOL

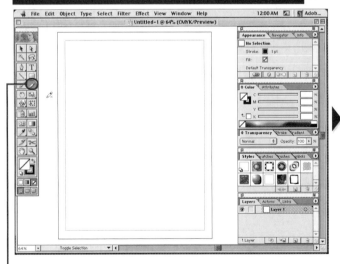

1 Click the Pencil tool in the Toolbox ( ).

■ The mouse ( ) changes to a pencil with a small x ( ).

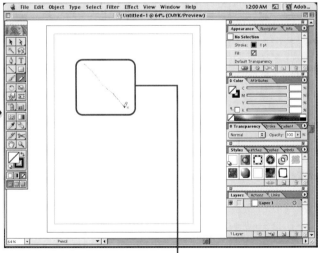

2 Place over the page.

3 Click and drag over the page.

The paths I draw with the Pencil tool seem kind of bumpy; is there any way to change them?

Double-click the Pencil tool in the toolbox to bring up the tool's properties box. You can type values in the Fidelity and Smoothness boxes. *Fidelity* determines how closely the final curve follows the path you drew, while *Smoothness* determines how angular your paths are. The higher the smoothness, the smoother the curve and the fewer anchor points. Click **OK** to have Illustrator accept your changes.

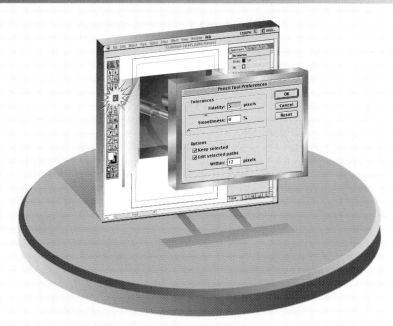

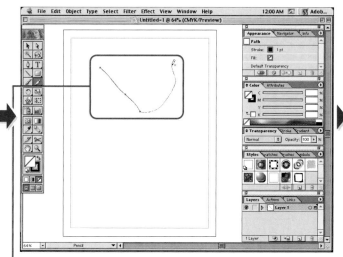

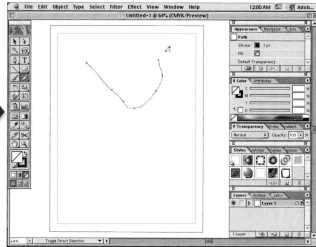

■ A freehand line is drawn on your artwork.

4 Release the mouse.

■ The line fills in with a solid color and anchor points.

DRAW CURVES WITH THE ARC TOOL

The Arc tool helps you easily draw smooth curves or parts of curves.

DRAW CURVES WITH THE ARC TOOL

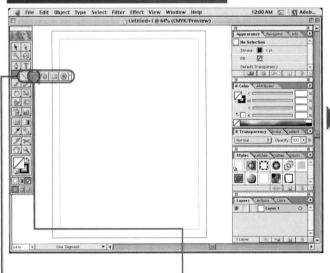

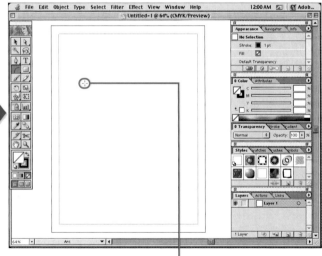

1 Click and hold ▸ on ▢.

■ A tearoff toolbar appears with several tools on it.

2 Drag ▸ over to the Arc tool (▱).

3 Release the mouse button.

■ The ▢ changes to ◰.

4 Position the ▸ over your artwork.

■ The ▸ changes to -¦-.

Is there a way to set my arc's properties without drawing and then adjusting them?

After you select the Arc tool, single-click the artboard. The Arc Segment Tool Options dialog box appears, where you can set your arc's length, type, convexity, and concavity. The values in the box are those of the last arc you drew.

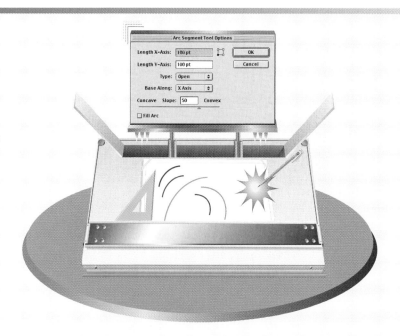

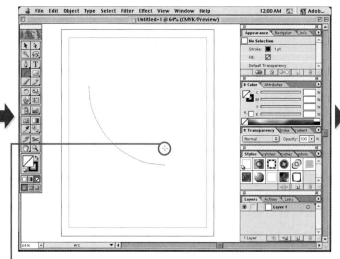

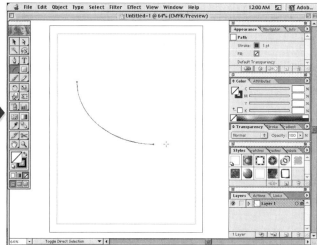

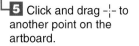 Click and drag –¦– to another point on the artboard.

6 Release the mouse.

■ An arc appears in your artwork.

DRAW STRAIGHT LINES WITH THE PEN TOOL

The Pen tool is the trickiest drawing tool in the Toolbox, and the most powerful. You can use the Pen tool to create paths of any type, and you have the most flexibility in your drawings when you use it. Straight lines are the easiest to draw.

DRAW STRAIGHT LINES WITH THE PEN TOOL

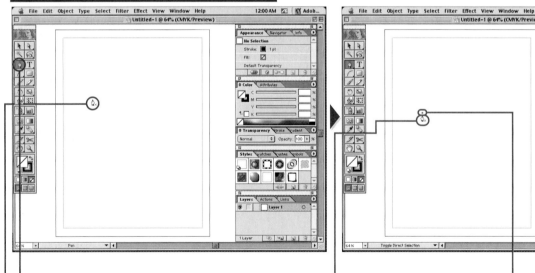

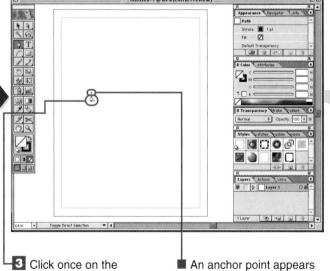

1 Click the Pen tool in the Toolbox (🖊).

2 Position the ▶ on the artboard.

■ The ▶ changes to a pen with an x (♙ₓ).

3 Click once on the artwork.

■ An anchor point appears on the page.

**Do I have to draw all my
continuous straight lines one at a
time?**

You do not have to draw one line
using the steps in this section,
then start all over again to draw
the next continuous line, and so
forth. You can draw continuous
straight lines by repeating steps **4**
and **5** in your artwork, much like
playing connect-the-dots.

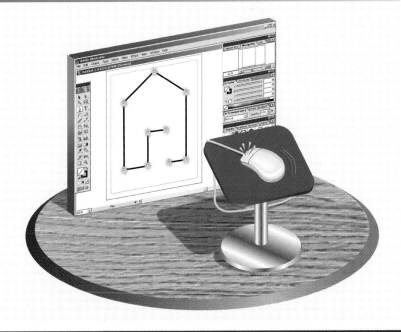

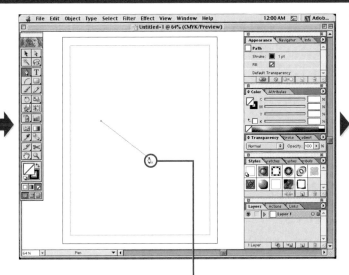

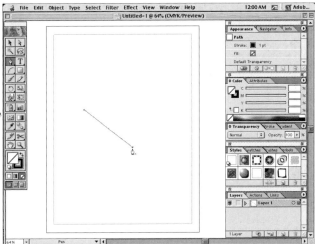

4 Position the ✐ on
another area on the
artboard.

Note: Do not drag the cursor.

5 Click again on the
artwork to create a second
anchor point.

■ A line appears between
your two anchor points.

■ To create a line in 45
degree increments, you can
hold down Shift .

■ To start a new line, press
⌘ or Ctrl and click a blank
area on the page. Then
repeat steps **1** through **5**.

DRAW CURVES WITH THE PEN TOOL

The Pen tool uses Bézier curves to create its paths, which you can scale to any size or shape without losing detail. For more on Bézier curves, see the section "Understanding Paths."

You may find drawing curved lines with the Pen tool counterintuitive at first. Practice drawing simple arcs, and then move on to more complex curves.

DRAW CURVES WITH THE PEN TOOL

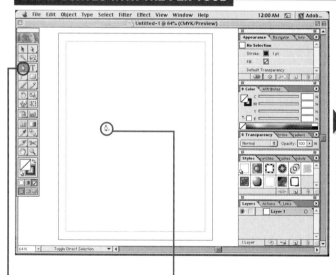

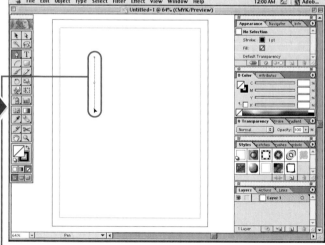

1 Click the 🖋 in the Toolbox.

■ You can also press the letter **P** to quickly switch to 🖋 .

2 Position ► to a point on your artwork.

■ The ► changes to ♦ₓ .

3 Click and drag the ♦ₓ .

■ An anchor point with control handles appears.

What techniques can I use to master drawing curves?

You can practice drawing "slalom" curves as a first step to working with curves. A more advanced technique is to try to draw a "figure eight" using as few anchor points as possible. If you can do this using only two overlapping anchor points, you have mastered the Pen tool.

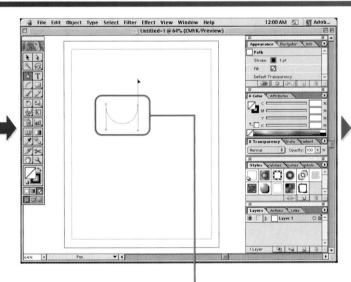

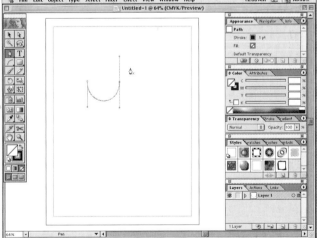

4 Release the mouse button.

5 Position ✒ a short distance away.

6 Click and drag ✒ in the opposite direction from step **2**.

■ A curve appears between the two anchor points.

7 Release the mouse button.

■ The final curve appears on the page.

■ To continue drawing curves, repeat steps **5** through **7**.

■ To start a new curve, press ⌘ or **Ctrl**, click a blank area on the page, and then repeat steps **1** through **7**.

RESHAPE A CURVE

You reshape curves using the control handles that appear from an anchor point, or by moving an anchor point. Use control handles to change a single curve; use anchor points to change both curve and length.

Control handles act like magnets that "attract" a line depending on the handle length and closeness to the line.

RESHAPE A CURVE

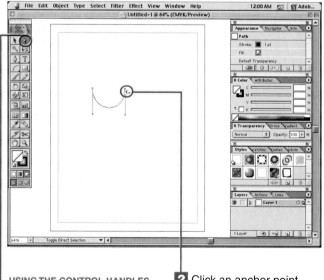

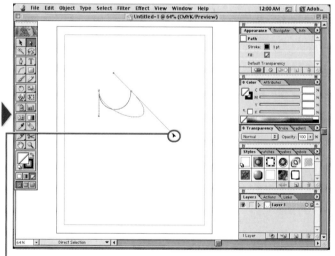

USING THE CONTROL HANDLES

■1 Click the Direct Selection tool in the Toolbox ( ).

■ You can also press **A** to switch to .

■2 Click an anchor point.

■ The control handles appear.

■3 Click and drag a control handle.

■ The curve changes shape.

■ When the curve is the proper shape, release the control handle.

**What if I use the
control handles, and
then cannot change my
curve back to its
original state?**

You can use the Undo
command to "back
out" the changes you
made with the control
handles. Click **Edit**,
then **Undo Move**, or
use the shortcut keys
⌘ + **Z** or **Ctrl** + **Z**,
to go back to your
original illustration.

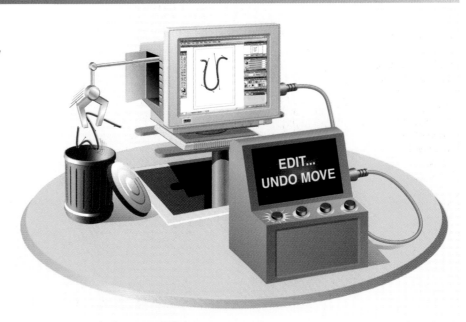

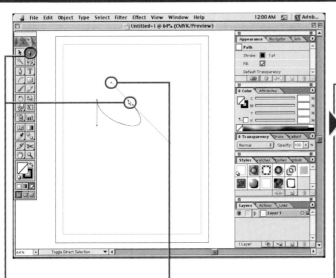

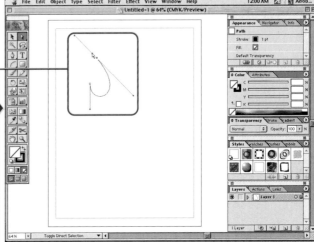

USING THE ANCHOR POINT

1 Click 🔳 in the Toolbox.

2 Click an anchor point.

■ The control handles
appear.

3 Click and drag an anchor
point.

■ The curve changes
shape.

■ When the curve is the
proper shape, release the
anchor point.

RESHAPE A LINE WITH THE RESHAPE TOOL

The Reshape tool changes the look of a line by inserting an anchor point in it. You can drag the new anchor point around to change the line's shape.

RESHAPE A LINE WITH THE RESHAPE TOOL

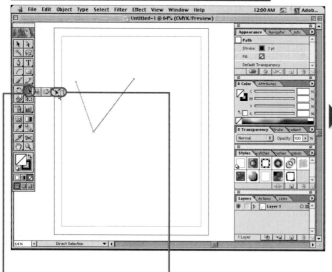

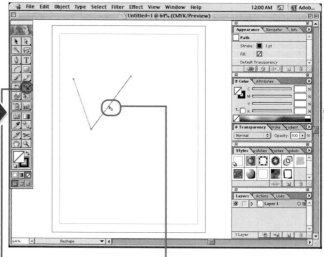

■ **1** Click and hold the Scale tool ( ).

■ A toolbar appears underneath .

■ **2** Drag ʞ over the Reshape tool ( ).

■ **3** Release the mouse.

■ The toolbox changes to show .

■ The ʞ changes to a gray arrow ( ).

■ **4** Position over a path segment.

■ **5** Click the mouse.

What if I do not like the new look I have drawn?

Switch to the Pen tool and move it over your new anchor point. When the Pen tool changes to a minus sign (✑), click the anchor point, and Illustrator deletes your anchor point. Your path returns to its original shape.

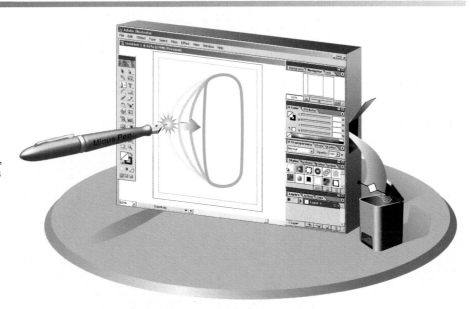

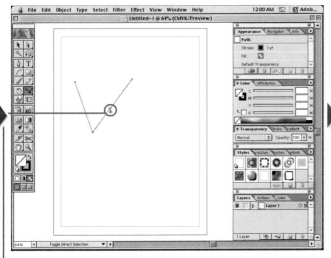

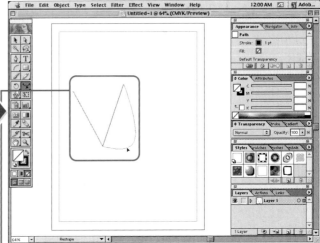

■ An anchor point with a box around it appears on the path.

Note: You must place the new anchor point within a segment; you cannot make the point an endpoint.

6 Click and drag the new anchor point.

■ The line changes shape.

CLOSE AN OPEN PATH

You can close an open path by connecting two anchor points together. The Pen tool gives you visual cues for when you can close off a path.

CLOSE AN OPEN PATH

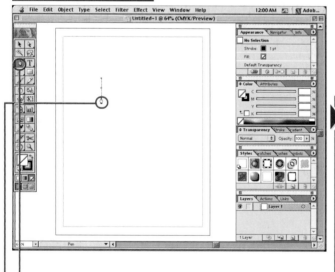

1 Click .

2 Click the artboard to create an anchor point.

■ The ▶ changes to ♦ₓ.

3 Drag ♦ₓ to another area on the artboard.

4 Click the artboard to create a second anchor point.

When do I close an open path?

Most of the time, you want to close paths in your artwork, because it makes it easier to work with paths and objects, especially when you select or move them. You can apply fills to open paths, and for artistic reasons you may want to do so; but in general, closed paths are better to work with.

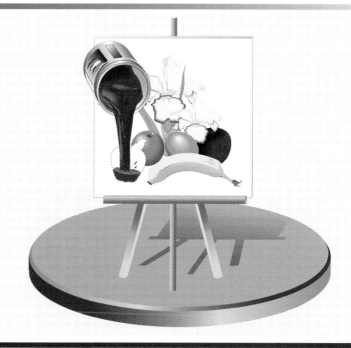

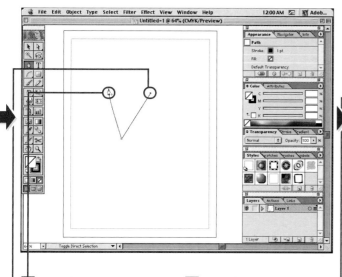

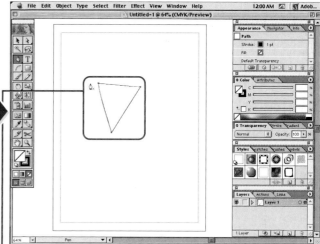

5 Click 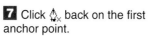 on another area on the artboard.

6 Click the artboard to create a third anchor point.

7 Click ⬧ back on the first anchor point.

■ The ⬧ changes to a pen with a small circle (⬧).

8 Click the first anchor point.

━ ■ A closed path is created.

■ This example uses straight lines; you can use the same procedure with curved lines.

OPEN A CLOSED PATH

You can use the Scissors tool to cut a path into two segments with overlapping anchor points. You can then move the two segments, delete them, or add to them.

OPEN A CLOSED PATH

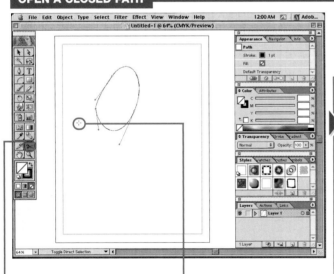

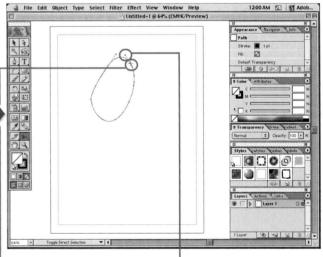

1 Click the Scissors tool (✂).

■ You can also press the letter **C** to quickly switch to ✂.

■ The ◦ changes to a crosshair (-¦-).

2 Position -¦- over a path you want to cut.

3 Click the mouse button.

4 An anchor point appears on the path.

Note: There are actually two anchor points directly overlapping each other.

What is the difference between the Scissors tool and the Knife tool?

The Scissors tool () is ideal for cutting through paths. The Knife tool (⬚) is best for cutting through shapes or cutting around irregular areas. See Chapter 5 for more information on the Knife tool.

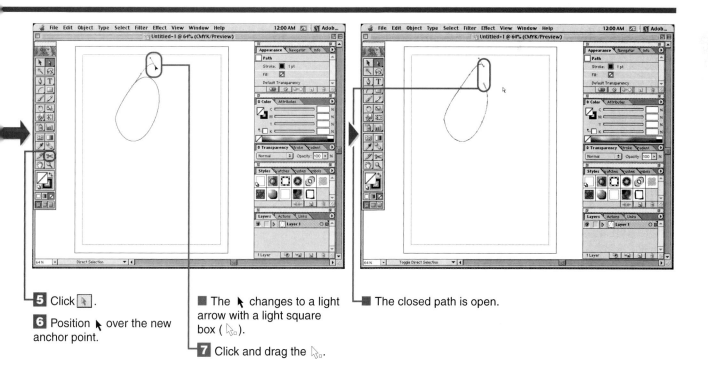

5 Click 🔺.

6 Position 🔺 over the new anchor point.

■ The 🔺 changes to a light arrow with a light square box (🔺₀).

7 Click and drag the 🔺₀.

■ The closed path is open.

DELETE PATHS

You can delete
an entire path
using the
Selection tool,
or part of a path
using the Direct
Selection tool.

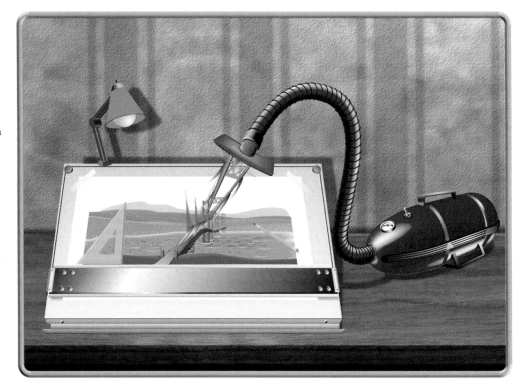

DELETE PATHS

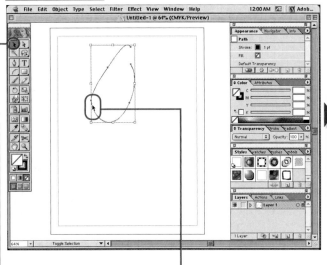

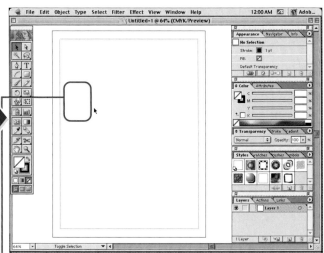

DELETE AN ENTIRE PATH

1 Click ▶.

■ You can also press **V** to
quickly switch to ▶.

2 Click any part of the path
you want to delete.

■ The path is selected and
displays a bounding box.

3 Press **Delete**.

■ The path is deleted.

■ You can also drag a
marquee box around all or
part of a path to select it.

Is there an easy way to select different parts of a path and delete them all at once?

You can add segments or paths by holding down Shift and then clicking with either the Selection or Direct Selection tool. You can then delete only the objects you select.

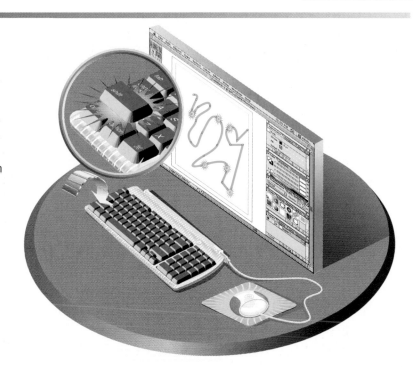

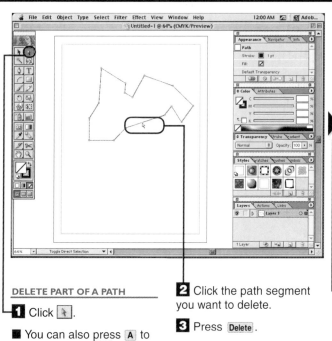

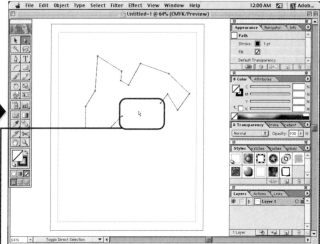

DELETE PART OF A PATH

1 Click ⬚.

■ You can also press **A** to quickly switch to ⬚.

2 Click the path segment you want to delete.

3 Press Delete.

■ The path segment is deleted.

■ You can also drag a marquee box around all or part of a path to select it.

ERASE PARTS OF A PATH

You can remove parts of a path with the Erase Tool. It works like a regular eraser, rubbing out as much or as little of a line segment as you want.

ERASE PARTS OF A PATH

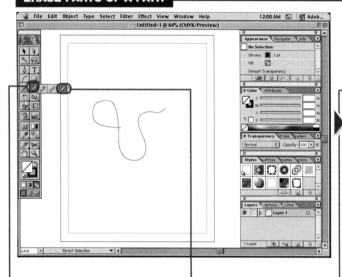

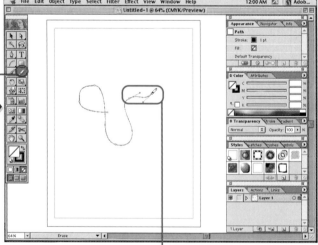

1 Click and hold ✏ in the toolbox.

■ A toolbar appears underneath ✏.

2 Drag ▶ over the Eraser tool (✏).

3 Release the mouse.

■ The toolbox changes to show ✏.

■ The ▶ changes to an upside-down pencil ✏.

4 Position the ✏ over a path segment.

5 Click and drag the ✏ repeatedly over the segment.

Can I use the eraser on lines drawn with the Pen tool?

You can use the Eraser tool () on many types of paths including ones drawn by the Pen tool (🖋). However, you should probably use it to edit freeform lines drawn with the Pencil tool (✏) instead. Pen-drawn paths are best edited using the Pen tool to place new anchor points or manipulate control handles.

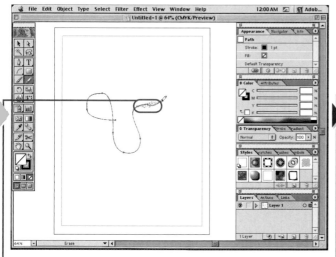

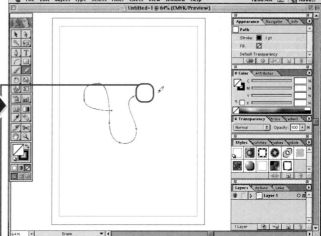

■ A dark area appears, showing where you are erasing.

6 Release the mouse.

■ The line segment you erased disappears.

■ Anchor points appear at the ends of the paths.

SMOOTH A PATH

The Smooth tool does just what it sounds like — smoothes out a line so it has a more flowing look and feel to it.

The smooth tool is especially effective on lines you draw with the Pencil tool, but you can use it with Pen-drawn paths too.

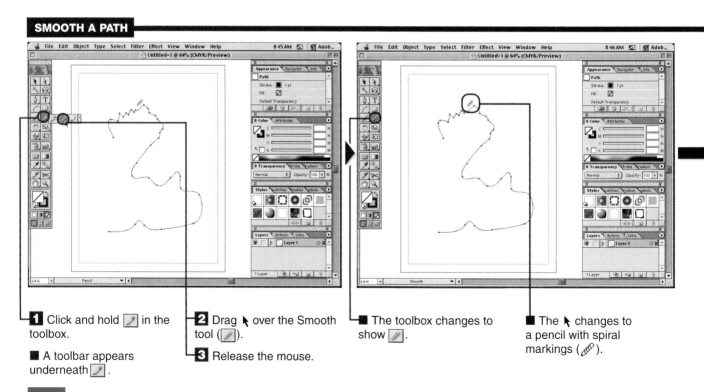

1 Click and hold 🖉 in the toolbox.

■ A toolbar appears underneath 🖉.

2 Drag ⬈ over the Smooth tool (✏️).

3 Release the mouse.

■ The toolbox changes to show ✏️.

■ The ⬈ changes to a pencil with spiral markings (✏️).

How can I change the Smooth tool properties?

You can set the Smooth tool's sensitivity to change how closely it keeps to the original line's shape. Click **Edit**, then **Preferences**, then **Type & Auto Tracing**. The Preferences dialog box appears; type values for the Auto Trace options to adjust the tool's sensitivity.

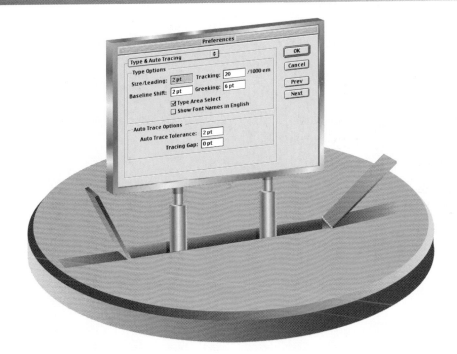

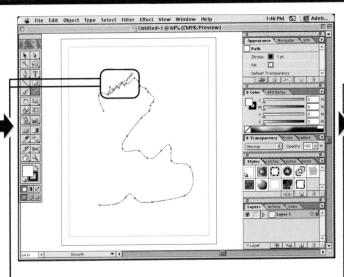

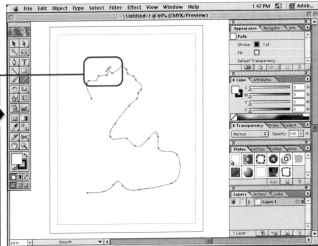

4 Position ✐ over a line segment.

5 Click and drag ✐ along the line segment.

6 Release the mouse.

■ The line smoothes out its appearance.

■ Repeat steps **4** through **6** to keep smoothing the line.

STRAY POINTS DETECTED

...EXCLUDE COMMAND IN PROGRESS...

JOINING ENDPOINTS

EXCLUDE

ADD ANCHOR POINT

CHAPTER 4

Using Advanced Path Techniques

Are you ready to move to the next level with your paths? Once you master drawing paths, you can change them using a variety of Illustrator commands. In this chapter, you learn how to add, remove, convert, average, and join points as well as how to apply certain commands to achieve the effect you want.

Add or Remove Anchor Points 74

Convert Anchor Point Type 76

Remove Excess Anchor Points 82

Clean Up Stray Anchor Points 84

Average Points 86

Join Points 88

Using Add and
  Subtract Commands 90

Using the Intersect Command.............92

Using the Exclude Command 93

Create a Compound Path 94

ADD OR REMOVE ANCHOR POINTS

You can add *anchor points* to give yourself better control over a path, or to extend an open path. Removing anchor points simplifies or changes the shape of the path. See Chapter 3 for more information about anchor points.

ADD ANCHOR POINTS

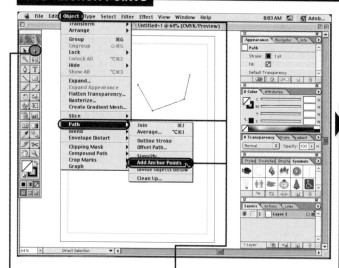

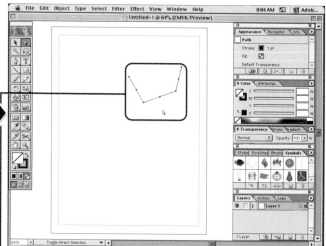

1 Select a path or group of paths with either the Direct Selection tool ( ) or Selection tool ( ).

Note: See Chapter 2 for more on selecting a path.

2 Click **Object**.

3 Click **Path**.

4 Click **Add Anchor Points**.

■ You can also click and hold on the Pen tool ( ), then select the Add Anchor Point tool ( ).

■ New anchor points appear equally between existing anchor points along each segment you selected.

■ If you use , you can add anchor points anywhere along a path.

How many anchor points does the Add Anchor Point tool add?

The Add Anchor Point tool (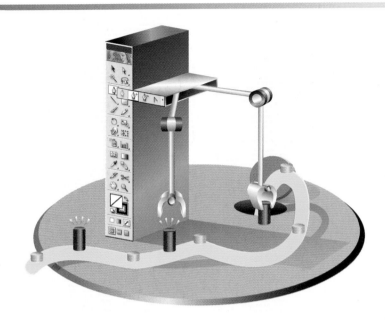) inserts a new anchor point between every pair of existing anchor points. If you select a single segment with two anchor points, Illustrator adds one new anchor point between them. If you select a square, Illustrator adds four new anchor points in the middle of each segment.

REMOVE ANCHOR POINTS

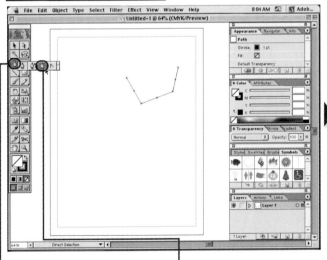

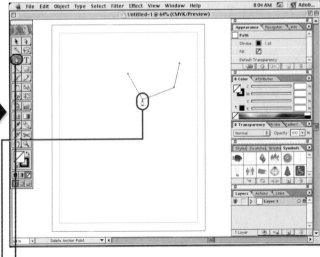

1 Select a path using ![cursor] or ![cursor].

Note: See Chapter 2 for more on selecting a path.

2 Click and hold ![tool] in the toolbox.

■ A toolbar appears underneath ![tool].

3 Drag the cursor (![pointer]) over the Remove Anchor Point tool (![tool]).

4 Release the mouse.

■ The ![pointer] changes to a pen with a minus sign ![tool].

5 Click the anchor point you want to remove.

■ The anchor point vanishes.

Note: Depending on where the anchor point is, your path changes shape.

CONVERT ANCHOR POINT TYPE

You may need to convert anchor point types as your drawing changes. Doing this gives you flexibility in using existing paths without having to redraw them just to change the anchor point type.

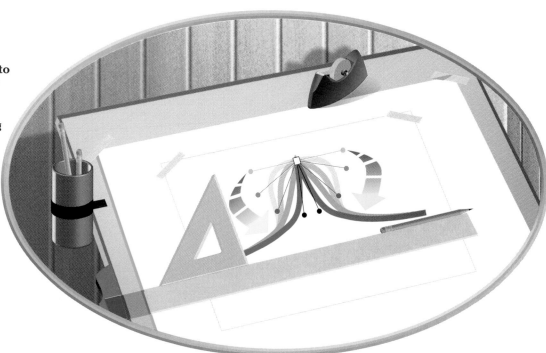

CONVERT ANCHOR POINT TYPE

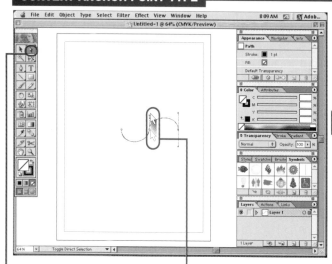

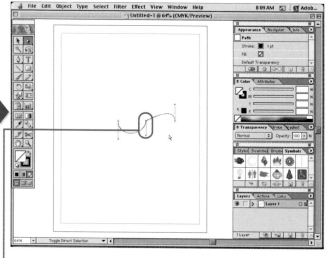

CONVERT A SMOOTH POINT TO A COMBINATION CORNER POINT

1 Click [ ].

■ The ▶ changes to a light arrow (▷).

2 Click and drag an anchor handle into the anchor point.

3 Release the mouse button.

■ A combination anchor point appears.

Note: You can also use this method to convert a curved corner point into a combination corner point.

What are the different kinds of anchor points?

You can identify anchor points by the types of lines they connect and the number of control handles.

A *smooth point* has a curved path flowing smoothly through it. It has two linked control handles.

A *straight corner point* has two straight lines meeting; it has no control handles.

A *curved corner point* has two curved lines that meet and suddenly change direction. It has two independent control handles.

A *combination corner point* has straight and curved lines meeting. It has one independent control handle.

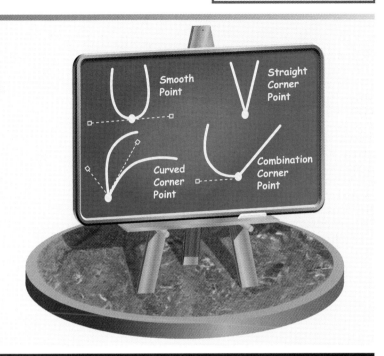

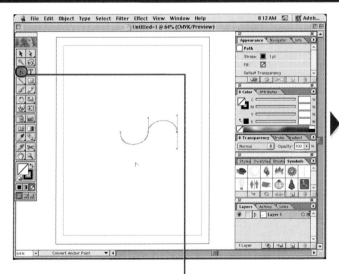

CONVERT A SMOOTH POINT TO A CURVED CORNER POINT

1 Press **Shift** + **C** to select the Convert Anchor Point tool.

■ The ▶ changes to the Convert Anchor Point tool (⌐).

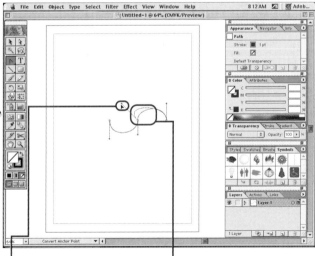

2 Click and drag a smooth anchor point control handle.

■ The smooth anchor point converts to a curved anchor point.

CONTINUED

CONVERT ANCHOR POINT TYPE

You may want to convert straight or curved corner points to smooth points if you are sketching and need to smooth out sudden changes in direction. The easiest way is to select the corner point and drag it; this converts the corner point to a smooth point.

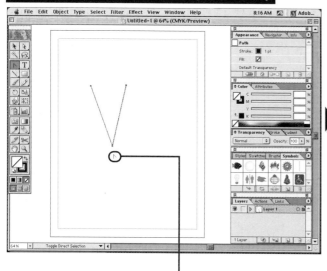

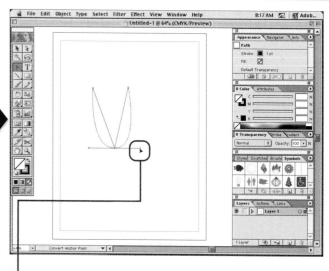

CONVERT A STRAIGHT CORNER POINT TO A SMOOTH POINT

1 Press **Shift** + **C** to select ⌐.

■ The ▸ changes to ⌐.

2 Click and drag a straight corner point.

■ The anchor point changes to a smooth corner point with linked control handles.

Note: You can also use this method to convert a curved corner point into a smooth corner point.

Where can I find all the Anchor Point tools?

The Pen tool in the toolbox has all the pen tools: the Pen tool , Add Anchor Point, Delete Anchor Point, and Convert Anchor Point tool. In some cases, you do not need to select them from the toolbox; Illustrator makes a best guess as to what tool you want to use and changes to that tool automatically.

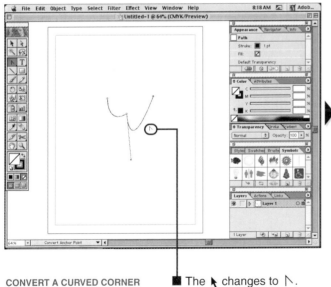

CONVERT A CURVED CORNER POINT TO A SMOOTH POINT

1 Press **Shift** + **C** to select ⌐.

■ The ▶ changes to ⌐.

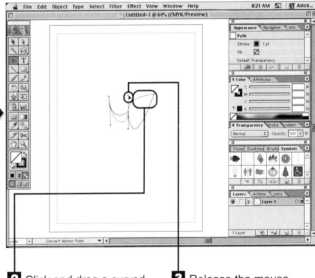

2 Click and drag a curved anchor point.

3 Release the mouse.

■ The curved corner point converts to a smooth point.

CONTINUED

CONVERT ANCHOR POINT TYPE

You can switch between curved corner and straight corner point types using the Convert Anchor Point tool. This lets you sharpen soft curves, or soften sharp angles, depending on what looks best for your illustration.

CONVERT ANCHOR POINT TYPE (CONTINUED)

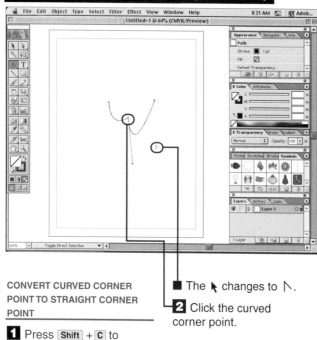

CONVERT CURVED CORNER POINT TO STRAIGHT CORNER POINT

1 Press `Shift` + `C` to select ⌐.

■ The ▸ changes to ⌐.

2 Click the curved corner point.

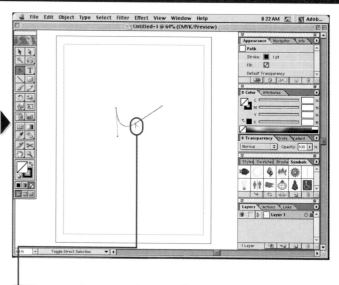

■ The curved corner point changes to a straight corner point.

Note: You can also use this method to convert combination corner points to straight corner points.

How can I more quickly switch modes with the Pen tool?

Pressing `option` or `Alt` toggles between modes on the Pen tool. Experiment moving the Pen tool over different points and paths, and pressing `option` or `Alt`. The status area tells you which tool is active.

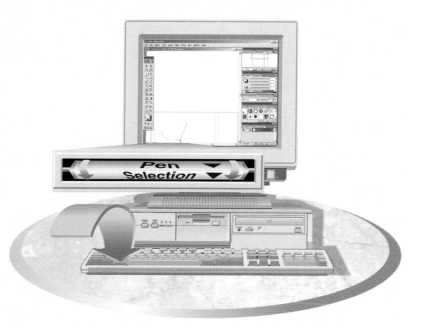

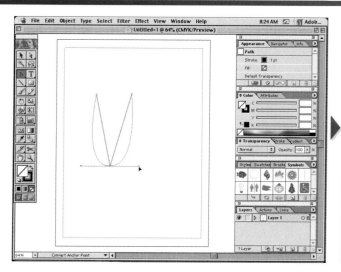

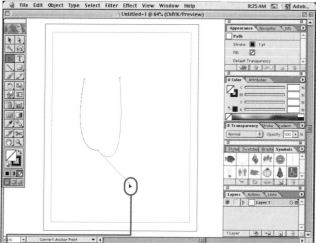

CONVERT STRAIGHT CORNER POINT TO CURVED CORNER POINT

1 Repeat steps **1** through **2** of "Convert a Straight Corner Point to a Smooth Point."

2 Click and drag one of the control handles.

■ The corner point is converted to a curved corner point.

■ You can move both control handles independently of one another.

Illustrator can remove excess anchor points from a series of paths you select, which makes the paths less complex while still retaining their shapes.

REMOVE EXCESS ANCHOR POINTS

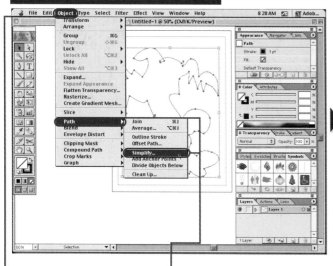

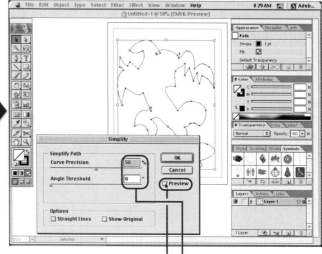

1 Select a path or group of paths using ![cursor] or ![cursor].

Note: See Chapter 2 for more about selecting paths.

2 Click **Object**.

3 Click **Path**.

4 Click **Simplify**.

■ The Simplify dialog box appears.

■ Curve Precision affects how closely the new paths should match the old.

■ Angle Threshold preserves angles less than the value selected.

5 Type your Curve Precision or Angle Threshold values.

6 Click **Preview** (□ changes to ☑).

What causes excess anchor points?

You can obtain excess anchor points when you use the Auto Trace or Streamline tools. You can also create a lot of anchor points when you use the Pencil tool to draw freehand lines.

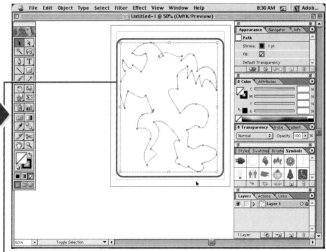

■ The dialog box displays the old and new anchor point counts.

7 Click **OK**.

■ You can see a preview of your paths.

■ Excess anchor points disappear, leaving simpler paths.

CLEAN UP STRAY ANCHOR POINTS

Stray anchor points occur when you delete line segments or paths and do not select the end points, or when you click the Add Anchor Point tool. Stray anchor points can cause printing problems later.

You should clean up stray points after every work session, and before you print.

CLEAN UP STRAY ANCHOR POINTS

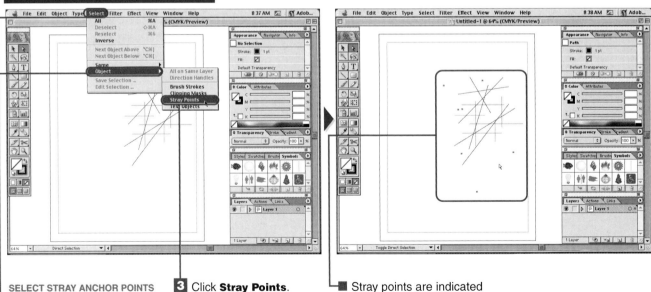

SELECT STRAY ANCHOR POINTS

1 Click **Select**.

2 Click **Object**.

3 Click **Stray Points**.

■ Stray points are indicated by a solid blue square on the artboard.

Can I use the Clean Up tool on other strays?

The tool cleans up stray anchor points, unpainted objects, and empty text paths. All of these objects are "invisible" but still exist in your artwork, and can cause problems later.

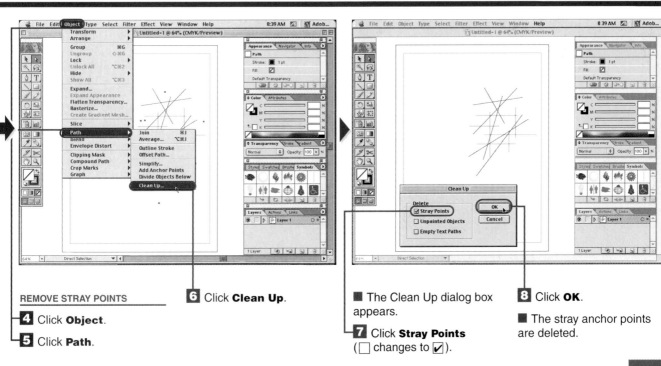

REMOVE STRAY POINTS

4 Click **Object**.

5 Click **Path**.

6 Click **Clean Up**.

■ The Clean Up dialog box appears.

7 Click **Stray Points** (☐ changes to ☑).

8 Click **OK**.

■ The stray anchor points are deleted.

AVERAGE POINTS

The Average command lets you move two or more anchor points — on the same path or on different paths — vertically, horizontally, or both, to a position that is the average of their current locations. This lets you quickly overlap anchor points or align them precisely with each other.

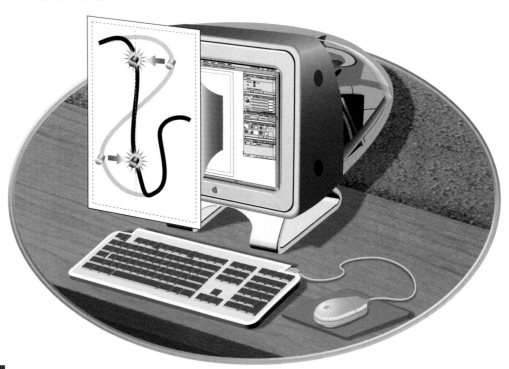

AVERAGE POINTS

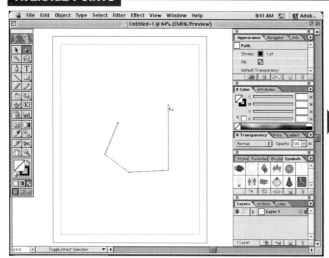

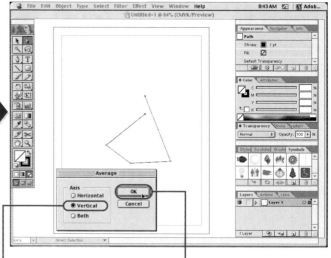

SELECT POINTS

1 Select two points by pressing **Shift** + ↖.

■ You can select points on the same path or different paths.

Note: See Chapter 2 for more on selecting paths.

2 Press ⌘ + **option** + **J** or **Ctrl** + **Alt** + **J** .

AVERAGE POINTS VERTICALLY

■ The Average dialog box appears.

3 Click **Vertical** (○ changes to ◉).

4 Click **OK**.

■ The selected points align vertically.

**Can I use the Group
Selection tool to
average the points?**

You can, but it is
not recommended.
If you use either
the Selection or the
Group Selection
tool, Illustrator
averages every
point on all the
paths, which may
result in something
that you do not
want, especially if
you average both
horizontally and
vertically.

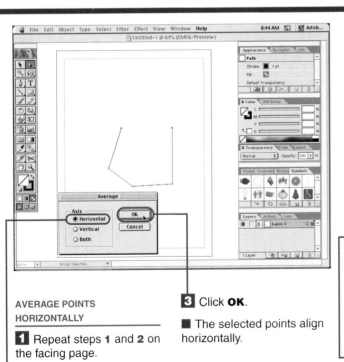

**AVERAGE POINTS
HORIZONTALLY**

1 Repeat steps **1** and **2** on
the facing page.

2 Click **Horizontal**
(○ changes to ◉).

3 Click **OK**.

■ The selected points align
horizontally.

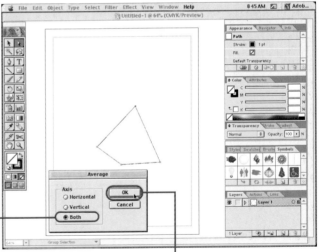

AVERAGE POINTS TOGETHER

1 Repeat steps **1** and **2** on
the facing page.

2 Click **Both** (○ changes
to ◉).

3 Click **OK**.

■ The selected points align
on top of each other.

JOIN POINTS

You can combine two points to create a single point when you place one on top of another. This acts both to close a path and reduce the number of anchor points, making it easier to work with the object.

JOIN POINTS

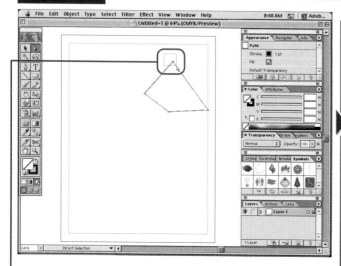

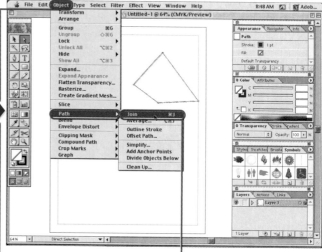

■ If you do not have overlapping points, click ![arrow] to click and drag one end point over the other.

1 Click and drag a marquee box around the two end points.

Note: See Chapter 2 for information about selecting objects, paths, and anchor points.

■ The two end points are selected.

2 Click **Object**.

3 Click **Path**.

4 Click **Join**.

■ You can also press ⌘ + **J** or **Ctrl** + **J** to join points.

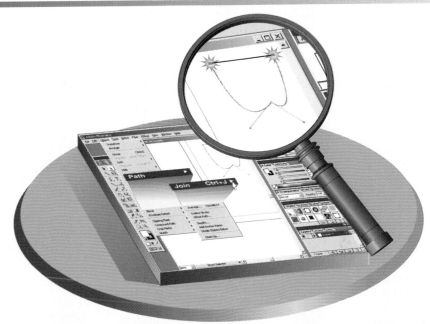

Can I join two end points with a line segment?

Yes. The Join function also links two end points with a line segment. Select two end points with 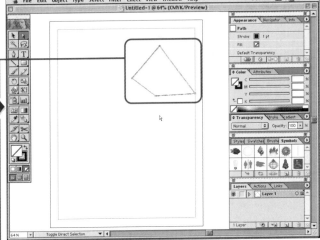, then click **Object**, **Path**, and then **Join** to make a line segment form between the points.

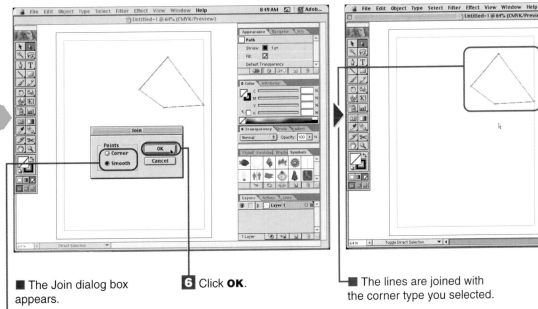

■ The Join dialog box appears.

5 Click the anchor point corner type for your joined lines (○ changes to ⦿).

6 Click **OK**.

■ The lines are joined with the corner type you selected.

USING ADD AND SUBTRACT COMMANDS

The Pathfinder Add command lets you add the area of two overlapping paths, and the Subtract command removes the non-overlapping areas. Using these commands, you can easily join shapes without drawing the individual paths.

For more on different uses for the Pathfinder tool, see Chapter 9.

USING ADD AND SUBTRACT COMMANDS

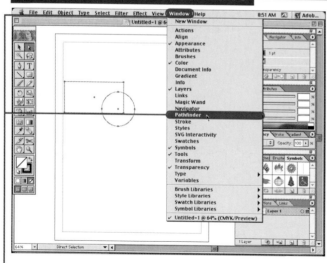

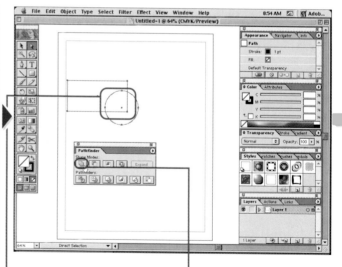

OPEN THE PATHFINDER PALETTE

1 Click **Window**.

2 Click **Pathfinder**.

■ The Pathfinder palette appears.

■ You can also press **Shift** + **F9** to open the palette.

USING THE PATHFINDER ADD COMMAND

3 Select two overlapping paths with .

4 Click the Add to Shape Area button ( ).

**Is it important
which shape
overlaps another?**

It makes a
difference when
determining which
shape you want to
add or subtract
from another one.
Try working with
different
overlapping
situations to
determine which
areas Illustrator
adds or subtracts
depending on
overlap.

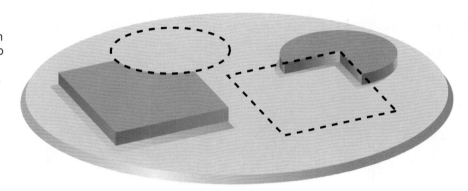

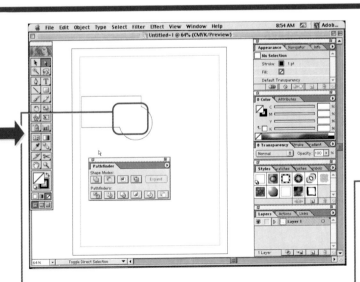

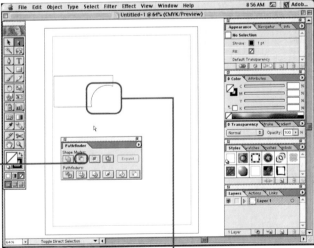

■ The overlapping area is
added to the underlying
area.

*Note: This does not delete the other
paths; you can still work with them
by selecting them again.*

**USING THE PATHFINDER
SUBTRACT COMMAND**

1 Repeat steps **1** through **3**
on the previous page.

2 Click the Subtract from
Shape Area button (⬜).

■ The overlapping area is
subtracted from the
underlying area.

*Note: This does not delete the other
paths; you can still work with them
by selecting them again.*

The Pathfinder
Intersect command
removes all parts
of paths that do
not intersect,
leaving only the
intersecting paths
remaining. This is a
quick way to
remove extraneous
or overhanging
areas without
having to edit and
redraw the paths.

USING THE INTERSECT COMMAND

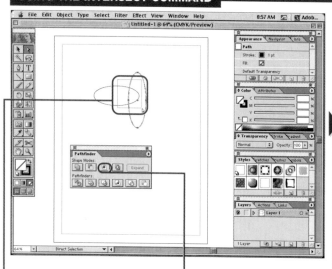

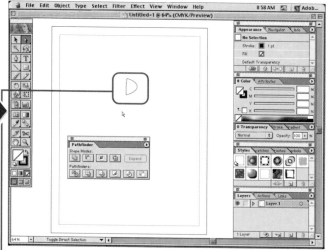

1 Use 🔲 to select
intersecting paths.

*Note: See Chapter 2 for more on
selecting paths.*

2 Click the Intersect Shape
Areas button (🔲).

■ Only the intersecting
areas remain.

*Note: This action does not delete the
other paths; you can still work with
them by selecting them again.*

The Pathfinder Exclude command removes intersecting areas that you have selected. It works as the opposite of the Intersect command. You often use the Exclude command to join together closed areas, such as overlapping text that you have converted to paths.

The Exclude effect is most noticeable if you have applied a fill to a path area.

USING THE EXCLUDE COMMAND

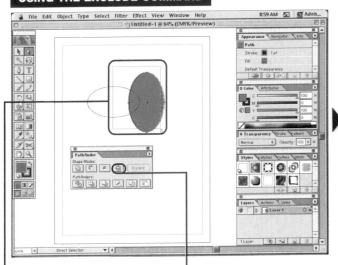

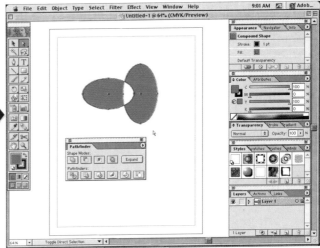

1 Use ![cursor] to select intersecting paths.

2 Click the Exclude Shape Areas button (![button]).

■ The selected areas remain.

Note: See Chapter 2 for more on paths.

CREATE A COMPOUND PATH

A compound path contains two or more paths that Illustrator fills so that holes appear where paths overlap, like rivet holes in a metal beam.

You commonly use compound path effects for text, such as the capital letter *O* or lowercase *g*.

CREATE A COMPOUND PATH

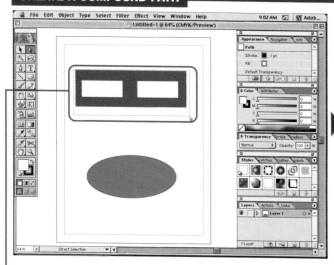

1 Select a group of paths using ▶ or the Group Selection tool (▶).

Note: See Chapter 2 for more on selecting objects.

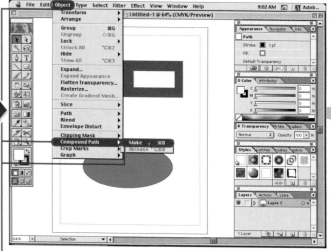

2 Click **Object**.

3 Click **Compound Path**.

4 Click **Make**.

■ The objects become grouped as a compound path.

Note: Fill was added for clarity.

Where can I find out more about compound paths?

An excellent resource that goes into depth about compound paths is the *Illustrator 10 Bible* (Hungry Minds, Inc., 2002), and we highly recommend it if you want to understand the complex details on compound paths.

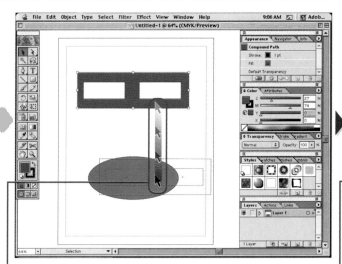

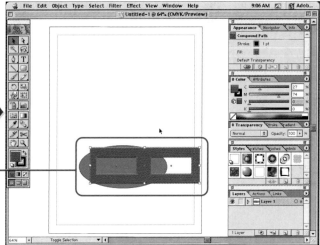

5 Click and drag the compound path over another object.

6 Release the mouse button.

■ The compound path has holes that enable you to see the object underneath.

CHAPTER 5

Working with Objects

Working with objects is one of the easiest and quickest ways to create new and interesting artwork. This chapter shows you how to create, manipulate, and group objects using the powerful tools you find in Illustrator.

Draw a Rectangle or
   Rounded Rectangle 98

Draw an Ellipse or Circle 100

Draw Regular Polygons 102

Draw Stars 103

Create a Spiral 104

Create a Rectangular Grid 106

Create a Polar Grid 108

Rotate an Object 110

Reflect an Object 111

Scale an Object 112

Apply Shear to an Object 114

Align Objects 116

Move Objects Forward and Back 118

Group and Ungroup Objects 120

Cut Objects with the Knife Tool 122

DRAW A RECTANGLE OR ROUNDED RECTANGLE

Rectangles are one of the most frequently used objects in artwork. Fortunately, with Illustrator they are also the easiest to draw.

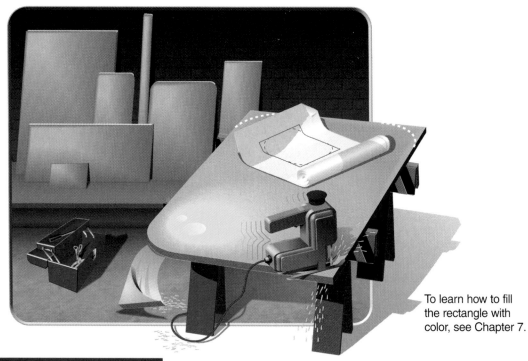

To learn how to fill the rectangle with color, see Chapter 7.

DRAW A RECTANGLE OR ROUNDED RECTANGLE

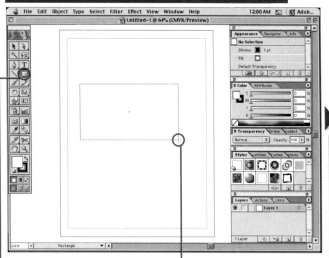

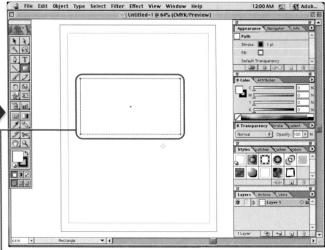

DRAW A RECTANGLE

1 Click the Rectangle tool (▢).

■ The cursor changes to crosshairs (-¦-).

2 Click and drag -¦- on your artwork.

■ You can drag -¦- to size and resize the rectangle.

3 Release the mouse.

■ A rectangle appears.

■ To draw a square, hold the Shift key (**Shift**) while you drag the mouse.

How do I create exact dimensions for rectangles?

You can create exact dimensions for rectangles by selecting a rectangle tool then clicking once on the artboard. A dialog box appears, and you can type exact dimensions. The Rounded Rectangle tool also lets you specify the rounded corner's radius.

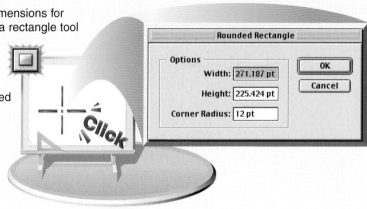

Rounded Rectangle

Options
Width: 271.187 pt
Height: 225.424 pt
Corner Radius: 12 pt

OK
Cancel

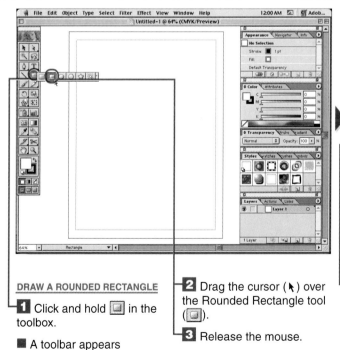

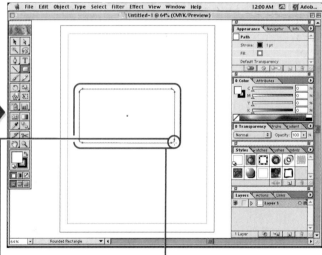

DRAW A ROUNDED RECTANGLE

1 Click and hold 🔲 in the toolbox.

■ A toolbar appears underneath 🔲.

2 Drag the cursor (➤) over the Rounded Rectangle tool (🔲).

3 Release the mouse.

■ The ➤ changes to ⊹.

4 Click and drag ⊹ on your artwork.

■ You can drag ⊹ to size and resize the rectangle.

■ A rounded rectangle appears.

■ To draw a rounded square, hold Shift while you drag the mouse.

DRAW AN ELLIPSE OR CIRCLE

You can draw simple ellipses and circles for use in your artwork.

To fill your newly created shape with color, see Chapter 7.

DRAW AN ELLIPSE OR CIRCLE

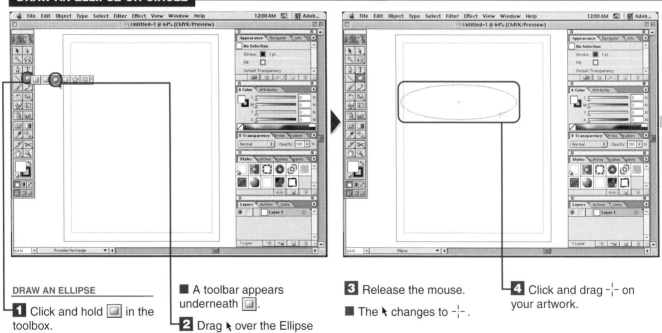

DRAW AN ELLIPSE

1 Click and hold ▣ in the toolbox.

■ A toolbar appears underneath ▣.

2 Drag ▶ over the Ellipse tool (◯).

3 Release the mouse.

■ The ▶ changes to -¦-.

4 Click and drag -¦- on your artwork.

How do I create exact dimensions for ellipses and circles?

You can create exact dimensions for ellipses and circles by selecting the Ellipse tool (⬭) then clicking once on the artboard. A dialog box appears, and you can type exact dimensions for your ellipse. A circle has equal dimensions in the Height and Width boxes.

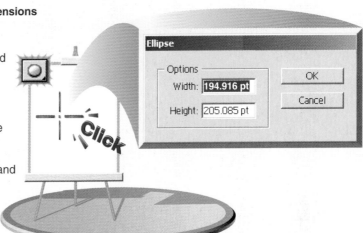

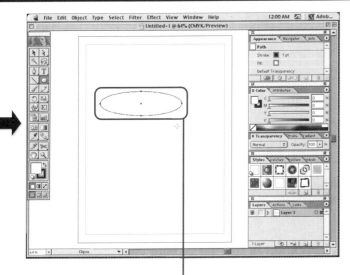

■ You can drag -¦- to size and resize the ellipse.

5 Release the mouse.

■ An ellipse appears.

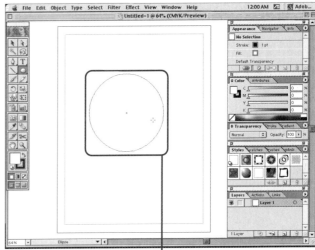

DRAW A CIRCLE

1 Repeat steps **1** through **4** from the previous page.

2 Press Shift while you drag the mouse.

■ A circle appears.

DRAW REGULAR POLYGONS

You can draw regular polygons quickly with Illustrator. You create a regular polygon by making its sides and angles of equal length.

To create a polygon, you must specify the radius — the distance from the center to a vertex — and the number of sides.

DRAW REGULAR POLYGONS

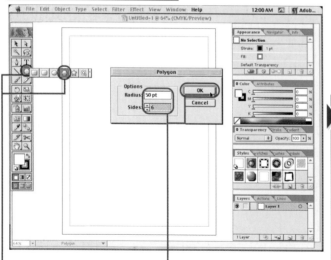

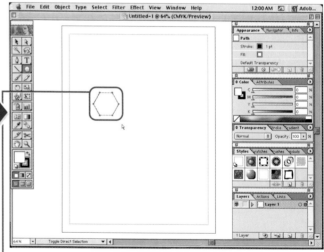

1 Click and hold 🔲.

2 Drag and release ➤ over the Polygon tool (🔲) from the toolbar that appears.

3 Click once on the artboard.

■ The Polygon dialog box appears.

4 Type the radius and number of sides.

5 Click **OK**.

■ The regular polygon appears.

Note: You can draw irregular polygons with the Line or Pen tools. For more on these tools, see Chapters 3 and 4.

You can draw stars with nearly any number of points and of any size using the Star tool.

To create a star, you must specify two radii and the number of points for the star.

Radius 1 is closest to the center, and radius 2 is the farthest point from the center.

DRAW STARS

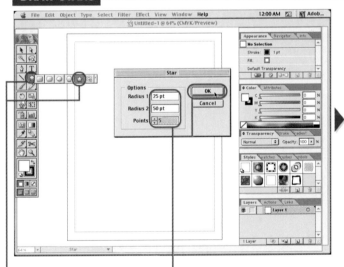

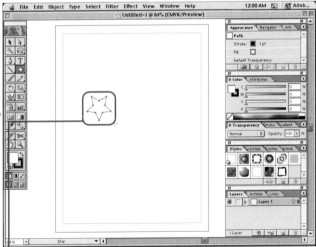

1 Click and hold ▣.

2 Drag and release ▸ over ☆ in the toolbar that appears.

3 Click once on the artboard.

■ The Star dialog box appears.

4 Type both radii and number of points.

5 Click **OK**.

■ The star appears.

CREATE A SPIRAL

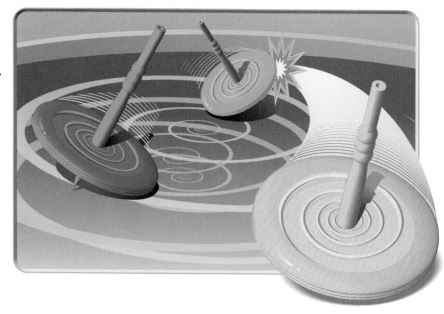

Illustrator has a great tool for drawing smooth, evenly spaced spirals. Spirals add a festive, creative flair, and are useful for producing paths for text to follow.

See Chapter 8 for information about creating text paths.

CREATE A SPIRAL

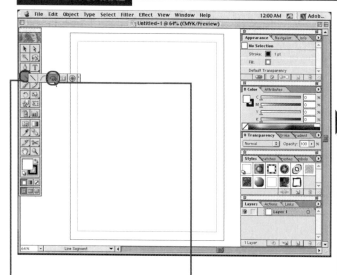

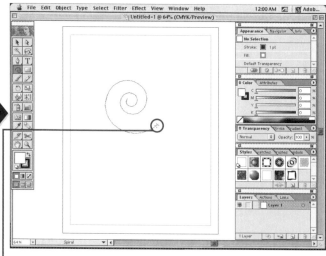

1 Click and hold the Line Segment tool (⬚) in the toolbox.

■ A toolbar appears underneath ⬚.

2 Drag ▶ over the Spiral tool (◎).

3 Release the mouse.

■ The ▶ changes to ‐¦‐.

4 Click and drag ‐¦‐ on the artboard.

■ A spiral appears on the artboard.

Can I draw different types of spirals?

Yes. Click the Spiral tool (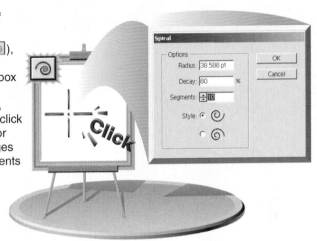), and then click once on the artboard. The Spiral dialog box appears, and you can type values for the radius, decay, and segment. You can also click a style — either clockwise or counterclockwise (O changes to ⦿). There are four segments in each full turn of a spiral; decay controls how each wind of the spiral decreases relative to the previous wind.

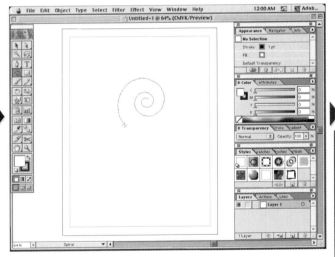

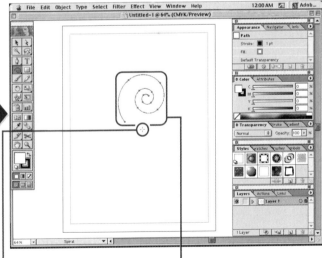

■ You can rotate -¦- to change the spiral's orientation.

■ You can press **Shift** while dragging to constrain the spiral to 45° increments.

5 Release the mouse.

■ A spiral is drawn on your artboard.

CREATE A RECTANGULAR GRID

Grids are handy for organizing other objects or elements in your artwork. You can quickly configure the Rectangular Grid for the number of rows and columns you need.

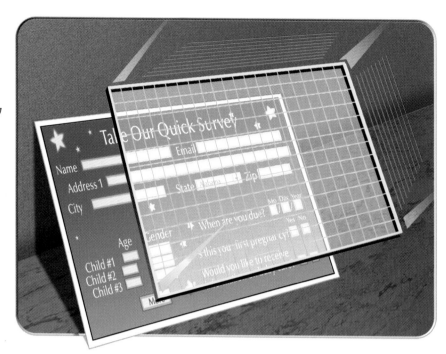

CREATE A RECTANGULAR GRID

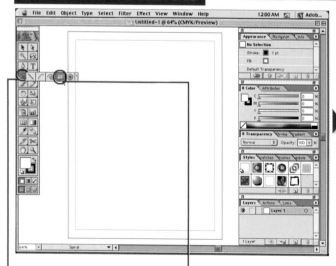

1 Click and hold ▨ in the toolbox.

■ A toolbar appears underneath ▨.

2 Drag ▸ over the Rectangular Grid tool (▦).

3 Release the mouse.

■ The ▸ changes to -¦-.

4 Click once on the artboard.

■ The Rectangular Grid Tool Options dialog box appears.

Do I have to type the new grid settings every time?

Like most of the other tools in the Toolbox, the Rectangular Grid tool remembers the last settings you used. You can click and drag on the artboard to create a grid with the same dimensions as the previous grid.

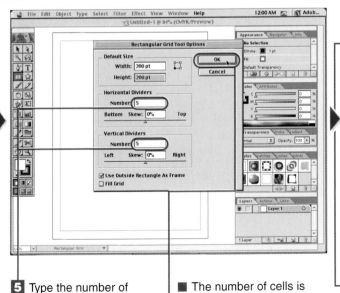

5 Type the number of horizontal and vertical cells.

■ The number of cells is one more than the number of dividers.

6 Click **OK**.

■ A rectangular grid appears in your artwork.

CREATE A POLAR GRID

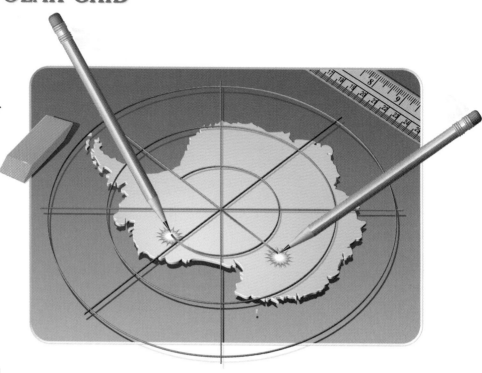

You can use polar grids to create fun effects, such as radar screens, or useful illustrations like maps of Antarctica.

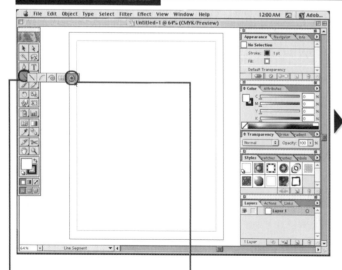

1 Click and hold ◺ in the toolbox.

■ A toolbar appears underneath ◺.

2 Drag ▶ over the Polar Grid tool (⊕).

3 Release the mouse.

■ The ▶ changes to ⁻ᵢ⁻.

4 Click once on the artboard.

■ The Polar Grid Tool Options dialog box appears.

Is the Properties dialog box the only way to change my polar grid's appearance?

No. You can use keyboard shortcuts to change the grid's appearance. The Polar Grid tool uses a number of keyboard keys to adjust the look and drawing method that the Polar Grid Properties dialog box does not list. You can press the `Spacebar` to move the grid while drawing, change the number of radials and concentric rings with the keyboard arrow keys, and several other shortcuts. Check the online help for more information.

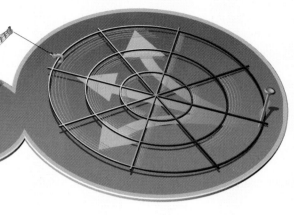

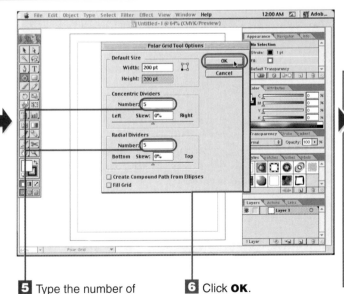

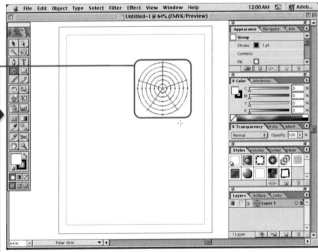

5 Type the number of concentric dividers and radial dividers.

6 Click **OK**.

■ A polar grid appears in your artwork.

■ You can also click ⊞ and then click and drag on the artboard to automatically create a polar grid.

ROTATE AN OBJECT

You can rotate an object using the Rotate tool to align it with other elements in your artwork. You can also rotate paths or grouped objects with the Rotate tool.

ROTATE AN OBJECT

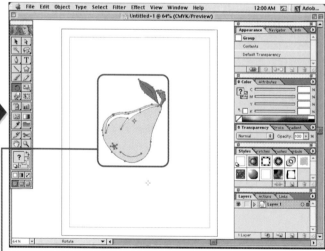

1 Draw an object with an Illustrator tool.

Note: See the previous sections in this chapter to draw shapes.

2 Click the Rotate tool (⟳) in the toolbox.

3 Click and drag an object on the artboard.

■ The object rotates around its center.

4 Release the mouse.

■ The object keeps its new orientation.

■ To rotate around a different point than the object's center, first click a point on the artboard, then click and drag the object.

You can reflect an
object to align it with
other elements in
your artwork.

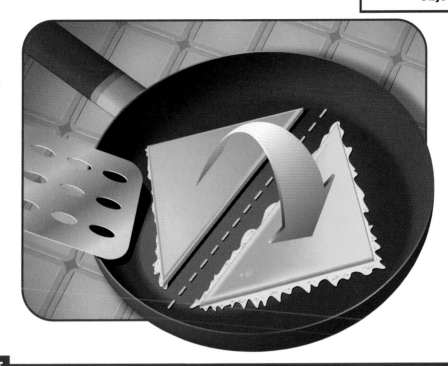

REFLECT AN OBJECT

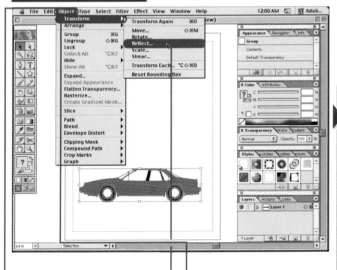

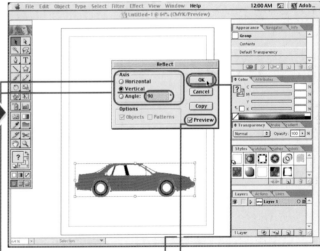

1 Select an object using
the Selection tool (▶).

Note: See Chapter 2 to select an object.

2 Click **Object**.

3 Click **Transform**.

4 Click **Reflect**.

■ The Reflect properties
dialog box appears.

5 Select a reflection axis
(○ changes to ◉).

■ Alternatively, you can type
a specific reflection angle.

6 Select **Preview** to see
how your reflection will look
(□ changes to ☑).

7 Click **OK**.

■ The object is reflected
along the axis you selected.

SCALE AN OBJECT

You may find, after drawing an object in one size, that you need to resize to make it fit your artwork. You can resize your objects by setting scaling properties or by dragging the bounding box.

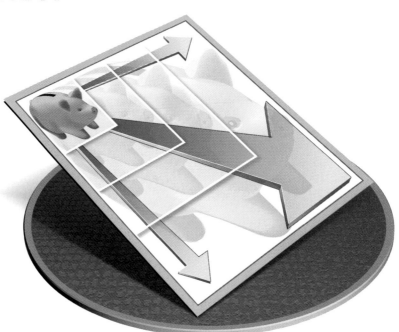

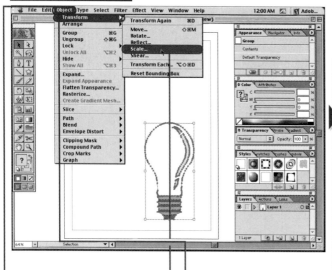

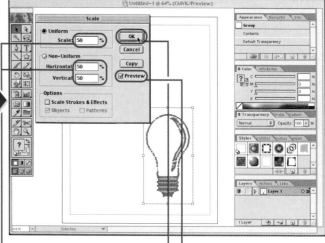

SCALE USING OBJECT PROPERTIES

1 Select an object using ▶.

Note: See Chapter 2 to select an object.

2 Click **Object**.

3 Click **Transform**.

4 Click **Scale**.

■ The Scale properties dialog box appears.

5 Type the scaling percentage you want to apply to the object.

■ You can apply non-uniform scaling by clicking that option (○ changes to ●) and typing values into the boxes.

■ You can click **Preview** (☐ changes to ☑) to see how your scaled object will look.

6 Click **OK**.

Can I use the bounding box to scale objects?

The bounding box resizes but does not scale objects — in other words, dragging a bounding box handle does not maintain a precise relationship among all of an object's component parts. If you need precision, you should scale instead of using the bounding box.

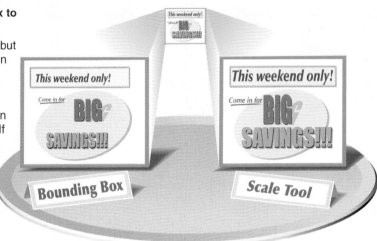

Bounding Box

Scale Tool

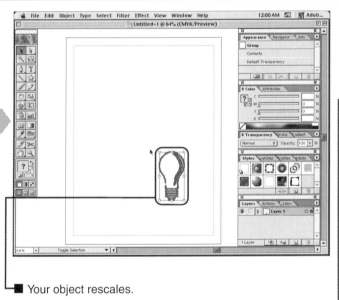

■ Your object rescales.

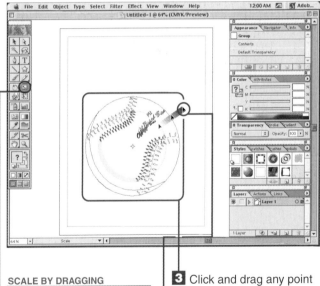

SCALE BY DRAGGING

1 Click the Scale tool (🔲).

2 Click the artboard to set the scaling point.

3 Click and drag any point on the object.

4 Release the mouse.

■ Your object rescales.

APPLY SHEAR TO AN OBJECT

You can apply shear to an object to make it tilt or slant in a different direction. You can do this to help force perspective or to add a feeling of motion to objects.

APPLY SHEAR TO AN OBJECT

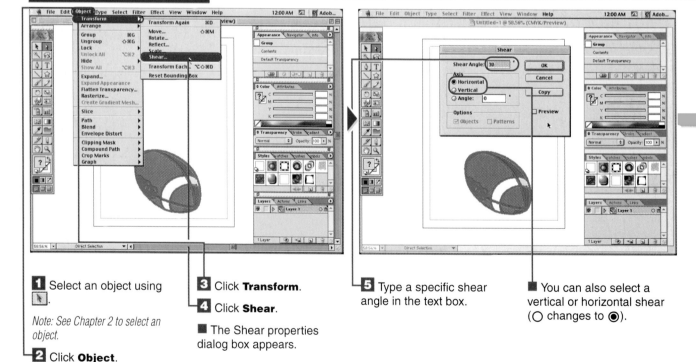

1 Select an object using [cursor].

Note: See Chapter 2 to select an object.

2 Click **Object**.

3 Click **Transform**.

4 Click **Shear**.

■ The Shear properties dialog box appears.

5 Type a specific shear angle in the text box.

■ You can also select a vertical or horizontal shear (○ changes to ●).

Is there another way to apply shear?

You can use the Shear tool to apply shear freehand. Click and hold the Scale tool (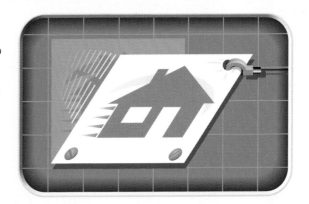), then drag over the Shear tool (   ). You can then click and drag anywhere on an object and apply shear to it; Illustrator applies the last Shear settings you used.

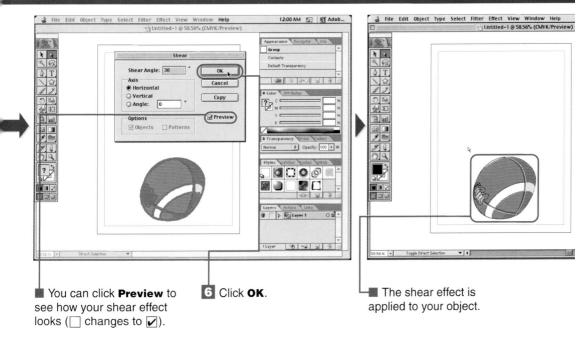

■ You can click **Preview** to see how your shear effect looks (☐ changes to ☑).

6 Click **OK**.

■ The shear effect is applied to your object.

ALIGN OBJECTS

Often in artwork you need to align objects with an imaginary line, or distribute them evenly in your artwork. The ability to do this is controlled by the Align palette.

ALIGN OBJECTS

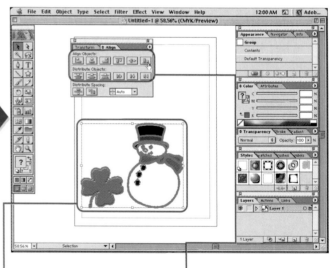

ALIGN OR DISTRIBUTE OBJECTS

1 Click **Window**.

2 Click **Align**.

■ The Align palette appears.

3 Select the objects you want to align using 🔺 or 🔺.

Note: See Chapter 2 to select an object.

4 Click an alignment option.

■ The selected objects align per your specifications.

How do I specify an exact alignment amount?

The Align palette has a Distribute Spacing setting. You can leave it on Auto, or you can type in a distribution spacing value, either positive or negative. Alternatively, you can click ▣ to increment your values. Illustrator uses the new value as your spacing setting. You can access this new value, as well as the Auto setting, by clicking ▾ to the right of the box.

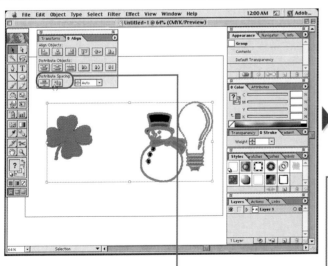

DISTRIBUTE OBJECTS EVENLY

1 Repeat steps **1** through **3** on the previous page.

2 Click a Distribute Spacing option.

■ The objects distribute per your specifications.

MOVE OBJECTS FORWARD AND BACK

Sometimes you have overlapping objects and need to change the order in which the layers stack. You can use commands to move objects forward and back within the same layer to change overlap order.

MOVE OBJECTS FORWARD AND BACK

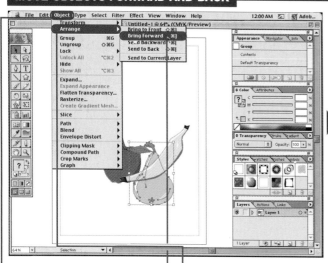

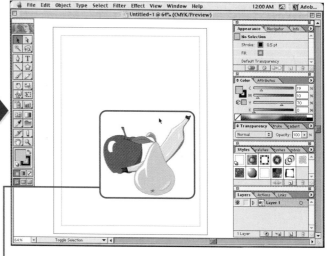

MOVE AN OBJECT FORWARD

1 Select an object that is overlapped by another using ![] or ![].

Note: See Chapter 2 to select an object.

2 Click **Object**.

3 Click **Arrange**.

4 Click **Bring Forward**.

■ The selected object moves forward one position in the stack.

■ You can press ⌘ + **]** or **Ctrl** + **]** to quickly move the object forward.

■ You can press ⌘ + **Shift** + **]** or **Ctrl** + **Shift** + **]** to quickly move the object to the front.

When I apply the Bring Forwards or Send Backwards command, my object does not move. Why not?

You may have your objects on different layers, rather than overlapping in the same layer. See Chapter 11 for more information on moving objects between layers.

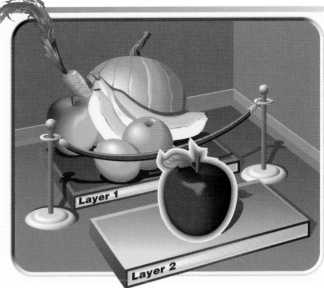

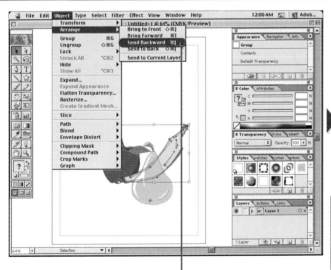

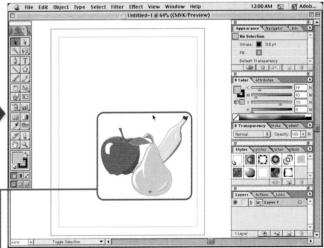

MOVE AN OBJECT BACK

1 Repeat steps **1** through **3** on the previous page.

2 Click **Send Backward**.

■ The selected object moves back one position in the stack.

■ You can press ⌘ + [or Ctrl + [to quickly move the object backward.

■ You can press ⌘ + Shift + [or Ctrl + Shift + [to quickly send the object to the back.

GROUP AND UNGROUP OBJECTS

Frequently you want to treat separate objects as a group, either for moving them or applying effects to them. You do this by grouping objects. You can also ungroup objects to work with them individually.

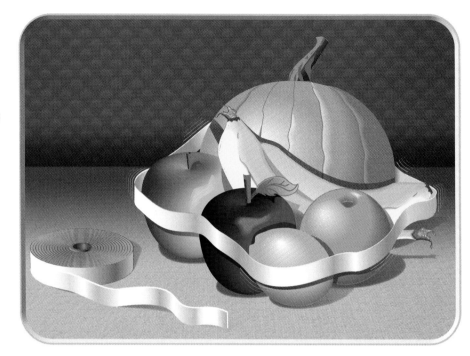

GROUP AND UNGROUP OBJECTS

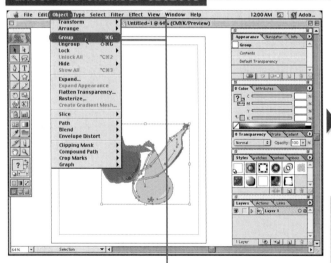

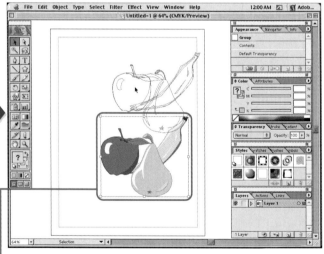

Note: See Chapter 2 to select an object.

GROUP OBJECTS

1 Select the objects you want to make part of the group using any of the selection tools.

2 Click **Object**.

3 Click **Group**.

■ The objects are linked together as a group.

■ You can also press ⌘ + **G** or **Ctrl** + **G** to group selected objects together.

What happens when I group together objects from different layers?

When you group together objects from different layers, they all move to the top layer and form a group there. This means that the stacking order may change and your artwork's appearance may rearrange. You can click Undo (⌘ + Z) when you do not intend to group objects from different layers.

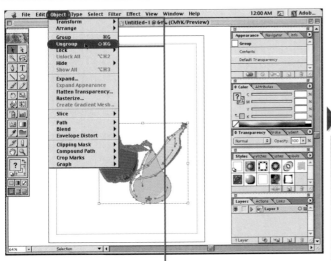

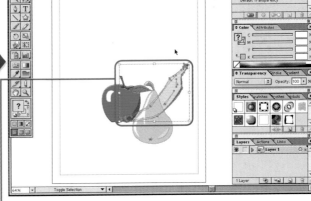

UNGROUP OBJECTS

1 Select the group of objects using any of the selection tools.

Note: See Chapter 2 to select an object.

2 Click **Object**.

3 Click **Ungroup**.

■ The individual objects are ungrouped.

■ You can also press ⌘ + Shift + G or Ctrl + Shift + G to quickly ungroup a selected group of objects.

CUT OBJECTS WITH THE KNIFE TOOL

The Knife tool cuts objects along a freehand path, leaving separate objects with closed paths behind. You use the Knife tool when you need to cut through path areas, not just a single path.

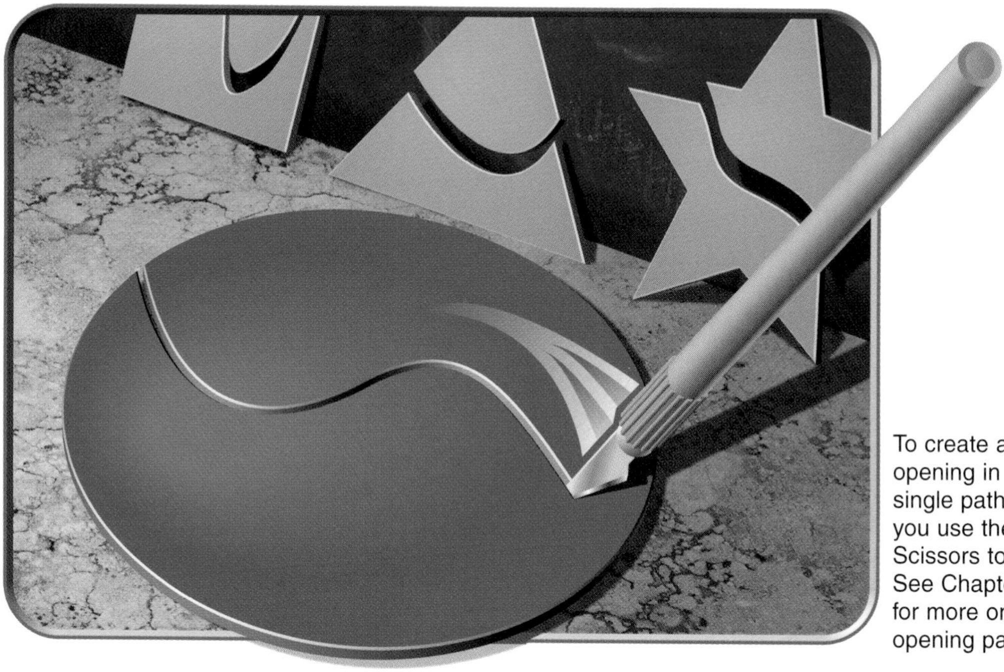

To create an opening in a single path, you use the Scissors tool. See Chapter 3 for more on opening paths.

CUT OBJECTS WITH THE KNIFE TOOL

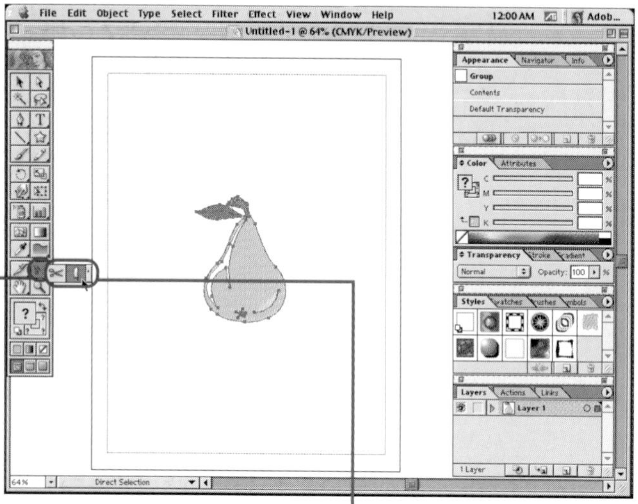

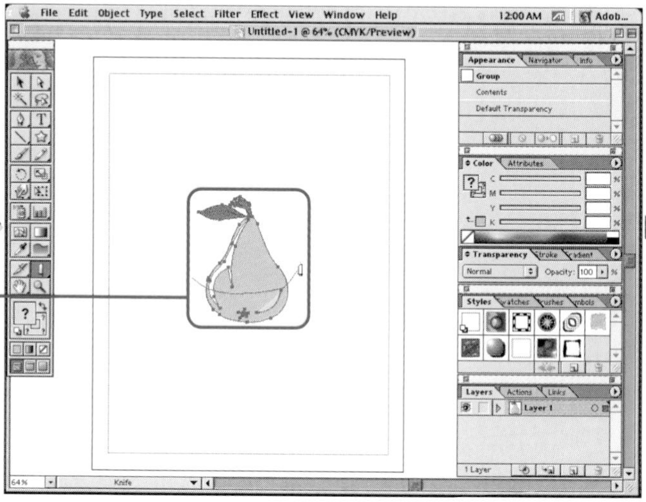

1 Click and hold the Scissors tool ( ) in the toolbox.

■ A toolbar appears underneath .

2 Drag the over the Knife tool ( ).

3 Release the mouse.

■ The changes to .

4 Click and drag the through the objects you want to cut apart.

■ Release the mouse.

■ A path appears along the knife cut.

Is there a way to use the Knife tool to cut straight lines?

You can make straight cuts through path areas by pressing `option` + `Shift` or `Alt` while dragging the mouse.

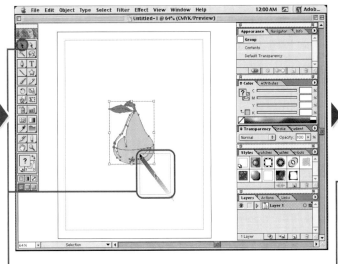

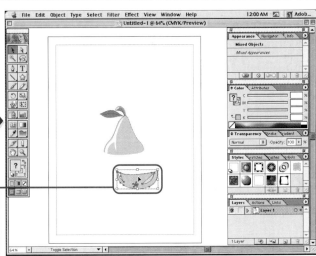

5 Click 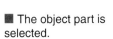.

6 Click and drag through one part of the object.

■ The object part is selected.

7 Click and drag the selected object.

■ The two objects separate.

CHAPTER 6

Advanced Object Effects and Symbols

Illustrator has a variety of tools to alter your artwork with a click of a button. In this chapter, you learn how to give your artwork that added creative flare, by applying and creating your own effects or symbols.

Understanding Object Effects and Symbols 126

Warp Objects 128

Using the Free Transform Tool 130

Apply the Envelope Distort Tool 132

Using the Liquify Tools.....................134

Create a Flare 136

Create a Symbol 138

Insert and Delete Symbols 140

Edit and Update Symbols 142

Apply Symbol Effects 144

Object effects and symbols are at the core of Illustrator's power as a design tool. By experimenting with various effects, you can discover how much you can do with Illustrator to enhance your artwork. And with the addition of symbol support, Illustrator 10 is the premiere tool for print and Web-based artwork.

What are Object Effects?

Object effects are specialized tools that produce transformations or alterations to objects in Illustrator. These effects do in seconds what would otherwise take hours to hand-draw using other tools.

Distortion Effects

Distortion effects geometrically distort an image, reshaping it or making it appear warped or crunched by gravity, water, or other "invisible" medium. You may find these some of the most interesting effects with which to work; like all effects, however, less is sometimes more.

Symbols and Illustrator

Symbols are reusable objects that you can edit and save in a palette. After you save it, you can repeatedly use that symbol in your artwork without having to create it again. Symbols also have the benefit of reducing your illustration's file size significantly, depending on how many symbols you use in your artwork.

When to Use Symbols

You should use symbols whenever you have a repeating design element or motif in your artwork, especially Web-based art. Symbols give you the flexibility of changing the underlying design and automatically applying that change to all other occurrences in your art. This is a great benefit when you need to make small changes, and you do not want to open and modify every illustration.

Best Types of Symbols

The best types of symbols are graphic elements that you can easily reuse throughout your artwork. This includes simple geometric objects, like stars or circles, and button images that you can reuse with different actions associated with the same button.

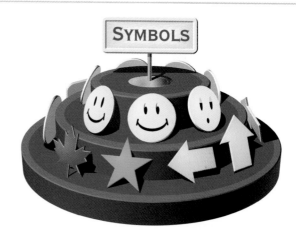

WARP OBJECTS

The Warp tool provides a wide variety of easy-to-apply effects for objects. You can quickly add bulge, flag, fish, or shell-like effects to your objects.

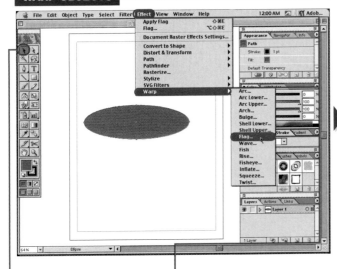

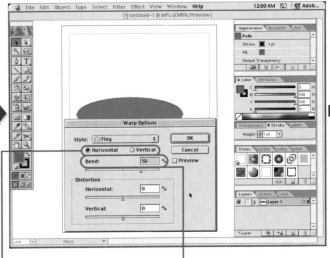

1 Select an object using the Selection tool (🔖).

Note: For more on selecting objects, see Chapter 2.

2 Click **Effect**.

3 Click **Warp**.

4 Click **Flag**.

■ The Warp Options dialog box appears.

5 Click the alignment you want (○ changes to ◉).

■ The alignment determines whether the object "waves" up or down.

6 Type the amount of bend in the object.

■ The bend determines whether the object "waves" to the left or the right.

Which effects can I apply to objects?

All of the Warp effects are available from the Effects menu, which you access by clicking **Effect** and then **Warp**. The effects appear in a submenu. You can also access effects by clicking ⬍ or ⬍ in the Style box located on the Warp Options dialog box.

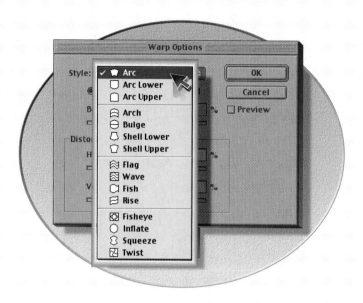

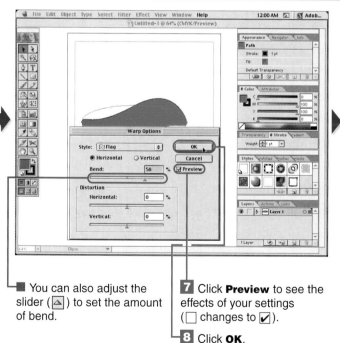

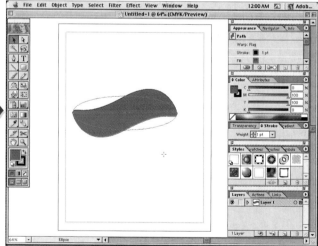

■ You can also adjust the slider (△) to set the amount of bend.

7 Click **Preview** to see the effects of your settings (☐ changes to ☑).

8 Click **OK**.

■ Illustrator applies the Flag effect to your object.

Note: The original object paths are still present, enabling you to change the object's shape without changing the effect applied to it.

USING THE FREE TRANSFORM TOOL

The Free Transform tool enables you to rotate, scale, reflect, and shear all at once.

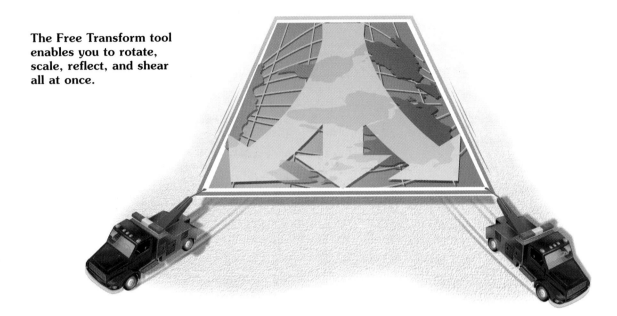

USING THE FREE TRANSFORM TOOL

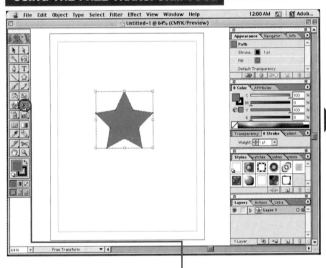

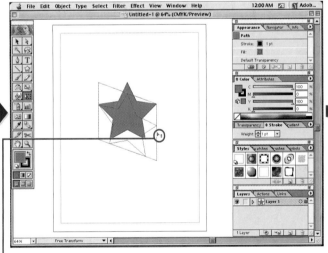

1 Select an object or group of objects.

Note: For more on selecting objects, see Chapter 2.

2 Click the Free Transform tool (▦).

3 Click and drag a side handle (▸) on the bounding box.

4 Press and hold ⌘ or Ctrl.

Illustrator does not distort an object when I first hold down a key on the keyboard then click and drag the mouse ⤢. Why not?

This is another one of Illustrator's quirks. Instead of holding down a key and then dragging the ⤢, you must start dragging first, then press and hold a key on the keyboard. You can then distort objects.

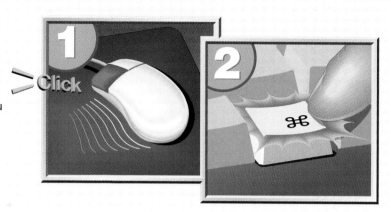

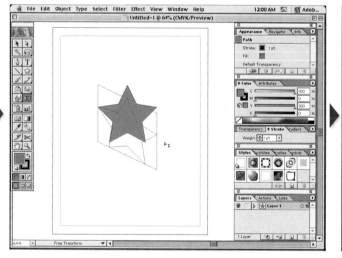

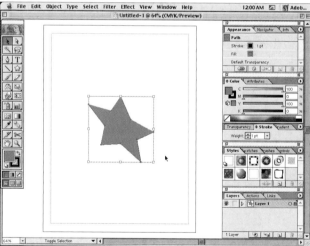

■ The object distorts only the selected edge.

5 Release the mouse button.

■ The object remains distorted.

Note: The original object paths are still present, enabling you to change the object's shape without changing the effect applied to it.

APPLY THE ENVELOPE DISTORT TOOL

The Envelope Distort tool is new in Illustrator 10. It enables you to create an envelope out of any path you draw, so you can warp text, images, or other elements with the envelope.

APPLY THE ENVELOPE DISTORT TOOL

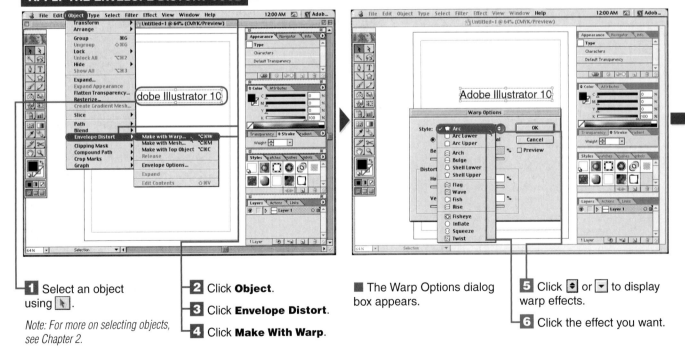

1 Select an object using ▢.

Note: For more on selecting objects, see Chapter 2.

2 Click **Object**.

3 Click **Envelope Distort**.

4 Click **Make With Warp**.

■ The Warp Options dialog box appears.

5 Click ▢ or ▢ to display warp effects.

6 Click the effect you want.

What other settings can I adjust for the Envelope Distort tool?

You can change a number of other Envelope Distort settings:

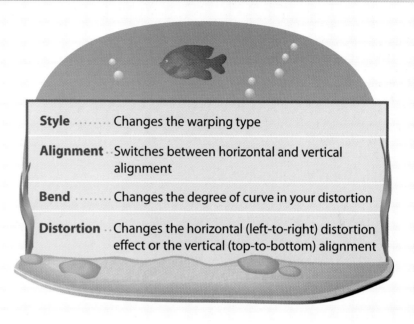

Style	Changes the warping type
Alignment ..	Switches between horizontal and vertical alignment
Bend	Changes the degree of curve in your distortion
Distortion ..	Changes the horizontal (left-to-right) distortion effect or the vertical (top-to-bottom) alignment

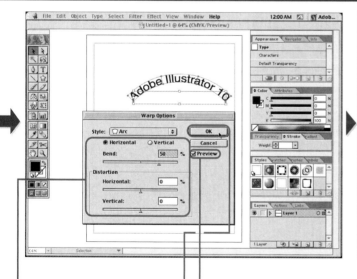

7 Select your warp settings.

Note: For more information on the various warp settings, see the section "Warp Objects," earlier in this chapter.

8 Click **Preview** to see the effects of your settings (○ changes to ●).

9 Click **OK**.

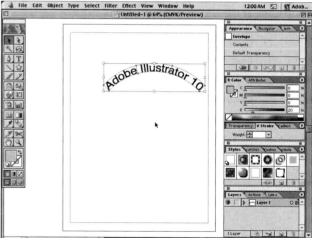

■ Your Envelope Distort settings take effect.

Note: You can edit the underlying object without having to delete and reapply the Envelope Distort effect.

USING THE LIQUIFY TOOLS

The Liquify tool is new in Illustrator 10 and provides seven new warping effects, from twirls to crystallization or wrinkles.

USING THE LIQUIFY TOOLS

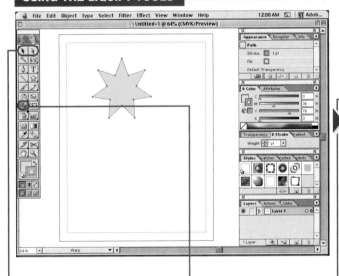

USING THE WARP TOOL

1 Select an object using or .

Note: For more on selecting objects, see Chapter 2.

2 Click the Warp tool ().

3 Click and drag over the object.

■ Illustrator warps the object.

What other liquify tools are available?

Illustrator provides seven different liquifying effects:

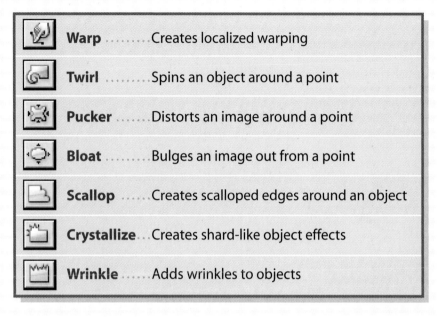

	Warp	Creates localized warping
	Twirl	Spins an object around a point
	Pucker	Distorts an image around a point
	Bloat	Bulges an image out from a point
	Scallop	Creates scalloped edges around an object
	Crystallize	Creates shard-like object effects
	Wrinkle	Adds wrinkles to objects

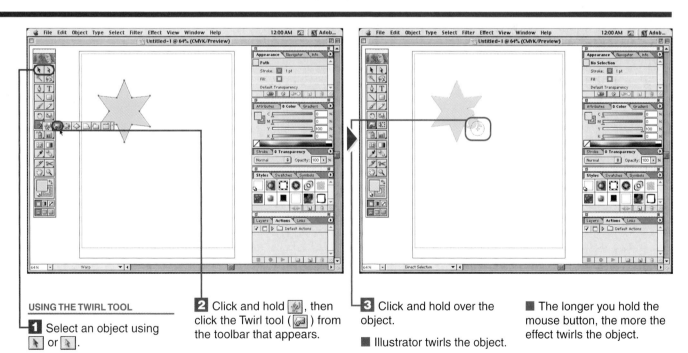

USING THE TWIRL TOOL

1 Select an object using ![arrow] or ![arrow].

Note: For more on selecting objects, see Chapter 2.

2 Click and hold ![icon], then click the Twirl tool (![icon]) from the toolbar that appears.

3 Click and hold over the object.

■ Illustrator twirls the object.

■ The longer you hold the mouse button, the more the effect twirls the object.

CREATE A FLARE

Flares are those star-like ghost images that can appear when using photographic equipment. You can add those effects to an illustration to make it look like it was shot with a camera. Flares also make great stars.

CREATE A FLARE

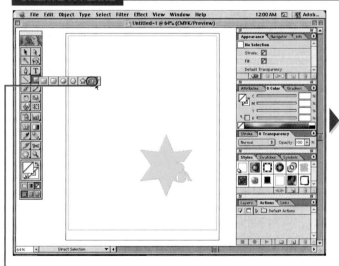

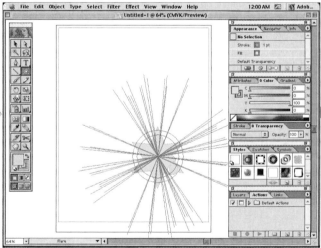

1 Select an object.

Note: For more on selecting objects, see Chapter 2.

2 Click and hold the Rectangle tool (▣), then, while dragging, click the Flare tool (▦) from the toolbar.

■ The ▶ changes to ⊹.

3 Click and drag the tool across the object.

■ The Flare paths appear.

What options does Illustrator provide for the Flare tool?

You can set a number of options, including diameter, rays, rings, and halo effect. Click the Flare tool ( ) and then click the object to which you want to apply the effect. The Flare Tool Options dialog box appears. You can experiment with any of the options to achieve the effect you want.

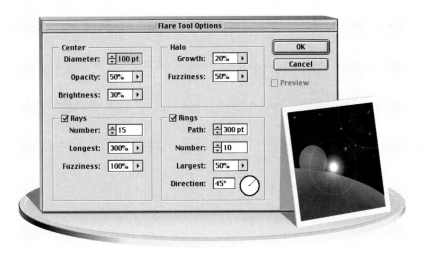

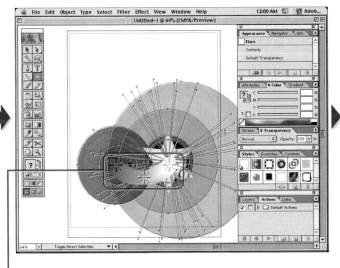

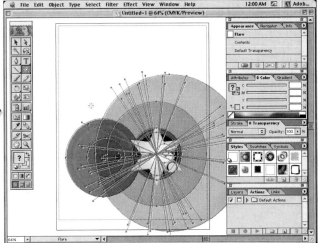

■ You can rotate ✛ to adjust the flare effect.

4 Release the mouse button.

5 Click the artboard.

■ The lens flare appears.

CREATE A SYMBOL

You can create symbols from any Illustrator art object, including paths, compound paths, text, images, objects, and groups of objects. Symbols help reduce file size and simplify making changes to image elements later.

CREATE A SYMBOL

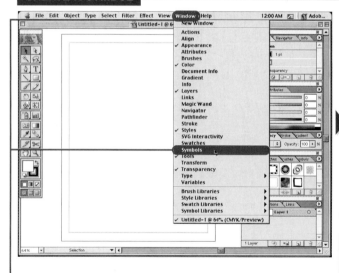

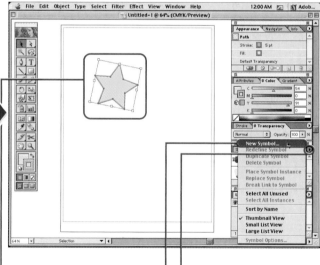

1 Click **Window**.

2 Click **Symbols**.

■ The Symbol palette appears.

■ You can also press **Shift** + **F11** to open the Symbols palette.

3 Select an object you want to use as a symbol.

Note: See Chapter 2 to learn about selecting objects.

4 Click ▶ in the Symbols menu.

5 Click **New Symbol**.

How can I tell what the different palette symbols are?

You can switch the palette view from thumbnail — the default — to a small or large list view. Click 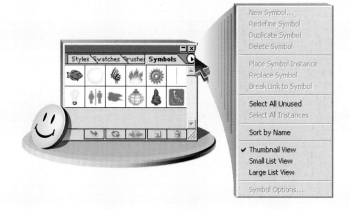 and then click the appropriate view from the list. A check mark ☑ appears next to the currently selected view.

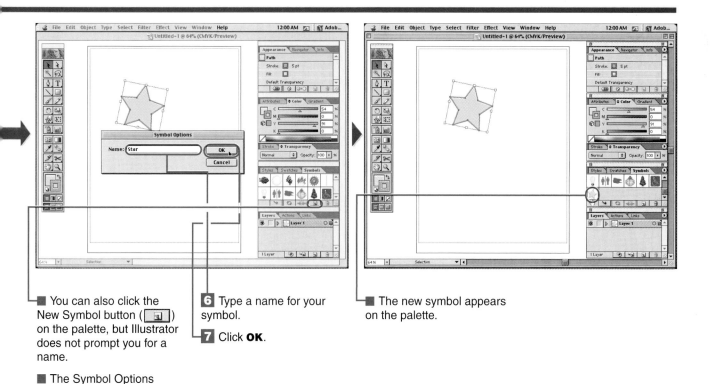

■ You can also click the New Symbol button (🔳) on the palette, but Illustrator does not prompt you for a name.

■ The Symbol Options dialog box appears.

6 Type a name for your symbol.

7 Click **OK**.

■ The new symbol appears on the palette.

INSERT AND DELETE SYMBOLS

You can easily insert symbols into your artwork or delete unused ones from the Symbols palette.

When you insert a symbol from the Symbols palette into your artwork, you are creating a *symbol instance* in your art.

INSERT A SYMBOL

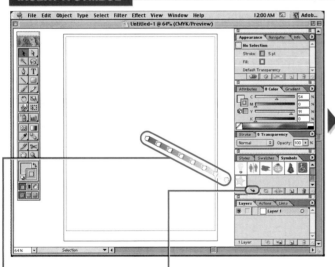

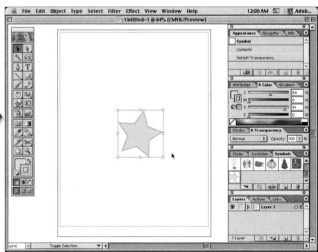

1 Click and drag a symbol from the Symbols palette onto your artwork.

2 Release the mouse button.

■ You can also click a symbol and then click the Place Symbol Instance button ( ) on the palette.

■ Your symbol appears on the artwork.

Note: Illustrator maintains a link between the symbol instance and the original symbol on the Symbols palette.

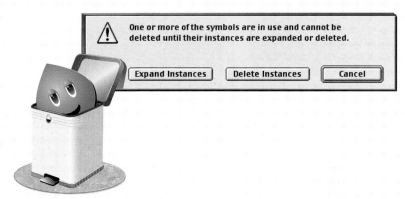

What if there are still symbol instances in my artwork when I delete a symbol from the Symbols palette?

A warning dialog box displays your available options. Click **Expand Instances** if you want to break the symbol links and leave the symbols in your art as stand-alone objects, or **Delete Instances** if you want to get rid of the symbol instances altogether. Click **Cancel** if you do not want to delete the symbol from the palette.

> One or more of the symbols are in use and cannot be deleted until their instances are expanded or deleted.
>
> [Expand Instances] [Delete Instances] [Cancel]

DELETE A SYMBOL

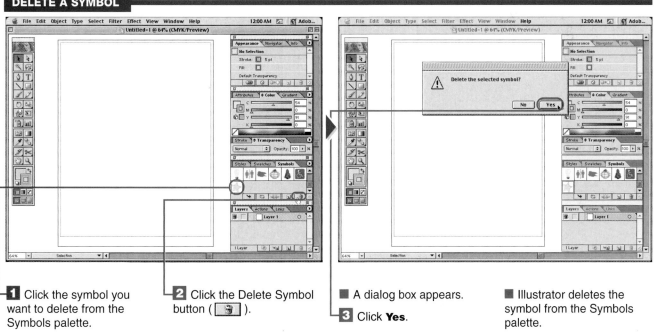

1 Click the symbol you want to delete from the Symbols palette.

2 Click the Delete Symbol button (🗑).

■ A dialog box appears.

3 Click **Yes**.

■ Illustrator deletes the symbol from the Symbols palette.

EDIT AND UPDATE SYMBOLS

You can edit and update symbols to keep them current. To edit symbols in your artwork, you must first break the link between the symbol and its source in the Symbols palette. Then you can edit your symbol using any of the editing tools. If you want your changes to affect the original symbol, you can update it.

EDIT A SYMBOL

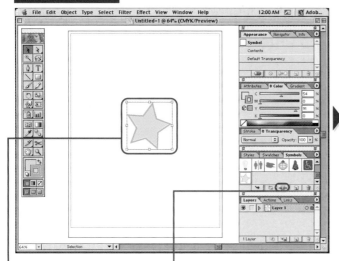

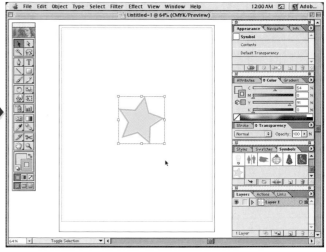

1 Click the symbol you want to edit.

■ A bounding box appears.

2 Click the Break Link button ( ) on the Symbols palette.

■ Illustrator breaks the link between the symbol instance in your artwork and the symbol in the palette.

■ You can now edit the symbol using any of the editing tools.

Do I have to update the original symbol if I modify an instance?

You do not have to update the original symbol each time you modify an instance. But if you are working on a symbol that you use frequently, such as a company logo, you may want to create a new symbol from the modified one, so that you can switch between them easily.

UPDATE A SYMBOL

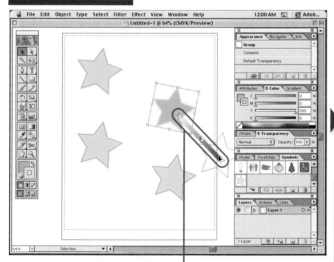

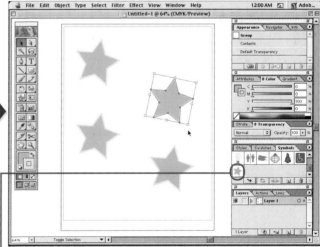

1 Press and hold `option` or `Alt`.

2 Click and drag an edited symbol onto the original symbol in the Symbols palette.

3 Release the mouse.

■ The original symbol updates.

■ Any symbol instances in your artwork also update.

APPLY SYMBOL EFFECTS

Illustrator has several symbol effects that you can apply to give your work an artistic flare. These range from spraying symbols onto your artwork to resizing symbols on the fly.

APPLY SYMBOL EFFECTS

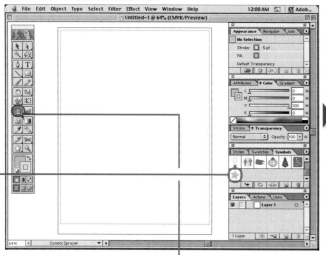

USING THE SYMBOL SPRAYER

1 Click a symbol on the Symbols palette.

2 Click the Symbol Sprayer tool ( ) in the toolbox.

3 Click and drag the mouse ( ) over your artwork.

■ The symbol sprays onto the artwork.

What symbol effects can I apply?

The specialized symbol effects include:

⟳	**Symbol Sizer**	Increases or decreases the symbol
	Symbol Stainer	Colorizes your symbols
	Symbol Screener ...	Adjusts symbol transparency
⊘	**Symbol Styler**	Applies a graphic style as a painted effect
	Symbol Shifter ...	Moves symbol instances around
	Symbol Scruncher ..	Pulls symbols together or apart
	Symbol Sprayer ...	Applies multiple instances of the symbol
	Symbol Spinner	Changes the rotation of a symbol instance

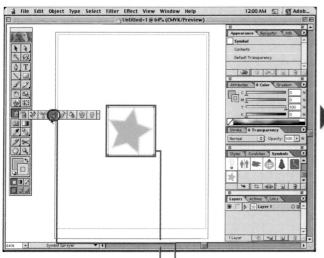

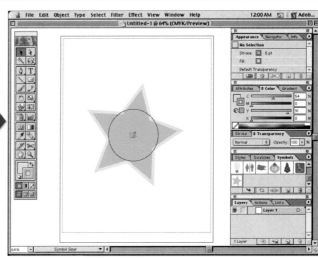

USING THE SYMBOL SIZER

1 Select a symbol on your artwork.

Note: For more on selecting objects, see Chapter 2.

2 Click and hold 🖼, then drag and select the Symbol Sizer (⟳) from the toolbar that appears.

3 Click and hold the ⟳ over the symbol.

■ The symbol grows in size.

4 Release the mouse.

■ Your symbol takes on its new size.

■ To shrink a symbol, press and hold **option** or **Alt** before clicking the symbol.

CHAPTER 7

Applying Color

Illustrator gives you a variety of ways to create colors and colorful patterns, which you can then apply to your artwork to make it stand out. You can apply these colors and patterns using different tools, including Illustrator's many types of paintbrushes and the Paint Bucket tool.

An Introduction to Color 148

Create and Save a CMYK Color 150

Create and Save an RGB Color 152

Fill an Object with Color 154

Stroke an Object 156

Paint with a Calligraphic Brush 158

Customize a Calligraphic Brush 160

Apply and Customize
  a Scatter Brush.............................162

Paint with an Art Brush 164

Fill an Object with a Gradient 166

Create a Multicolor Gradient............168

Fill an Object with a Pattern 170

Save Colors with the Eyedropper 172

Apply Colors with the Paint Bucket 173

Adjust Opacity of an Object 174

Adjust Blending of an Object............175

AN INTRODUCTION TO COLOR

Illustrator offers a variety of ways to spice up your artwork by creating and applying colors and patterns.

Color Spaces

Illustrator lets you choose colors to apply to your artwork using several different color spaces, including CMYK, RGB, and grayscale. The *color space* determines the range of colors available as well as how you go about defining your custom colors. When selecting a color model, consider how you want to use your art. Are you going to print your art or view it on a computer? Also consider what types of colors you need to access, such as color or grayscale. The Illustrator Color palette menu allows you to select from a variety of color spaces.

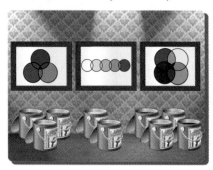

CMYK

In the CMYK color space, when you select your colors you mimic how printers create them, which is by mixing cyan, magenta, yellow, and black inks. "K" stands for black in CMYK, to avoid confusion with "B," which could stand for blue. You are most likely to work with the CMYK color space when you create artwork for print. See Chapter 13 for more about printing art.

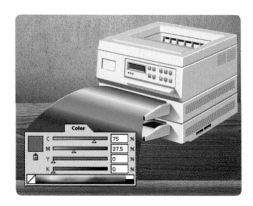

RGB

In the RGB mode color space, you select your colors based on how a computer monitor displays them, which involves mixing red, blue, and green light. You commonly work with RGB when you create art for display on a computer. *Web Safe RGB* is a subset of the RGB space that includes the 216 Web-safe colors that display consistently across different monitors and browser types. For more about creating art for the Web, see Chapter 14.

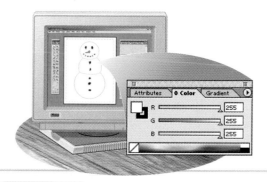

Apply Color

After you select a color space and define a color, you can apply the color in different ways. You can *fill* an object by coloring its interior. You can also *stroke* an object, which involves outlining it with color. You can also place color to your art with a variety of paintbrushes, which apply color along a path. After you apply color by filling, stroking, or painting, you can adjust or remove the color using the Color or Swatches palettes.

Color Patterns

You are not limited to solid colors in Illustrator. You can also apply multicolor patterns to your artwork, using fill, stroke, or paintbrush techniques. Illustrator has predefined patterns in the Swatches or Brushes palettes. You can create various effects yourself by saving artwork as a pattern. You can also apply *gradients* to your objects, which are patterns that gradually blend from one color to another.

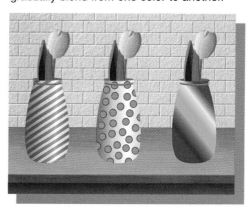

Blending Colors

You can specify how overlapping colors interact with one another. By changing the opacity of applied colors, you can make objects transparent to elements below them. You can also apply blending modes to your objects, which can cause colors to change brightness or hue depending on what colors they overlap.

CREATE AND SAVE A CMYK COLOR

You can define a custom CMYK color by mixing cyan, magenta, yellow, and black in the Color palette. You can save that color in the Swatches palette for later use.

You generally use CMYK colors when creating printed art. See Chapter 13 for more information on printing.

CREATE A CMYK COLOR

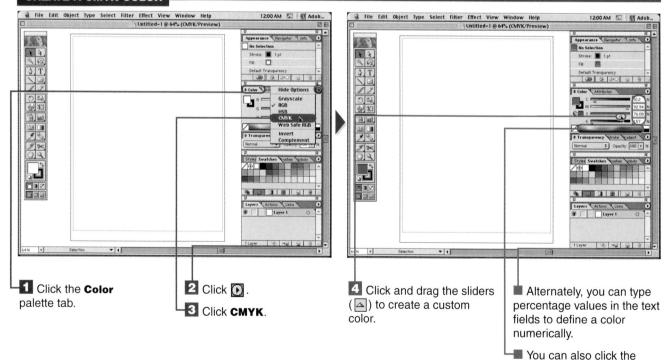

1 Click the **Color** palette tab.

2 Click 🔘.

3 Click **CMYK**.

4 Click and drag the sliders (△) to create a custom color.

■ Alternately, you can type percentage values in the text fields to define a color numerically.

■ You can also click the Spectrum to specify a color.

How do I manage the colors I have created in my Swatches palette?

The Swatches palette menu lets you duplicate or delete a selected color swatch, sort your swatches, or view your swatches at different sizes. You can also click the buttons on the bottom of the swatch menu to control which types of swatches are visible.

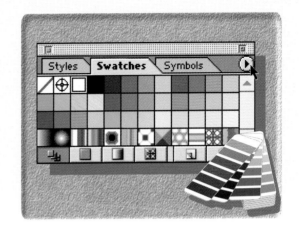

SAVE A CMYK COLOR

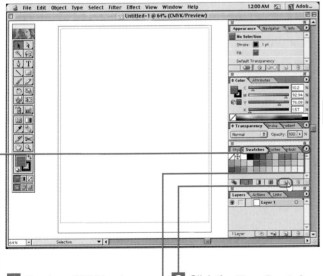

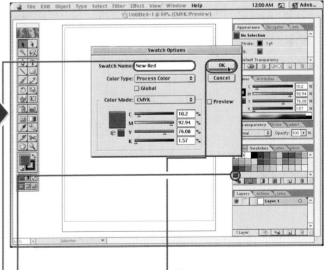

1 Create a CMYK color.

Note: See steps 1 through 4 on the previous page to create a color.

2 Click the **Swatches** palette tab.

3 Click the **New Swatch** button (▢).

■ You can also click ▶ on the Swatches palette and click **New Swatch**.

■ Illustrator adds the color to the Swatches palette.

4 Double click the new swatch.

■ The Swatch Options dialog box opens.

5 Type a name for the new swatch.

6 Click **OK**.

■ Illustrator saves the CMYK Color name.

■ You can roll your ▶ over the swatch to see the name.

CREATE AND SAVE AN RGB COLOR

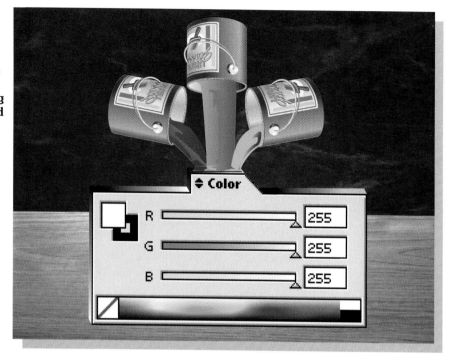

You can define a custom RGB color by mixing red, green, and blue in the Color palette. You can save that color in the Swatches palette for later use.

You generally use RGB colors when creating art for computers, such as Web images. See Chapter 14 for more information on preparing images for the Web.

CREATE AN RGB COLOR

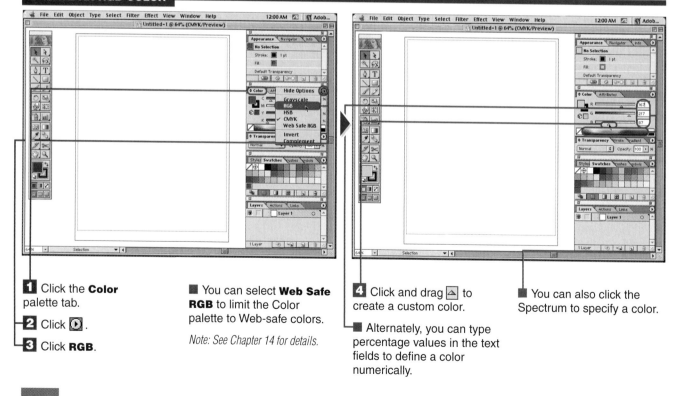

1 Click the **Color** palette tab.

2 Click ▣.

3 Click **RGB**.

■ You can select **Web Safe RGB** to limit the Color palette to Web-safe colors.

Note: See Chapter 14 for details.

4 Click and drag △ to create a custom color.

■ Alternately, you can type percentage values in the text fields to define a color numerically.

■ You can also click the Spectrum to specify a color.

Is there another way to select a specific color other than with the Color palette?

If you double-click the Fill box (☐) in the Color palette, the Color Picker dialog box appears. You can select a custom color by changing the settings and then clicking **OK**.

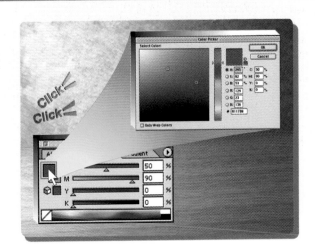

SAVE A COLOR

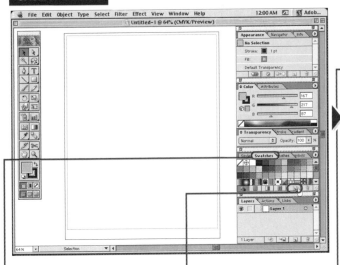

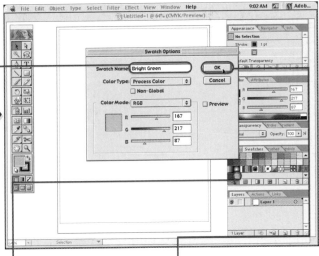

1 Create the color you want to save in the Color palette.

Note: See steps 1 through 4 on the previous page to create an RGB color.

2 Click the **Swatches** palette tab.

3 Click ▣.

■ You can also click ▶ and click **New Swatch** from the Swatches palette.

■ Illustrator adds the color to the Swatches palette.

4 Double click the new swatch.

■ The Swatch Options dialog box appears.

5 Type a name for the new swatch.

6 Click **OK**.

■ Illustrator saves the RGB color name.

■ You can roll your ▶ over the swatch to see the name.

FILL AN OBJECT WITH COLOR

You can fill an object with color using the Swatches palette, and then fine-tune your color choice with various tools. Filling creates areas of solid color, as opposed to outlines, in your art.

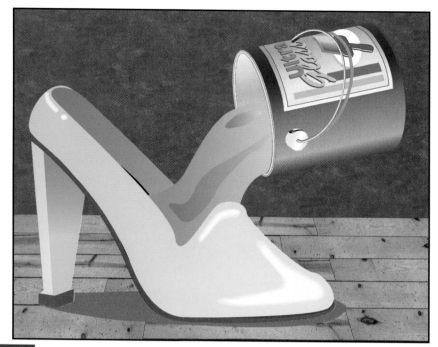

FILL AN OBJECT WITH COLOR

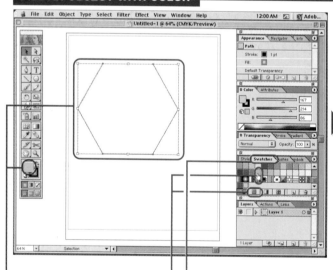

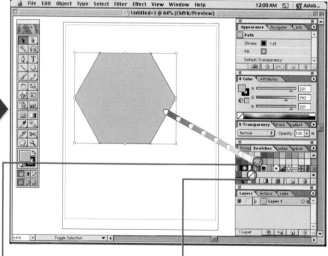

SELECT AND FILL AN OBJECT

1 Select an object using a Selection tool.

Note: See Chapter 2 to select an object.

2 Click the **Fill** box ( ).

3 Click the **Swatches** palette tab.

4 Click a color swatch.

■ You can click the Show Color Swatches button ( ) to display only the color swatches, not the gradients or patterns.

■ Illustrator fills the object with the selected color.

■ You can also apply color by clicking and dragging a color swatch onto an object.

■ You can remove an applied color by clicking the "none" swatch ( ).

How can I find more predefined colors with which to fill objects?

Illustrator comes with dozens of predefined colors for filling objects. Click **Window**, click **Swatch Libraries**, and then click a swatch set in the list. The set of swatches opens in a new palette.

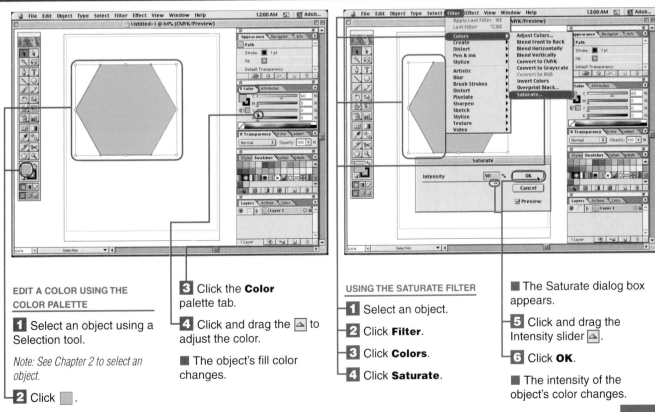

**EDIT A COLOR USING THE
COLOR PALETTE**

1 Select an object using a Selection tool.

Note: See Chapter 2 to select an object.

2 Click ▨.

3 Click the **Color** palette tab.

4 Click and drag the △ to adjust the color.

■ The object's fill color changes.

USING THE SATURATE FILTER

1 Select an object.

2 Click **Filter**.

3 Click **Colors**.

4 Click **Saturate**.

■ The Saturate dialog box appears.

5 Click and drag the Intensity slider △.

6 Click **OK**.

■ The intensity of the object's color changes.

STROKE AN OBJECT

You can stroke an object to outline it. You may find this useful when you want to highlight an object, or when an object has no fill color. You can adjust the outline using the Stroke palette.

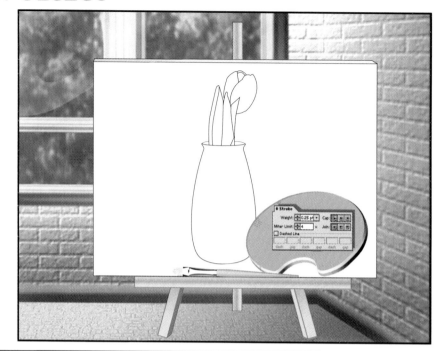

STROKE AN OBJECT

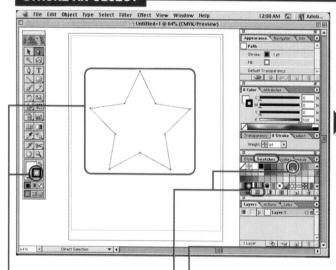

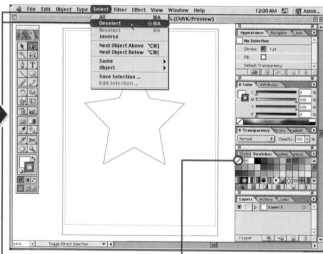

ADD A STROKE TO AN OBJECT

1 Select the object using a selection tool.

Note: See Chapter 2 to select an object.

2 Click the Stroke box (▣).

3 Click the **Swatches** palette tab.

4 Click a color swatch.

■ You can click ▦ to display only the color swatches, not the gradients or patterns.

■ Illustrator strokes the object with the selected color.

■ You may have to deselect the object by clicking **Select**, and then **Deselect**, to see the stroke.

■ You can remove the stroke by selecting the object and clicking ⟋.

How can I customize the corners of my stroked lines?

You can customize corners by adjusting the options in the Stroke palette. Clicking the Round Join button (⬚) rounds the corners of a stroke, while clicking the Bevel Join button (⬚) squares off your corners. With a Miter Limit, you can determine at what point Illustrator makes a standard corner beveled.

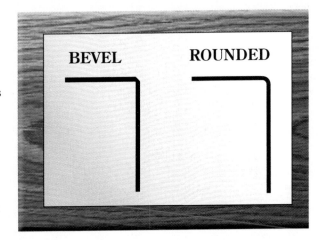

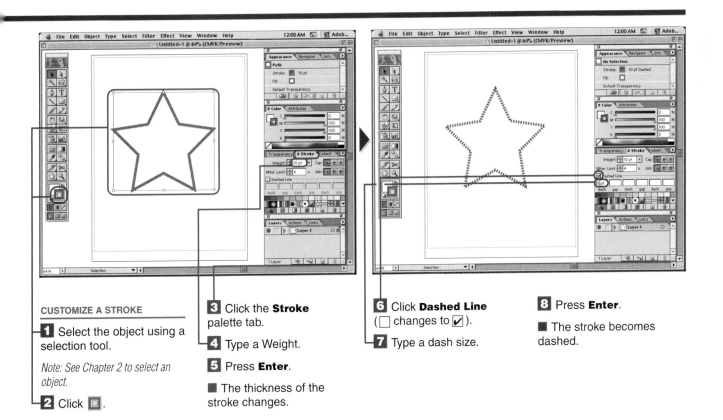

CUSTOMIZE A STROKE

1 Select the object using a selection tool.

Note: See Chapter 2 to select an object.

2 Click ▣.

3 Click the **Stroke** palette tab.

4 Type a Weight.

5 Press **Enter**.

■ The thickness of the stroke changes.

6 Click **Dashed Line** (☐ changes to ☑).

7 Type a dash size.

8 Press **Enter**.

■ The stroke becomes dashed.

PAINT WITH A CALLIGRAPHIC BRUSH

You can use a calligraphic brush to paint even- or variable-width lines. You can use this brush to create a line drawing, or to apply color to an object.

PAINT WITH A CALLIGRAPHIC BRUSH

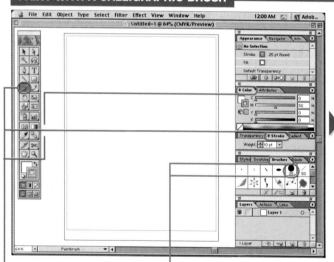

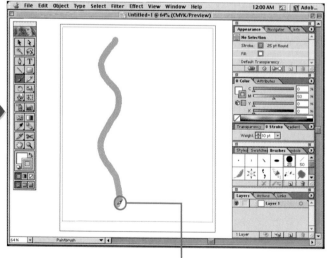

PAINT EVEN-WIDTH LINES

1 Click the **Paintbrush** Tool ().

2 Click the **Stroke** palette tab.

3 Click the **Color** palette tab and select a color to paint.

Note: See the section "Create and Save a CMYK Color" for more information.

4 Click the **Brushes** palette tab.

5 Click a round brush style.

■ The ▶ changes to a paint brush ( ).

6 Click and drag to paint a line.

■ A round brush style creates an even-width line.

158

How do I avoid filling in the curves of my painted lines?

If you have a fill color defined as you paint with a brush, you may see fill color in places where your line curves, especially if the fill color is different from the background. You can avoid this by turning off the fill color. To turn off the color, click the Fill box (☐) in the Toolbox and then click ☑ in the Color palette.

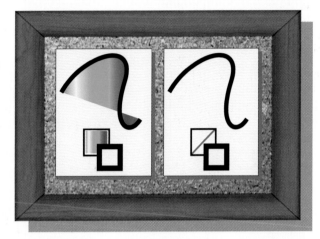

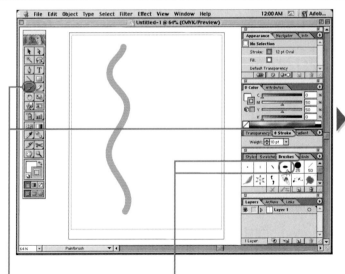

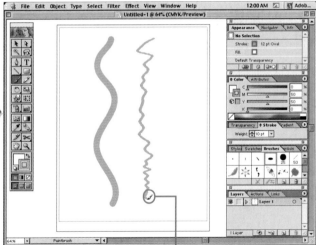

PAINT VARIABLE-WIDTH LINES

1 Click ✏.

2 Click the **Stroke** palette tab.

3 Click a color in the Color palette.

Note: See "Create and Save a CMYK Color" for more information.

4 Click the **Brushes** palette tab.

5 Click an oval brush style.

■ The ▶ changes to ✏.

6 Click and drag ✏ to paint a line.

■ An oval brush style creates a variable-width line.

CUSTOMIZE A CALLIGRAPHIC BRUSH

You can change the shape and orientation of a calligraphic brush to customize the types of lines it produces.

You can perform similar steps with scatter brushes and art brushes to customize those brush types as well.

CUSTOMIZE A CALLIGRAPHIC BRUSH

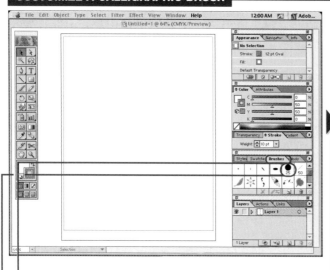

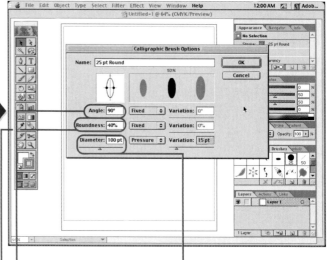

1 Click the **Brushes** palette tab.

2 Double-click a round or oval calligraphic brush.

■ You can click other brushes in the palette to customize other brush types.

■ The Calligraphic Brush Options dialog box appears.

3 Type a brush angle between –180 and 180 degrees.

4 Type a brush roundness between 0 and 100%.

5 Type a brush diameter between 0 and 1296 points (pt).

■ You can also click and drag the diagram inside the preview box to define your brush shape.

How do I create a new type of brush in the Brushes palette?

Click 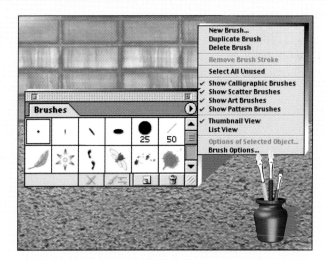 in the Brushes palette and then click **New Brush**. Alternately, you can click the New Brush button ( ). Illustrator prompts you to select a brush type and then the brush options. You can also duplicate an existing brush and customize that brush. Click a brush to duplicate in the Brushes palette, then click and click **Duplicate Brush**.

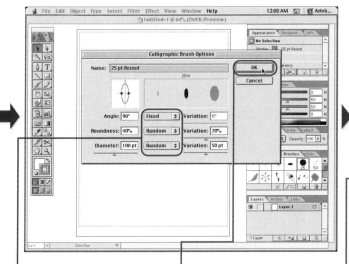

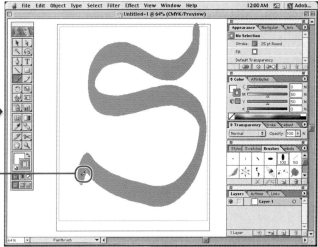

6 Choose how to vary the brush settings by clicking ◆ or ▼ and clicking a desired setting.

■ If you choose **Random** for any of the settings, specify a variation to define a range of randomness.

7 Click **OK**.

8 Click and drag to apply the customized calligraphic brush.

■ A custom line appears.

You can scatter copies of a
piece of art on your canvas
using a Scatter brush. With
this technique, you can
easily introduce repetition
and randomness to your
artwork.

APPLY A SCATTER BRUSH

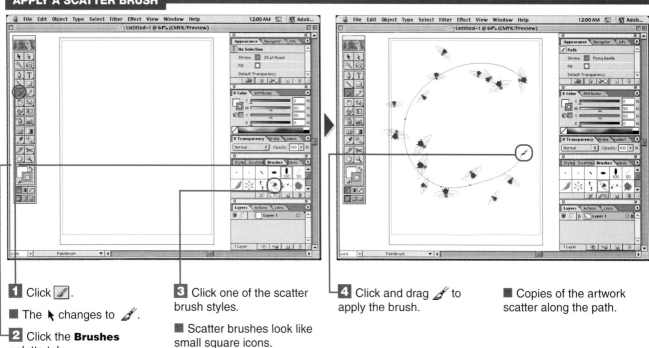

1 Click 🖌.

■ The ▶ changes to 🖌.

2 Click the **Brushes**
palette tab.

3 Click one of the scatter
brush styles.

■ Scatter brushes look like
small square icons.

4 Click and drag 🖌 to
apply the brush.

■ Copies of the artwork
scatter along the path.

How can I easily create a new scatter brush style?

Create the artwork that you want to scatter using the instructions in the earlier chapters of this book, and then click and drag the artwork onto the Brushes palette. Dialog boxes appear that allow you to specify the type and options for the new brush.

CUSTOMIZE A SCATTER BRUSH

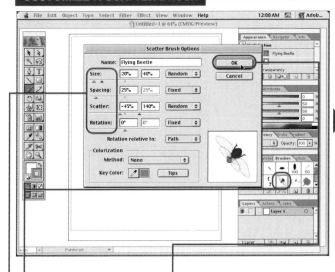

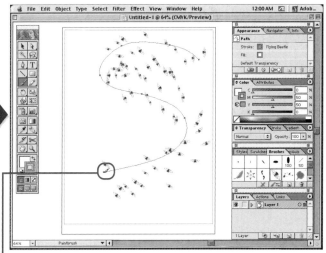

1 Double-click a scatter brush to open its dialog box.

2 Click and drag a slider (△):

Size sets the size of an item.

Spacing sets the distance between items on a path.

Scatter sets how far to the sides of the path the items fall.

Rotation sets how the items turn on the path.

3 Click **OK**.

4 Click and drag ✎ to apply the customized scatter brush.

■ Copies of the artwork scatter along the path according to your settings.

PAINT WITH AN ART BRUSH

You can paint with an art brush to stretch an object along the length of a path. You can make this object a simple stripe of color, or a detailed piece of artwork.

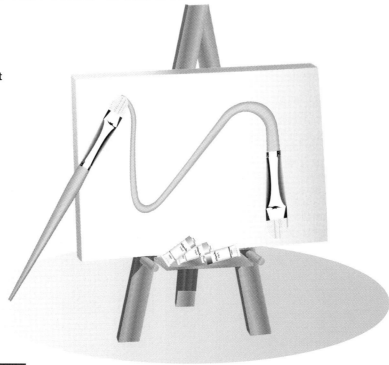

PAINT WITH AN ART BRUSH

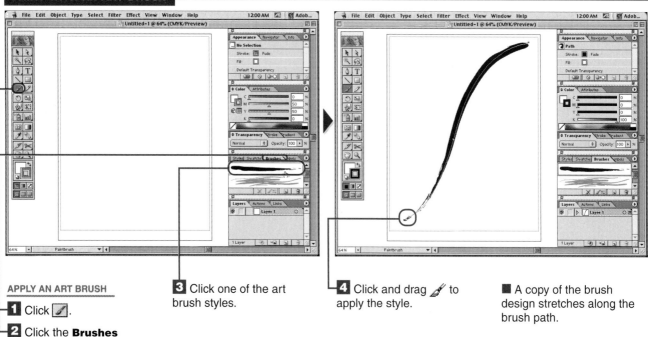

APPLY AN ART BRUSH

1 Click .

2 Click the **Brushes** palette tab.

3 Click one of the art brush styles.

4 Click and drag to apply the style.

■ A copy of the brush design stretches along the brush path.

How can I access more brush styles?

Illustrator comes with dozens of predefined brushes. Click **Window**, click **Brush Libraries**, and then click a brush set in the list. The set of brushes opens in a new palette.

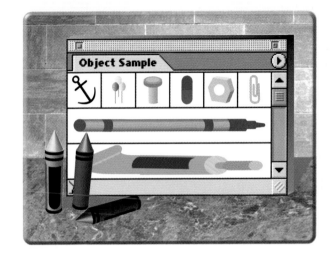

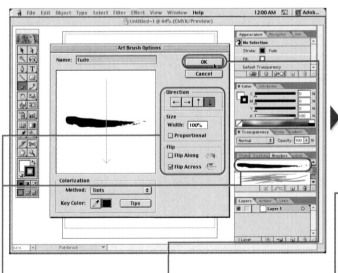

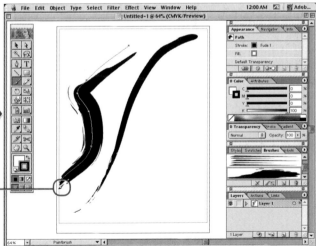

CUSTOMIZE AN ART BRUSH

1 Double-click an art brush to open its dialog box.

2 Set the brush options:

Direction buttons (←, →, ↑, ↓) set the orientation of the stroke.

Size specifies the art width.

Flip changes the orientation of the painted art (☐ changes to ☑).

3 Click **OK**.

4 Click and drag ✐ to apply the customized art brush.

■ The art stretches along the path according to your selected options.

FILL AN OBJECT WITH A GRADIENT

You can fill an object with a gradient to give your artwork a shaded or 3-D effect. You can create gradients that blend two colors, as illustrated in this section, or more than two colors.

See the section "Create a Multicolor Gradient" to fill artwork with more than two colors.

FILL AN OBJECT WITH A GRADIENT

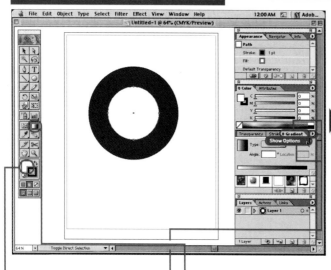

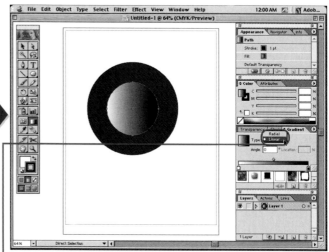

1 Select an object using a selection tool.

Note: See Chapter 2 to select an object.

2 Click ■.

3 Click the **Gradient** tool (▦).

4 Click the **Gradient** palette tab.

5 Click ▣ in the Gradient palette and click **Show Options**.

6 Click ◆ or ▾ and select a gradient Type.

■ A linear gradient blends colors along a straight line while a radial gradient blends them out from a center point.

How can I apply a predefined gradient?

Illustrator has several gradients predefined in the Swatches palette. Click to select an object, click ☐ in the Toolbox, then click a gradient in the Swatches palette. After applying a gradient fill, you can customize it using the Gradient palette. See the section "Create a Multicolor Gradient" for details on customizing a gradient.

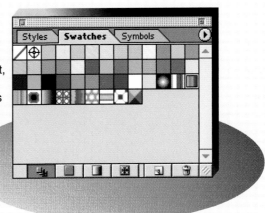

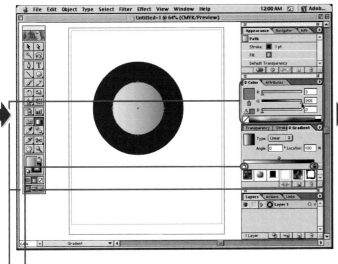

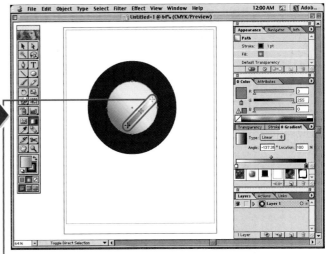

7 Click the starting color.

8 Define the starting color using the Color palette.

9 Click the ending color.

10 Define the ending color using the Color palette.

Note: For information on defining a color, see the section "Create and Save a CMYK Color."

11 Click and drag the ⊹ over the selected object to specify the angle and location of the gradient.

■ Illustrator fills the gradient per your specifications.

CREATE A MULTICOLOR GRADIENT

You can use the Gradient palette to build gradients that blend more than two colors. You can then apply the custom gradients to your art. Adding complex gradients can give your art rainbow-like radiance.

CREATE A MULTICOLOR GRADIENT

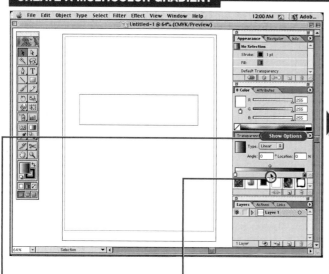

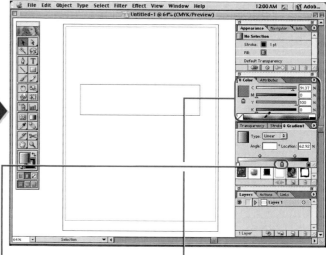

1 Click the **Gradient** palette tab.

2 Click ◆ or ▼ in the Gradient palette and click **Show Options**.

3 Click below the gradient slider to create a new color stop.

4 Click the new color stop.

5 Define the new color using the Color palette.

Note: See the section "Create and Save a CMYK Color" for details.

How can I edit a predefined gradient?

If you select a predefined gradient in the Swatches palette, its custom settings appear in the Gradient palette. You can adjust 🔒 to change the component colors of the gradient. You can drag ◇ to set how the colors blend with one another.

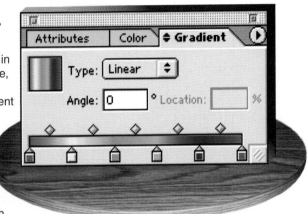

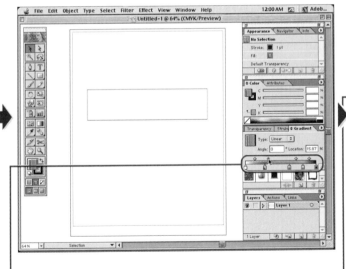

6 Repeat steps **3** through **5** to specify more colors.

7 Click and drag the diamond-shaped sliders (◈) to customize the transitions between the colors.

■ You can also click and drag the color stops (🔒).

8 Select an object with a selection tool.

Note: See Chapter 2 to select an object.

9 Click the Gradient Fill button (■).

■ The object displays the applied gradient.

FILL AN OBJECT WITH A PATTERN

You can fill an object with a pattern to add texture as well as color. You can also create your own custom pattern.

FILL AN OBJECT WITH A PATTERN

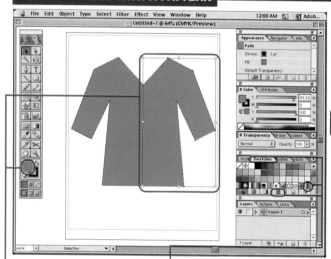

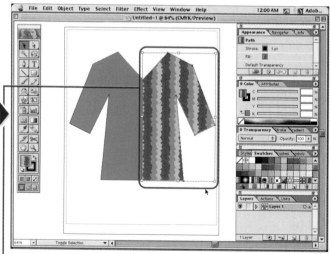

APPLY A PATTERN

1 Select the object using a selection tool.

Note: See Chapter 2 to select an object.

2 Click ☐.

3 Click the **Swatches** palette tab.

4 Click a pattern swatch.

■ You can click the Show Pattern Swatches button (田) to display only the pattern swatches and not the colors or gradients.

■ Illustrator fills the object with the selected pattern.

■ You can remove the pattern by clicking ☑.

Can I apply a pattern as a stroke?

Yes. Just click the Stroke box ( ) instead of in step 2 of the previous page. Illustrator adds the pattern as an outline around your object. For information about customizing an outline, see the section "Stroke an Object."

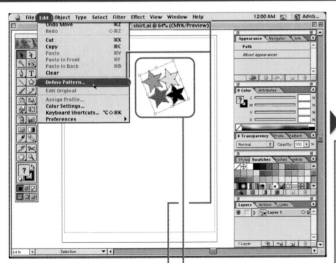

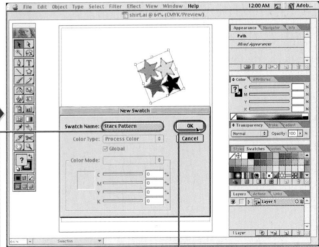

CREATE A CUSTOM PATTERN

1 Create artwork for the pattern using Illustrator's tools.

■ Remember, the smaller the pattern you create, the more it repeats when you apply it to an object.

2 Surround the artwork with a bounding box using the Rectangle Tool if you want to define the edges of the pattern.

3 Click **Edit**.

4 Click **Define Pattern**.

■ The New Swatch dialog box appears.

5 Type a name for the pattern.

6 Click **OK**.

7 Illustrator adds the pattern to the Swatches palette.

SAVE COLORS WITH THE EYEDROPPER

You can copy colors and other attributes with the Eyedropper Tool.

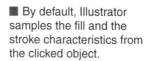

You can then apply these attributes with the Paint Bucket Tool. See the section "Apply Colors with the Paint Bucket" to apply attributes.

SAVE COLORS WITH THE EYEDROPPER

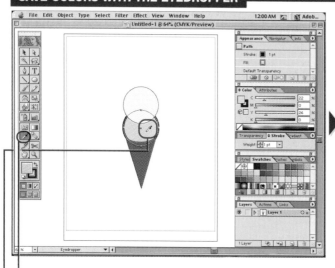

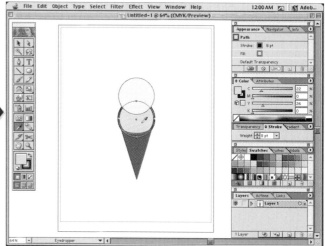

1 Click the **Eyedropper** tool (![eyedropper]).

2 Click an object.

■ By default, Illustrator samples the fill and the stroke characteristics from the clicked object.

■ You can hold Shift while you click to sample just the color.

■ Illustrator saves the fill and stroke attributes to the Fill and Stroke boxes in the Toolbox.

■ If you are just sampling a color, Illustrator saves the color to the Fill or Stroke box — whichever box is currently active.

■ You can customize what attributes you apply by double-clicking ![eyedropper] in the Toolbox.

APPLY COLORS WITH THE PAINT BUCKET

You can apply
colors and other
attributes with the
Paint Bucket Tool.
This gives you a
useful way to copy
attributes between
objects in your art.

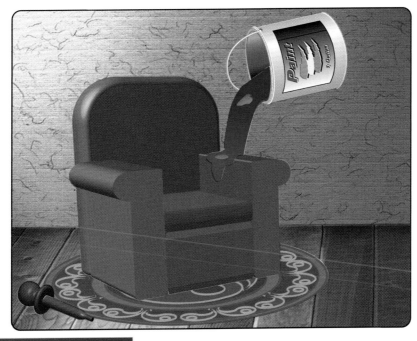

You can use the
Eyedropper Tool to
copy your attributes.
See the section
"Save Colors with
the Eyedropper" to
copy attributes.

APPLY COLORS WITH THE PAINT BUCKET

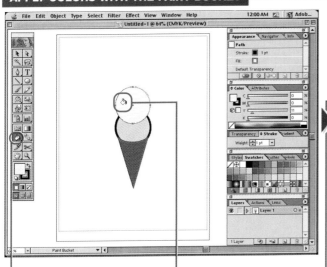

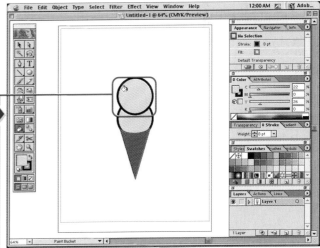

1 Click the Paint Bucket
tool (🖌️).

2 Click an object.

■ Illustrator applies the fill
and stroke attributes to the
object.

■ You can customize what
attributes you apply by
double-clicking 🖌️ in the
Toolbox.

ADJUST OPACITY OF AN OBJECT

You can adjust the opacity of an object to allow elements below it to show through. This can give glass or liquid elements in your artwork a transparent feel.

ADJUST OPACITY OF AN OBJECT

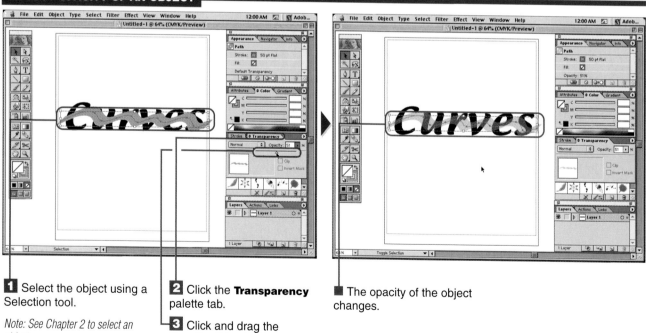

1 Select the object using a Selection tool.

Note: See Chapter 2 to select an object.

2 Click the **Transparency** palette tab.

3 Click and drag the Opacity slider (▲), or type a value from 0 to 100.

■ The opacity of the object changes.

You can adjust the
blending of an object
to control how its
colors combine with
elements below it.
You can use blending
to apply interesting
overlapping effects to
your art.

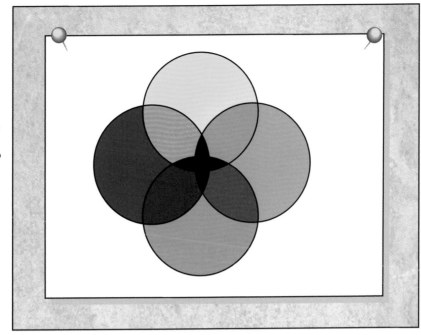

The blending
mode menu has
a variety of
settings, with
which you can
experiment to
create interesting
effects.

ADJUST BLENDING OF AN OBJECT

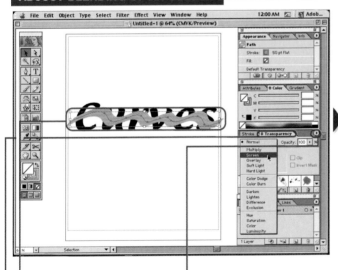

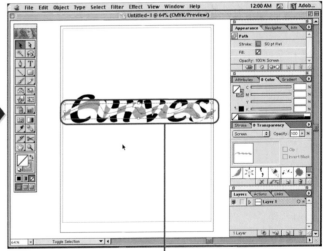

1 Select the object using a
Selection tool.

*Note: See Chapter 2 to select an
object.*

2 Click the **Transparency**
palette tab.

3 Click ▶ and click a blend
mode.

■ **Normal**, the default
mode, does not allow
overlapping layers to blend.

■ **Multiply** has a darkening
effect where colors overlap,
while **Screen** has a
lightening effect.

■ **Exclusion** creates a
photonegative effect where
light colors overlap.

■ The selected object
blends with objects below it.

CHAPTER 8

Working with Type

One of Illustrator's great strengths is that it allows you to add type in powerful, creative ways. In this chapter, you learn the basics of working with type in Illustrator, as well as how to convert type to outlines so that you can use path tools to manipulate them.

Understanding Type in Illustrator 178

Insert Point Type 180

Insert Area Type 181

Type Text Along a Path 182

Change Font and Font Size 184

Change Paragraph Alignment 186

Change Type Case 188

Using Smart Punctuation 189

Check Spelling 190

Link Type Blocks 192

Wrap Type Around an Object 194

Convert Type to Outlines 196

UNDERSTANDING TYPE IN ILLUSTRATOR

Illustrator handles type a little differently than you might expect. Instead of grafting a word processor onto a drawing application, Illustrator has sophisticated tools to meet the unique demands of placing type in artwork. These tools can help give you power and flexibility when managing type.

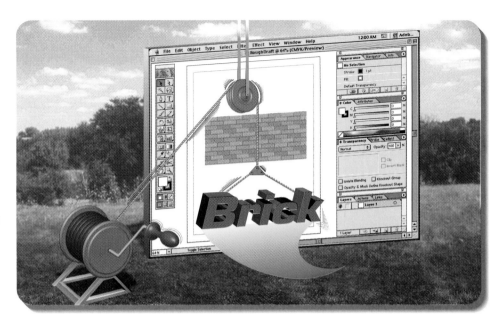

Type, Text, and Font

Sometimes people use "type", "text", and "font" interchangeably, but these terms actually represent different things. You use *type* to create text, and it has properties such as family, font, size, color, case, and alignment within a document. You can mix and match type within a document, a paragraph, or even a single word. *Text*, on the other hand, is the actual words and letters you insert in a document or on your illustration. *Font* is a complete collection of letters with a specific typeface, weight, posture, and size.

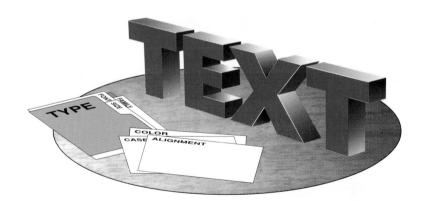

Raster and Vector Fonts

In the world of computers, fonts come in two types: raster and vector. *Raster* fonts are optimized for screen display technology and look best on a monitor. *Vector* fonts use mathematical scaling technology so they look the same on the screen as they do when you print them out on paper. You should use vector fonts for most of your work unless you have specific reasons to use raster fonts, such as placing them on a Web site. For more on creating illustrations for the Web, see Chapter 14.

PostScript and TrueType Fonts

Adobe PostScript and Microsoft TrueType fonts are two kinds of vector fonts that work differently and solve different technology problems. Many design professionals use PostScript font libraries for all their work; also most Macintosh and IBM-compatible PCs support TrueType fonts. Which kind of font you choose is up to you.

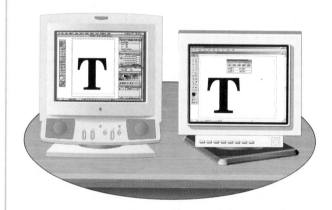

Type Outlines

Illustrator lets you create outlines from type, which enable you to make dramatic changes to the shape of the fonts in your art. Type outlines also let you increase the font size far beyond its supposed limit, so you can print building-size letters if your printer supports it. Because type outlines are paths, you can warp, change, or edit them with any of the path-editing tools available to you. To learn more about paths, see Chapter 3. For advanced path techniques, see Chapter 4.

Type Effects

You can apply simple type effects, such as filling it with solid color, forcing it to follow a path, or turning it into outlines. If you convert type to an outline, you can then apply wild and fanciful effects such as gradients and fills, masks, and distortion effects. These make your text come alive with color, life, and energy.

INSERT POINT TYPE

Point type is type that starts from a single point in the artwork, without shape boundaries. You can insert point type into any artwork with the Type tool without having to create a path first.

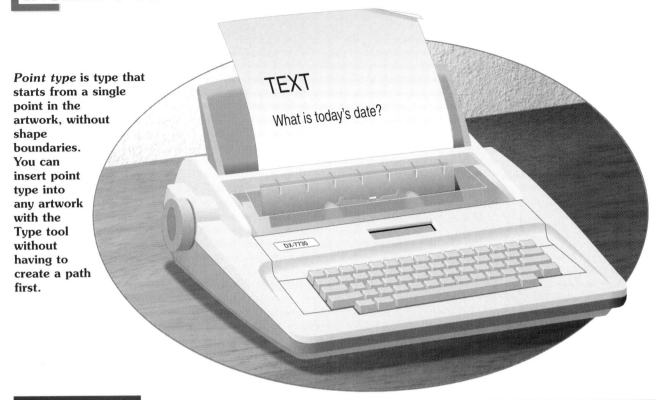

INSERT POINT TYPE

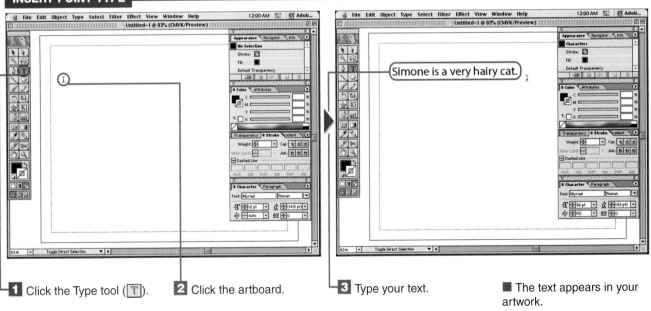

1 Click the Type tool ().

2 Click the artboard.

3 Type your text.

■ The text appears in your artwork.

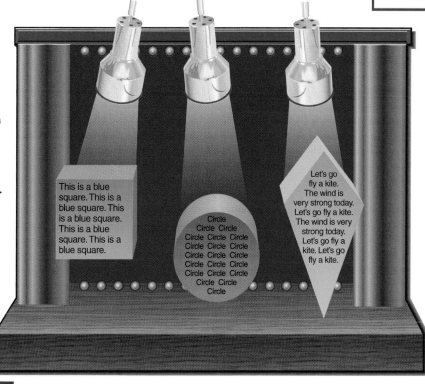

Area type **is type that you enter within a shape or object in your artwork. You often use area type in advertisement columns or for eyecatching newsletter designs.**

You can use almost any shape, but shapes with gentle changes of direction work better than narrow or sharp ones.

INSERT AREA TYPE

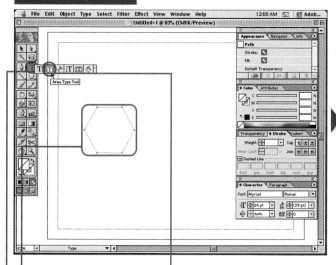

1 Create a shape or object.

Note: For more on creating objects, see Chapter 5.

2 Click and hold 🕂.

■ Several tool buttons appear.

3 Click 🕂 to select the Area Type tool.

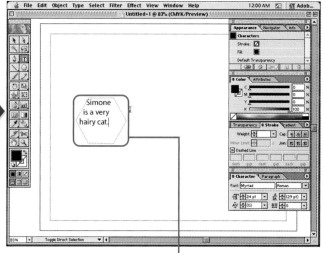

4 Click an object's path where you want to place text.

5 Type your text.

■ The text appears inside your object.

You can quickly create text that follows any path in your art, no matter how elaborate. This lets you curve or swoop your text around your illustration.

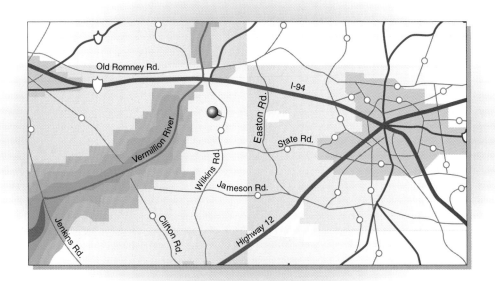

TYPE TEXT ALONG A PATH

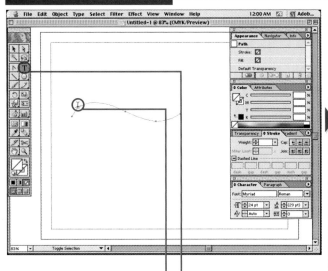

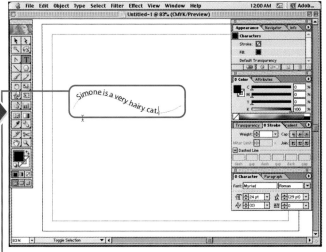

TYPE TEXT ABOVE A PATH

1 Draw or select a path in your artwork.

Note: See Chapters 3 and 4 for more about drawing and selecting paths.

2 Click T.

3 Position the ⬦ over your path.

■ The cursor automatically changes to the Type Path tool (⅃).

4 Click the ⅃ somewhere on your selected path.

5 Type your text.

■ The text follows the selected path.

How can I easily make type run vertically?

The Vertical Type tool  and the Vertical Path Type tool give you two different ways to create vertically aligned text. You can find them on the Type toolbar, which appears when you click ⟋ .

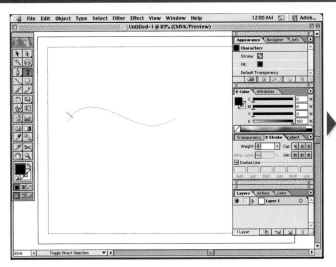

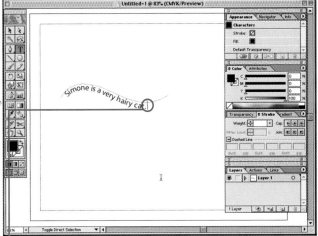

TYPE TEXT BELOW A PATH

1 Repeat steps **1** through **4** on the previous page.

2 Press `option` + `Shift` + `▼` or `Alt` + `Shift` + `▼`.

■ The ⟋ moves incrementally below the path.

3 Type your text.

■ The text follows the underside of the selected path.

CHANGE FONT AND FONT SIZE

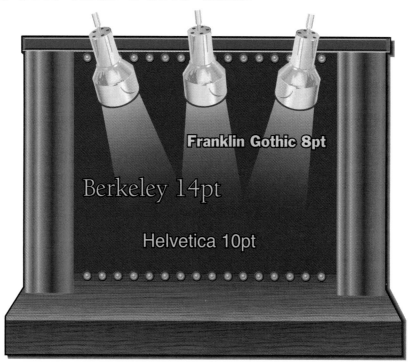

You can use any font that you have installed on your computer in your Illustrator art. You can also adjust the size of a font to make the text in your art more readable.

Franklin Gothic 8pt

Berkeley 14pt

Helvetica 10pt

CHANGE FONT AND FONT SIZE

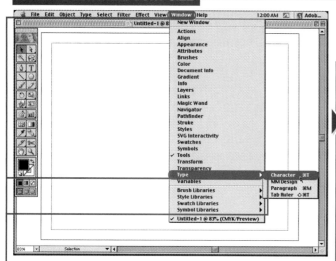

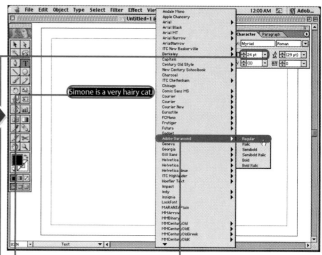

CHANGE THE FONT

■1 Click **Window**.

■2 Click **Type**.

■3 Click **Character**.

■ The Character palette appears.

■ You can also press ⌘ + T or Ctrl + T to bring up the Character palette.

■4 Select the text you want to change with the Selection tool (▶).

Note: See the Chapter 2 to learn about using the Selection tool.

■5 Click ⬍ or ▾ to display a list of fonts.

■6 Click the new font.

■ The font changes immediately.

■ This list lets you select bold, italic, or other font styles.

Where can I find a wider variety of fonts?

You can find some fonts downloadable for free over the Internet; you can also purchase entire font libraries along with dedicated font creators and editors from several companies, including Adobe.

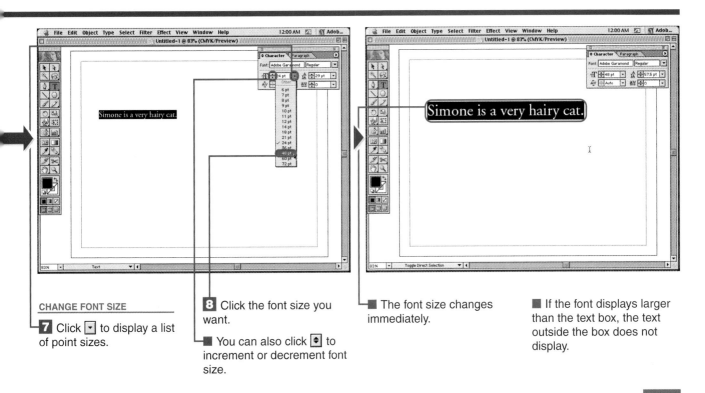

CHANGE FONT SIZE

7 Click ▾ to display a list of point sizes.

8 Click the font size you want.

■ You can also click ▾ to increment or decrement font size.

■ The font size changes immediately.

■ If the font displays larger than the text box, the text outside the box does not display.

CHANGE PARAGRAPH ALIGNMENT

Paragraph alignment helps you present text effectively in your art. Which alignment you choose for your text depends on the shape of the object in which it appears.

CHANGE PARAGRAPH ALIGNMENT

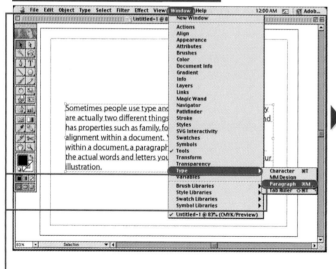

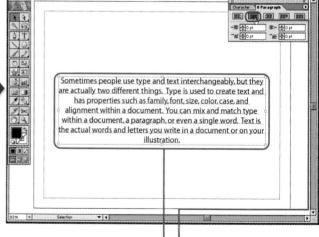

1 Click **Window**.

2 Click **Type**.

3 Click **Paragraph**.

■ You can also press ⌘ + M or Ctrl + M to bring up the Paragraph palette.

■ The Paragraph palette appears.

4 Select the paragraphs you want to align with ▶.

5 Click the Align Center button (▤) to center-align the text.

■ The text center-aligns immediately.

How do I set paragraph indents?

Open the Paragraph palette by clicking **Window**, **Type**, and then **Paragraph**. The lower half of the palette contains settings for paragraph indentations, hanging indents, and first-line indents.

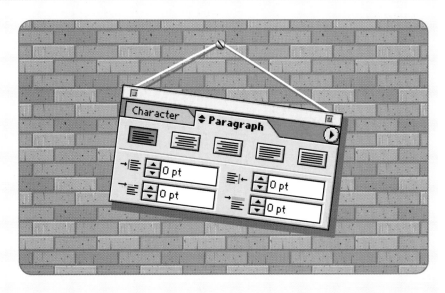

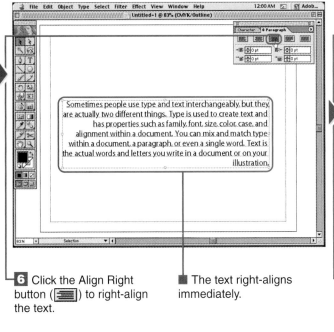

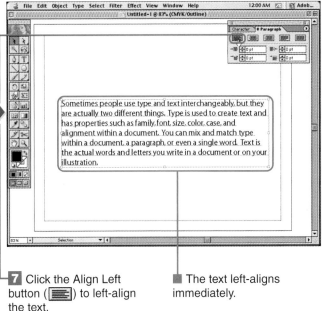

6 Click the Align Right button (▤) to right-align the text.

■ The text right-aligns immediately.

7 Click the Align Left button (▤) to left-align the text.

■ The text left-aligns immediately.

CHANGE TYPE CASE

You can quickly change type case without deleting and retyping text.

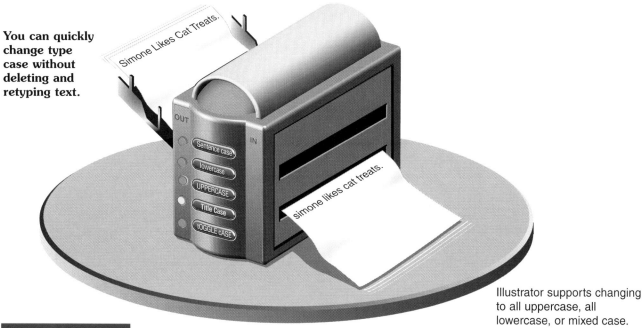

Illustrator supports changing to all uppercase, all lowercase, or mixed case.

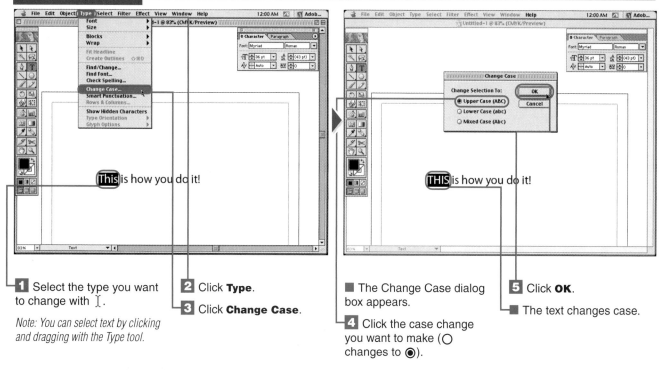

1 Select the type you want to change with ⌶.

Note: You can select text by clicking and dragging with the Type tool.

2 Click **Type**.

3 Click **Change Case**.

■ The Change Case dialog box appears.

4 Click the case change you want to make (○ changes to ◉).

5 Click **OK**.

■ The text changes case.

Smart Punctuation is Illustrator's way of converting some keyboard text into publishable text, giving your designs an attractive, professional appearance. Examples include replacing straight quotes (' or ") with curly quotes (' or "), or two dashes (--) with an em dash (—).

USING SMART PUNCTUATION

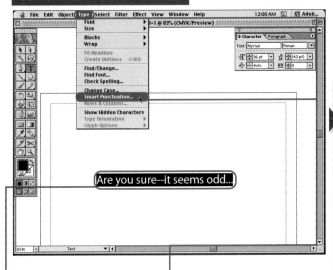

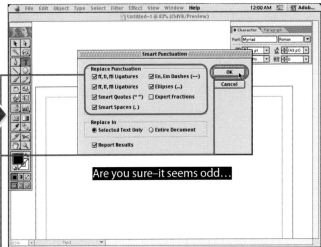

1 Select the text with which you want to use Smart Punctuation.

Note: You can select text by clicking and dragging with the Type tool.

2 Click **Type**.

3 Click **Smart Punctuation**.

■ The Smart Punctuation dialog box appears.

4 Click the Smart Punctuation options you want to apply to your selected text (☐ changes to ☑).

5 Click **OK**.

■ Illustrator immediately applies the Smart Punctuation.

■ If you have the Report Results option selected, a dialog box tells you what Illustrator changes.

CHECK SPELLING

The built-in spell checker lets you check your text for errors without copying it into a word processor.

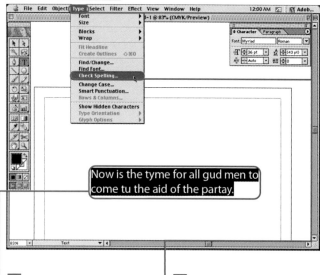

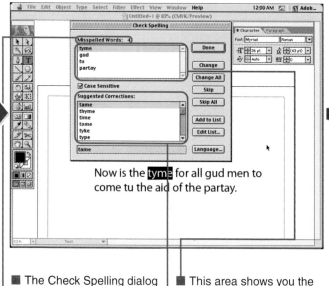

■1 Select the text you want to check for errors.

Note: You can select text by clicking and dragging with the Type tool.

■2 Click **Type**.

■3 Click **Check Spelling**.

■ The Check Spelling dialog box appears.

■ The spell checker reports on the number of words misspelled.

■ This area shows you the misspelled words.

■ This area lists the suggested corrections for the highlighted word.

Can I spell check text that I have turned into an outline?

Once you convert text to an outline, you can no longer run the spell checker on it. For this reason, you should perform a spell check before you covert text to an outline. For more on converting text to an outline, see the section "Convert Type to Outlines."

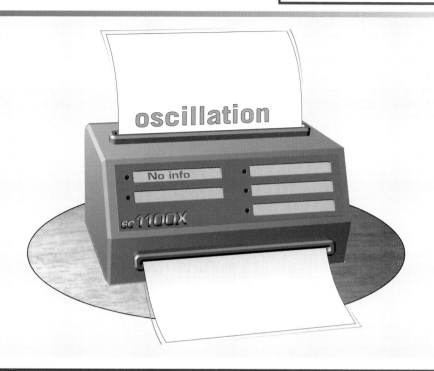

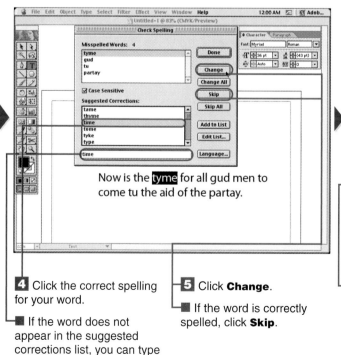

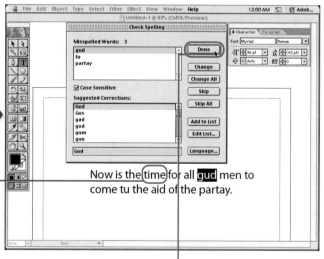

4 Click the correct spelling for your word.

■ If the word does not appear in the suggested corrections list, you can type in the correct spelling in this area.

5 Click **Change**.

■ If the word is correctly spelled, click **Skip**.

■ The word changes to the correct spelling in your text and the next misspelled word is highlighted.

■ Repeat steps **4** and **5** until you have corrected or skipped all of the words.

6 Click **Done**.

■ Your spell check is complete.

LINK TYPE BLOCKS

When you link type blocks, you flow type from one block to another. This lets you flow text around objects in your art. You use linking when you produce newsletters or other publications.

Skylights have been used to brighten up interior spaces for centuries, and today they're more popular than ever as more homeowners convert unfinished attics and bonus rooms into home offices, exercise studios, guest quarters, and playrooms. There

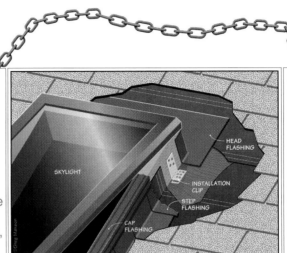

are a couple of other reasons to put in a skylight. Installing one is much easier and more affordable than building a dormer, and modern energy-efficient skylights are completely leakproof if they are properly installed.

LINK TYPE BLOCKS

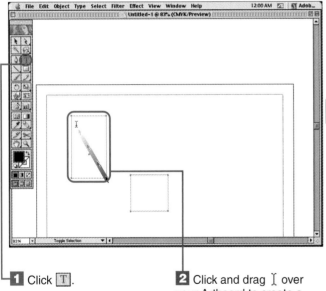

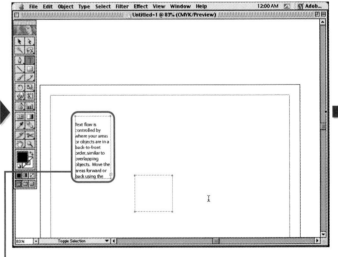

1 Click T.

■ The ↖ changes to I.

2 Click and drag I over your Artboard to create a text box.

3 Repeat step **2** to create additional text boxes.

4 Type the text you want to flow between the text boxes.

■ You can also copy and paste text by clicking **Edit**, then **Copy**, then **Edit**, then **Paste**.

Why does my text flow in a different order through my text areas?

Text flows differently depending on how you stack your objects from front to back in your art. If your text does not flow correctly, you can shuffle the order of your objects by clicking **Object**, **Arrange**, and then **Move Objects Forward** or **Move Objects Back**.

are a couple of other reasons to put in a skylight. Installing one is much easier and more affordable than building a dormer, and modern energy-efficient skylights are completely leakproof if they are properly installed.

Skylights have been used to brighten up interior spaces for centuries, and today they're more popular than ever as more homeowners convert unfinished attics and bonus rooms into home offices, exercise studios, guest quarters, and playrooms. There

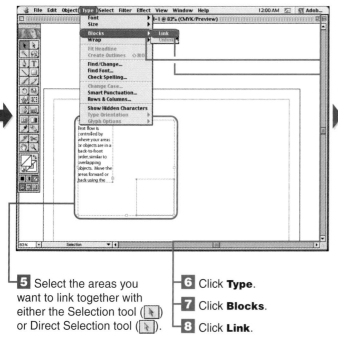

5 Select the areas you want to link together with either the Selection tool (⬚) or Direct Selection tool (⬚).

Note: See Chapter 2 to learn about using the Selection and Direct Selection tools.

6 Click **Type**.

7 Click **Blocks**.

8 Click **Link**.

■ The areas are linked as a single text block.

■ The text flows from one text box to another.

Note: You can use any shaped area for your text boxes.

WRAP TYPE AROUND AN OBJECT

You can make type flow around an object – for instance, around a photograph in a newspaper layout. You can use any object or closed path as a boundary.

WRAP TYPE AROUND AN OBJECT

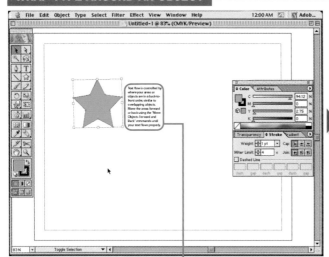

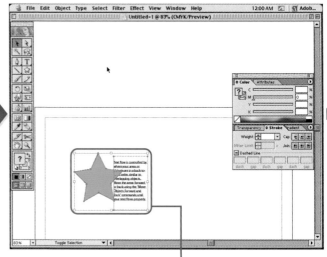

1 Create your object that you want your type to flow around.

2 Create a type area and type the text that you want to flow around the object.

3 Select the object and the text using .

Note: See Chapter 2 to learn more about using the Selection tool.

■ A bounding box appears around the selected object and text.

Why does my type not flow around the object?

You must place your object in front of your text. Click Object, then **Arrange**, then **Move Objects Forward** or **Move Objects Back** until your text flows properly.

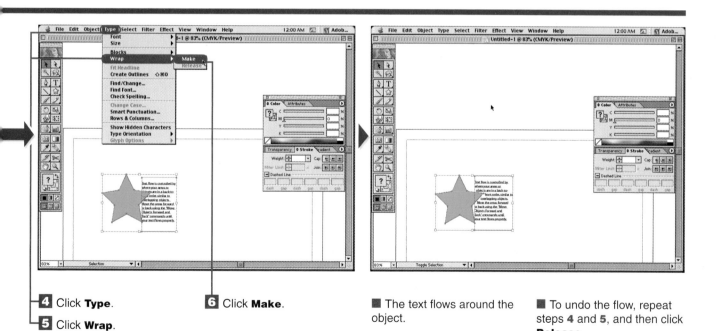

4 Click **Type**.

5 Click **Wrap**.

6 Click **Make**.

■ The text flows around the object.

■ To undo the flow, repeat steps **4** and **5**, and then click **Release**.

CONVERT TYPE TO OUTLINES

Converting type to an outline lets you apply many Illustrator features — such as fills, gradients, and effects — to the letters and words in your art. This can guarantee that your printed output looks exactly like what you see onscreen.

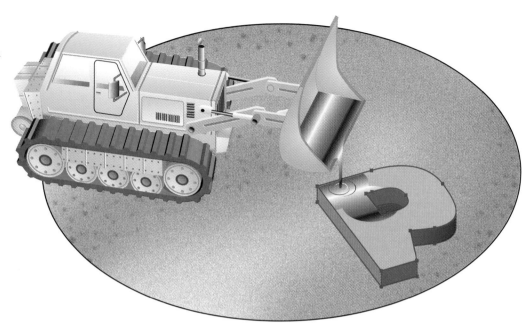

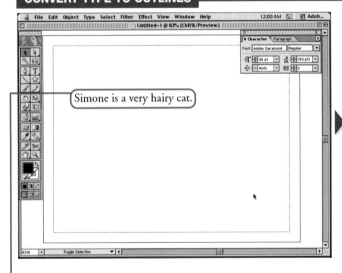

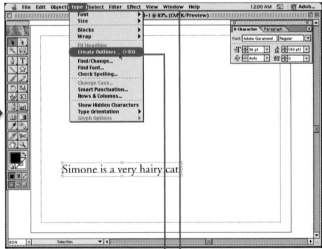

1 Create the text you want to turn into an outline.

Note: For more information, see the section "Insert Point Type."

2 Select your text using a selection tool.

Note: See Chapter 2 to learn about selecting text.

3 Click **Type**.

4 Click **Create Outlines**.

■ You can also press ⌘ + Shift + O or Ctrl + Shift + O to convert outlines on the fly.

Why does my type not convert to an outline?

The **Create Outlines** command works only with vector fonts such as Type 1 PostScript or TrueType; it does not work with raster or bitmapped fonts.

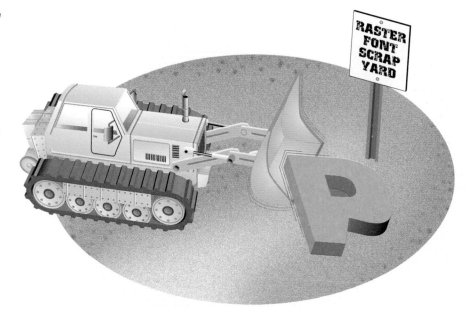

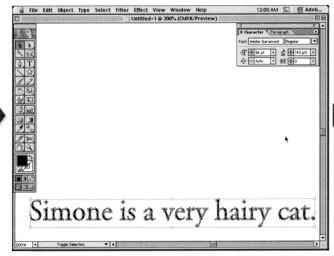

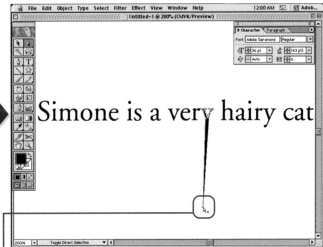

■ Illustrator converts the type to an outline.

■ You can click and drag the outlines to create different effects.

CHAPTER 9

Effects, Filters, and Styles

You can quickly make dramatic changes to your Illustrator artwork using effects and filters, or save often-used combinations of effects as styles. All of these features can save you time when trying to find the right look for your art.

An Introduction to Effects,
  Filters, and Styles 200

Apply the Roughen Effect 202

Apply the Feather Effect 204

Edit an Effect 206

Apply the Hatch Effects Filter 208

Apply the Pointillize Filter 210

Using the Appearance Palette 212

Apply a Style...................................214

Create a New Style 216

Using the Blend Tool 218

Using the Mesh Tool 220

AN INTRODUCTION TO EFFECTS, FILTERS, AND STYLES

You can make dazzling changes to your Illustrator artwork using dozens of effects and filters. You can save combinations of these effects as *styles,* which you can then use later on different artwork.

Effects let you radically alter the look of you artwork, without having to use a lot of different tools and go through a lot of complicated steps. Click an object, select a command from the Effects menu, and Illustrator applies the effect. Some effects, such as the Zig Zag effect, act on the shape of the paths of an object; others, such as many of the stylize effects, act on the colors of an object such as many of the Stylize effects. You can apply different effects to the same object to achieve interesting looks.

Effects and Filters Resources

Because there are many effects and filters available in Illustrator, this chapter covers the basics and shows you some of the most common ones. Besides the Roughen, Add, Subtract, and Stylize Effects, and the Hatch Effect and Pointillize Filter, the application offers numerous commands under the Effects and Filter menus that you can use to alter your artwork. For details on individual effects and filters, see Adobe's on-line help. A highly recommended resource that goes into depth about effects and filters is the *Illustrator 10 Bible* (Hungry Minds, Inc., 2002).

Applying Filters

Filters produce amazing effects — such as turning an object into something resembling an expressionist painting — that you would find very difficult to produce with Illustrator's other tools. Filters are actually add-on features in Illustrator, and you can find their corresponding files in the Plug-ins folder inside the Illustrator application folder. Illustrator gives you the option of applying a filter as an effect, or as a standard filter. Applying it as an effect lets you edit the feature later; applying it as a standard filter means the effects are permanent.

Saving Styles

Styles enable you to save an object's appearance, such as its fill color, stroke color, effects, and other characteristics, so you can easily apply it to other objects. Styles help you to maintain consistency across your Illustrator projects. You can access styles in the Styles palette. Illustrator comes with several styles predefined.

The Appearance Palette

The Appearance palette helps you keep track of what you have previously applied to your objects. When you select an object, the palette displays that object's fill color, stroke characteristic, transparency and blending, and any applied effects. When you apply a style to an object, the palette displays the fill, stroke, and other characteristics associated with that style.

APPLY THE ROUGHEN EFFECT

The Roughen effect skews the anchor points of an object to produce a jagged outline. It can give art a less formal feel.

APPLY THE ROUGHEN EFFECT

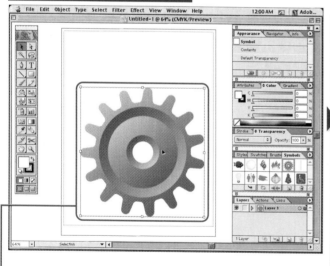

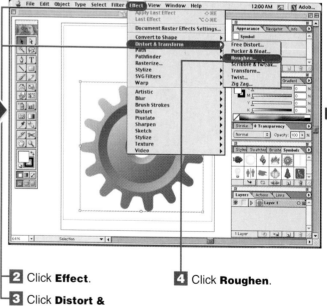

1 Select an object with a selection tool.

2 Click **Effect**.

3 Click **Distort & Transform**.

4 Click **Roughen**.

Besides using the Roughen effect, how else can I distort the edge of an object?

Many of the other effects under the Distort & Transform submenu distort the edge of an object. For example, when you click **Scribble & Tweak**, the Scribble & Tweak dialog box appears. You can change the various options in this dialog box and click **OK** to apply a more curved effect than Roughen. The Zig Zag effect, also under the Distort & Transform submenu, offers a less random option. It lets you apply evenly spaced distortion to an object's edge.

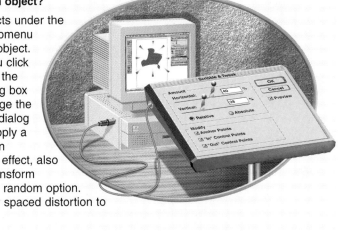

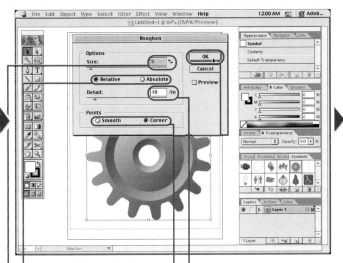

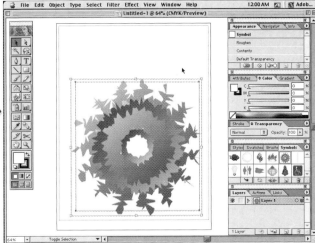

5 Click a sizing option (○ changes to ◉).

■ **Relative** applies a distortion amount relative to the object's size; **Absolute** applies a fixed amount of distortion.

6 Type a Size value to control the magnitude of the distortion.

7 Type a Detail value to control the density of the distortion.

8 Click to apply **Smooth** or **Corner** points (○ changes to ◉).

9 Click **OK**.

■ Your changes take effect.

■ You can also apply the Roughen effect as a filter.

■ Applying a filter takes less memory than an effect, but does not enable you to edit or remove the feature later.

APPLY THE FEATHER EFFECT

You can apply the Feather effect to soften the edges of an object.

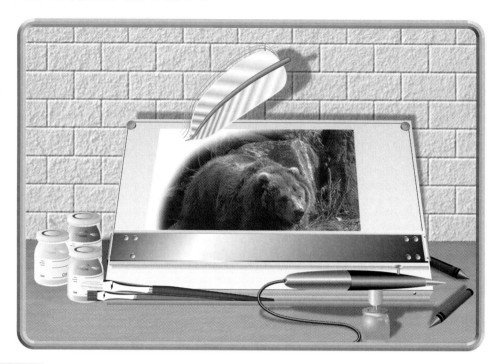

APPLY THE FEATHER EFFECT

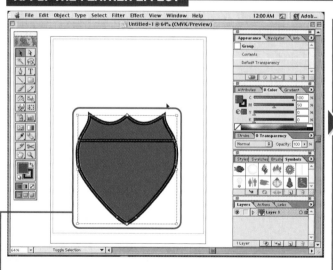

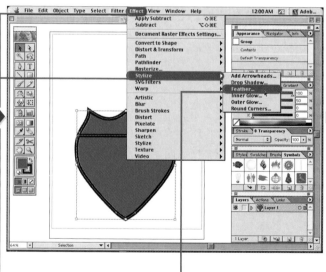

1 Select an object with a selection tool.

2 Click **Effect**.

3 Click **Stylize**.

4 Click **Feather**.

What are some other effects available under the Stylize submenu?

Add Arrowheads inserts arrowheads on the stroke of an object. You can specify where Illustrator applies the arrowheads, as well as their style and their direction. Drop Shadow places a blurred, offset shadow behind an object, giving it a 3-D look. Outer Glow adds diffuse color emanating out from the edges of an object. Inner Glow does the same, except the color emanates inward.

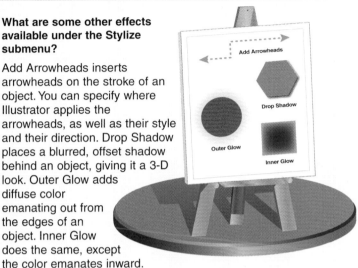

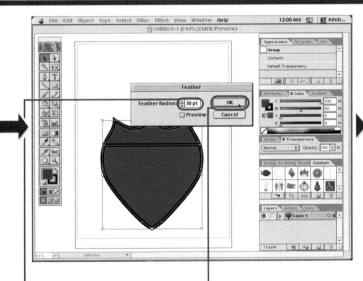

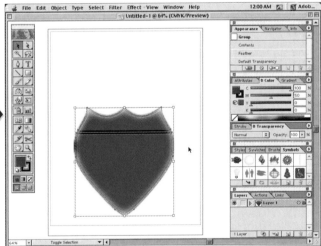

5 Type a Feather Radius to control the amount of softness applied.

6 Click **OK**.

■ The settings take effect in the object.

■ You can also apply the Feather effect as a filter.

■ Applying a filter takes less memory, but does not allow you to edit or remove the feature later.

EDIT AN EFFECT

You can edit or remove
Illustrator effects after
you apply them to an
object. This enables
you to experiment
more freely as you
design your artwork.

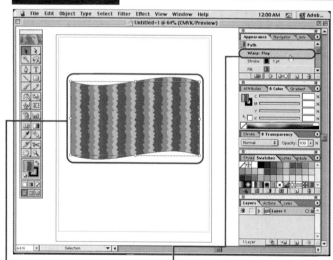

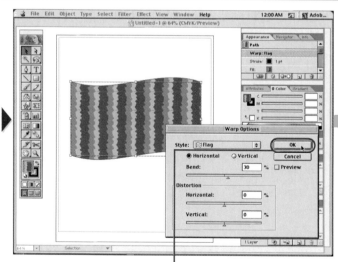

1 Select an object with a
selection tool.

*Note: See Chapter 2 for more on
selecting objects.*

■ Any applied effects
display in the Appearance
palette.

2 Double-click the effect.

■ The appropriate dialog
box appears.

3 Edit the settings in the
dialog box.

*Note: The options available in the
dialog box depend on what effect
you select in step 2.*

4 Click **OK**.

Does Illustrator offer a shortcut for reverting an object to its generic state?

You can select the object, click 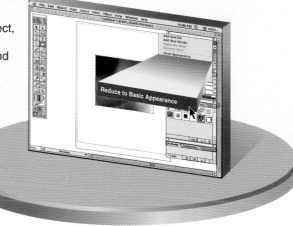 on the Appearance palette, and then click **Reduce to Basic Appearance**. This removes all appearance attributes except for Fill and Stroke.

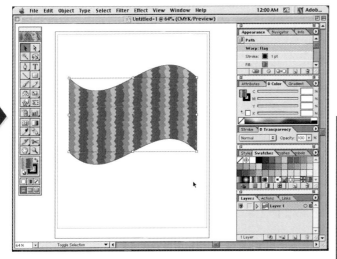

■ The new effect settings take effect.

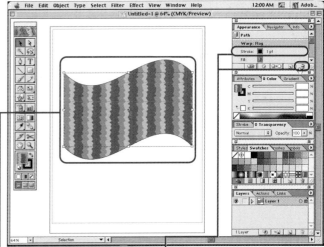

REMOVE AN EFFECT

1 Select an object with a selection tool.

Note: See Chapter 2 for more on selecting objects.

2 Click to select the effect in the Appearance palette.

3 Click Delete Selected Item (🗑).

■ Illustrator removes the effect.

APPLY THE HATCH EFFECTS FILTER

The Hatch Effects filter applies random textures such as crosshatching, which simulates a pen-and-ink drawing.

Hatch Effects is a vector-based filter, which means that you do not have to rasterize your artwork before you apply it.

For more about vector-based objects and rasterizing, see Chapter 12. Illustrator lists the vector-based filters in the top half of the Filter menu.

APPLY THE HATCH EFFECTS FILTER

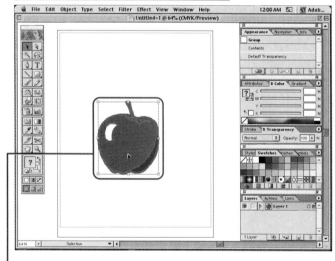

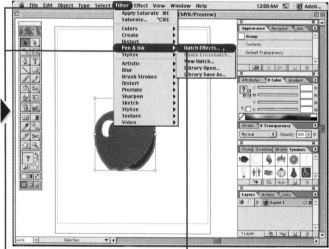

1 Select an object with a selection tool.

Note: See Chapter 2 for more on selecting objects.

2 Click **Filter**.

3 Click **Pen & Ink**.

4 Click **Hatch Effects**.

■ The Hatch Effects dialog box appears.

Can I apply hatch effects to a photographic object?

Yes, but you use a different command. You can apply the Photo Crosshatch filter to add hatch effects to any rasterized images on your artboard. To access the Photo Crosshatch filter, click **Filter**, click **Pen & Ink**, and then click **Photo Crosshatch**. A dialog box appears with various property settings, which you can change by clicking and dragging a specific slider △. You can then click **OK** to apply the effect.

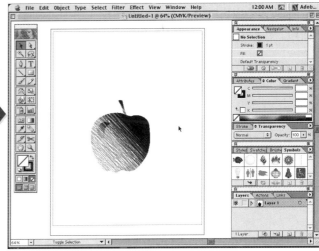

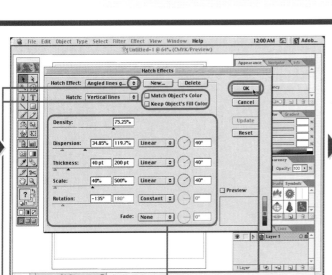

5 Click ◆ or ▼ to display predefined hatch effects and click the effect you want.

■ Click these options if you want to retain the object's current color (☐ changes to ☑).

■ You can optionally change the hatch shape applied in the Hatch menu.

■ You can also adjust other settings to fine-tune your design.

6 Click **OK**.

■ The hatch effect is applied to the object.

APPLY THE POINTILLIZE FILTER

Illustrator 10 comes with a number of Photoshop filters including the Pointillize filter, which makes your artwork look like it consists of small colored dots, like a pointillist painting.

Photoshop works with rasterized images, so you have to rasterize your artwork before you apply a Photoshop filter.

You also must work in RGB mode. You can find the Photoshop-based filters in the bottom half of the Filter menu.

APPLY THE POINTILLIZE FILTER

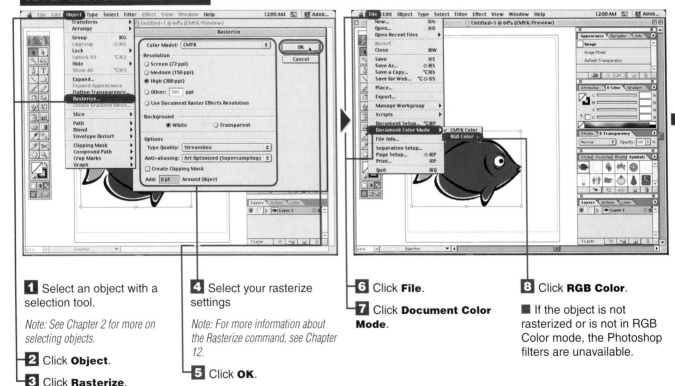

1 Select an object with a selection tool.

Note: See Chapter 2 for more on selecting objects.

2 Click **Object**.

3 Click **Rasterize**.

4 Select your rasterize settings

Note: For more information about the Rasterize command, see Chapter 12.

5 Click **OK**.

6 Click **File**.

7 Click **Document Color Mode**.

8 Click **RGB Color**.

■ If the object is not rasterized or is not in RGB Color mode, the Photoshop filters are unavailable.

How can I sharpen a blurry photo?

The Unsharp Mask filter is a great tool for sharpening photographic images. It enables you to precisely control the amount of sharpening that you apply. To apply it, select your object, click **Filter**, **Sharpen**, and then click **Unsharp Mask**. In the Unsharp Mask dialog box, type values or click and drag the sliders ▲ to adjust the Amount, Radius, and Threshold settings. Click **OK** to apply your changes. Amount controls the overall amount of sharpening. A low Radius setting limits the sharpening to the image's edge, while a high Radius setting adds sharpening to the entire image. Threshold determines how much contrast you must have before Illustrator sharpens the image.

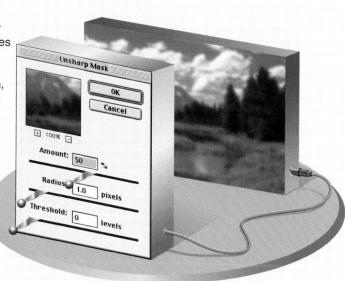

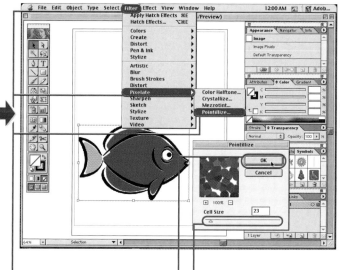

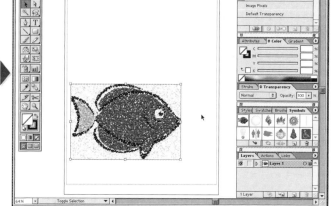

■⁹ Click **Filter**.

■¹⁰ Click **Pixelate**.

■¹¹ Click **Pointillize**.

■ The Pointillize dialog box appears.

■¹² Click and drag the slider to specify the size of the points.

■¹³ Click **OK**.

■ Illustrator applies the effect to the object.

You can view the
appearance attributes
for an object in the
Appearance palette.
Reordering the
attributes in the
palette can change
how Illustrator
displays an object.

USING THE APPEARANCE PALETTE

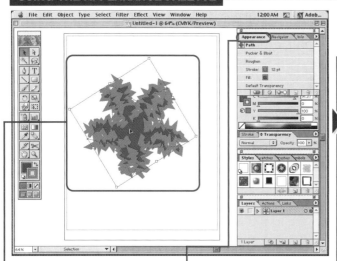

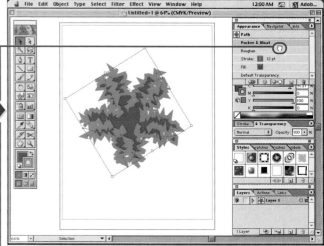

**VIEW ATTRIBUTES WITH THE
APPEARANCE PALETTE**

1 Select an object with a
selection tool.

*Note: See Chapter 2 for more on
selecting objects.*

2 Click the **Appearance**
palette tab.

■ Illustrator lists the
appearance attributes for
the object.

**REARRANGE APPEARANCE
ATTRIBUTES**

3 Click and drag to
rearrange the attributes.

■ The object changes
to reflect the rearranged
attributes. Illustrator applies
attributes from the top down
as listed in the Appearance
palette.

How can I edit a style using the Appearance palette?

If you apply a style to an object and then edit that object's attributes, you can replace the original style with the new attributes by clicking ▶ in the Appearance palette and then clicking **Redefine Style**. See the section "Apply a Style" for more information.

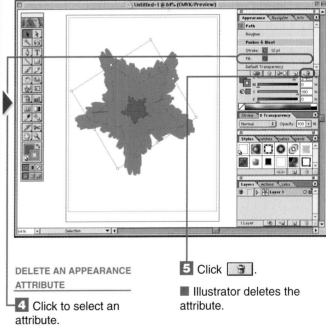

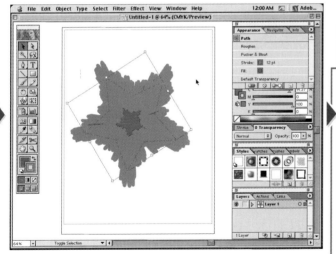

■ The object assumes its new appearance.

DELETE AN APPEARANCE ATTRIBUTE

4 Click to select an attribute.

5 Click 🗑.

■ Illustrator deletes the attribute.

APPLY A STYLE

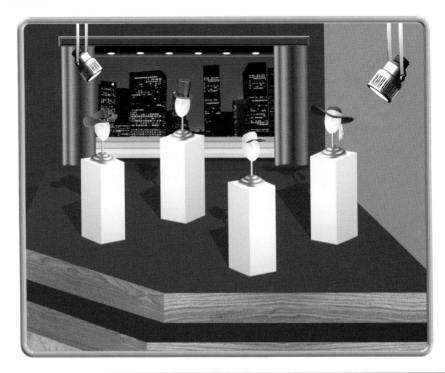

You can apply a style to an object to quickly and easily give it a predefined appearance. A style definition can include Fill and Stroke colors, pattern information, and other attributes.

APPLY A STYLE

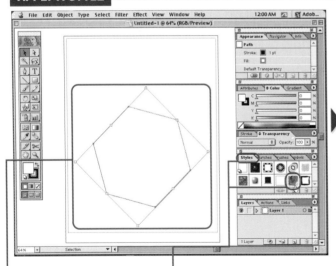

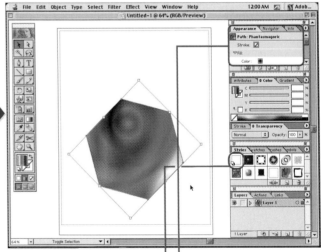

1 Select an object using a selection tool.

Note: See Chapter 2 for more on selecting objects.

2 Click the **Styles** palette tab.

3 Click a style.

■ Illustrator applies the style to the object.

■ This example shows a Fill style.

■ The attributes that define the style appear in the Appearance palette.

■ You can remove the style by clicking the Default style in the Styles palette.

How can I access more predefined styles?

Illustrator comes with dozens of predefined styles. Click **Window**, click **Style Libraries**, and then click a style set. The set of styles opens in a new palette.

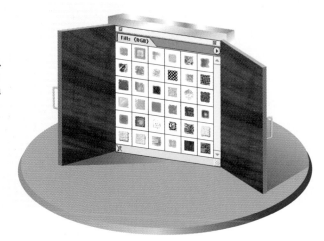

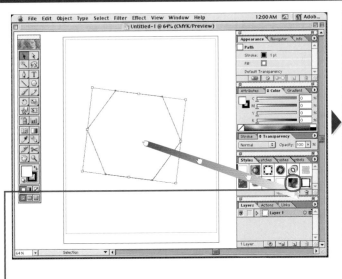

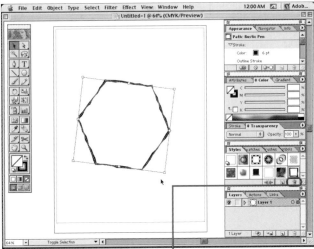

<u>DRAG AND DROP A STYLE</u>

1 Click a style.

2 Click and drag the style onto an object.

■ The ▶ changes to a ✋ or ▧.

■ Illustrator applies the style to the object.

■ This example shows a Stroke style.

■ To delete a style from the Styles palette, click the style and then click 🗑.

CREATE A NEW STYLE

You can save the appearance attributes for an object as a new style in the Styles palette. Then you can apply the style to other objects.

CREATE A NEW STYLE

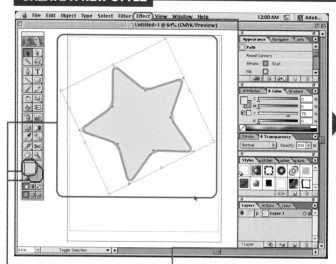

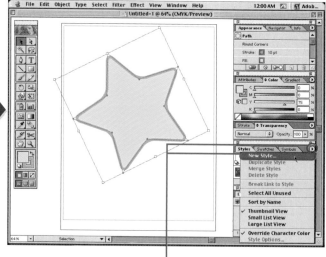

1 Select the object using a selection tool.

2 Specify a Fill color or pattern.

3 Specify a Stroke color or pattern.

Note: See Chapter 2 for more on selecting objects. To specify a Fill or Stroke color, see Chapter 7.

4 Specify any effects you want included in your style.

5 Specify any other appearance attributes, such as transparency.

6 Click the **Styles** palette tab.

7 Click the ▶.

8 Click **New Style**.

Does Illustrator provide a shortcut for creating a new style in the Styles palette?

Yes. Illustrator displays the appearance attributes of a selected object in the Appearance palette. To define those attributes as a new style, you can click and drag the thumbnail at the top of the Appearance palette onto the Styles palette.

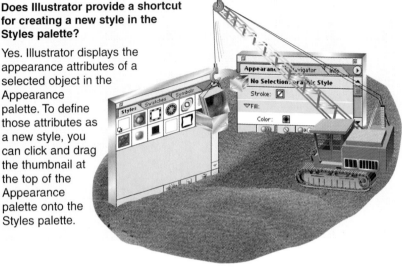

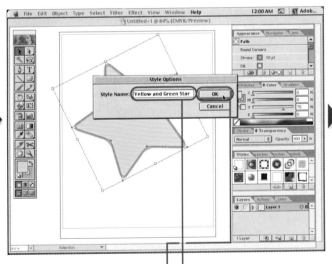

■ The Style Options dialog box appears.

9 Type a name for the new style.

10 Click **OK**.

■ The new style appears in the Styles palette.

Note: To use the new styles, see the section "Apply a Style," earlier in this chapter.

USING THE BLEND TOOL

You can create a
sequence of intermediate
objects between two
objects with the Blend
tool. Doing this can
imply motion or gradual
change in your artwork.

USING THE BLEND TOOL

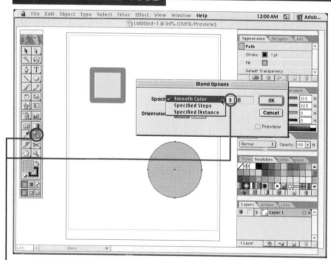

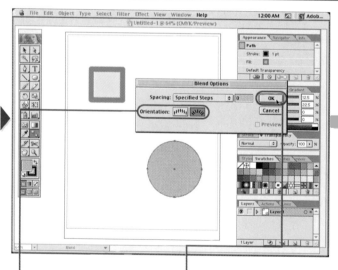

1 Double-click the Blend
tool (⬚).

■ The Blend Options dialog
box appears.

2 Click ⬚ or ⬚ to select
your spacing options.

■ You can specify that
intermediate steps between
the objects be based on
color, on a specific number
of steps, or on distance.

■ Specifying a number
of steps determines the
number of intermediate
objects that Illustrator
creates.

3 Click an option to
specify whether you want the
intermediate objects aligned
with the enclosing page ⬚
or with the path between the
objects ⬚.

4 Click **OK**.

How do I change the arrangement of a blend?

Select the blend, and then click **Object**, **Blend**, and then **Reverse Spline** to reverse the order of the blended objects along the path. You can also select **Reverse Front to Back** under the **Blend** menu to switch the stacking order of the objects.

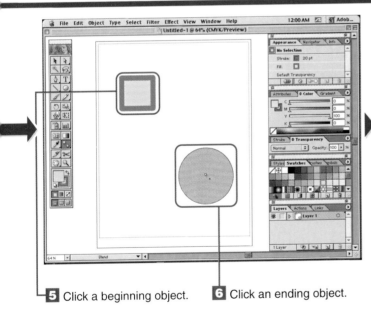

5 Click a beginning object.

6 Click an ending object.

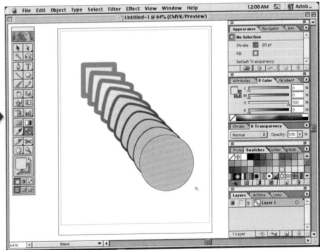

■ Illustrator creates intermediate objects between the selected objects.

■ You can also select more than two objects and Illustrator creates intermediate objects between each pair of objects in the sequence.

■ To remove a blend, select the group of objects and then click **Object**, **Blend**, and then **Release**.

USING THE MESH TOOL

You can create multicolored objects that have a three-dimensional appearance with the Mesh tool.

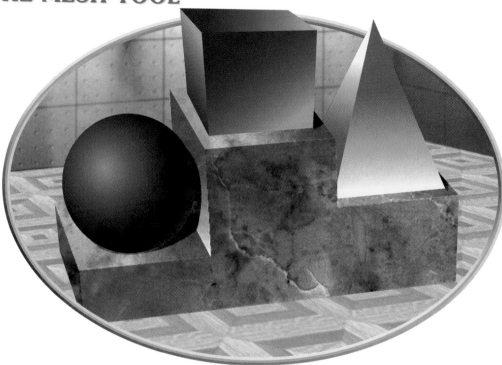

USING THE MESH TOOL

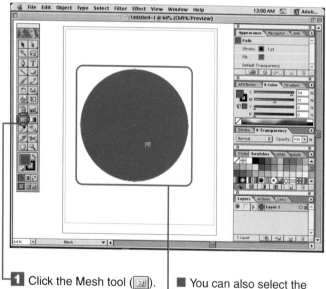

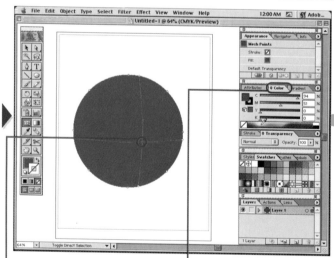

1 Click the Mesh tool (image).

■ You can also select the tool by pressing **U**.

2 Click an object.

■ The object converts into a mesh object, with a mesh of points laid atop it.

3 Click a point on the mesh object.

4 Click the **Color** palette tab.

5 Select a color.

Note: For more information about selecting colors, see Chapter 7.

How can I add or delete points on my mesh objects?

You can hold Shift while you click with the Mesh tool (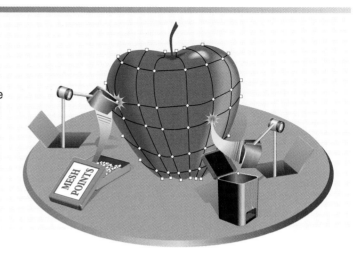) to add a point. You can hold option or Alt while you click to delete a point.

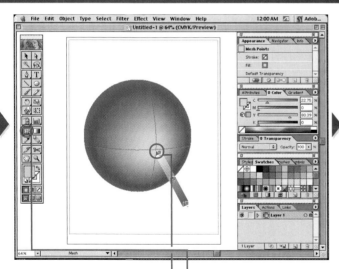

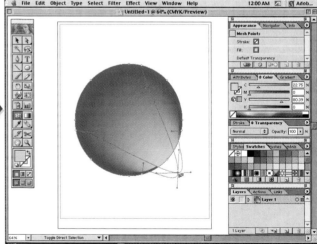

■ The color applies itself to the mesh around the selected point.

6 Press U to select the Mesh tool.

7 Click and drag a mesh point (📐).

■ The mesh overlay distorts and the color gradients on the object change to reflect the distortion.

■ You can continue to add colors and adjust the mesh by repeating steps **3** to **7**.

■ To create more complicated meshes, you can select an object and click **Object** and then **Create Gradient Mesh**.

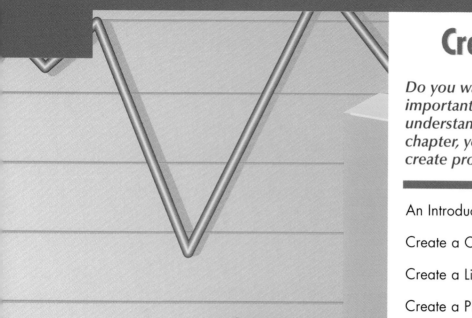

CHAPTER 10

Creating Graphs

Do you want to present your important information in an easy-to-understand and visual format? In this chapter, you learn to use Illustrator to create professional graphs.

An Introduction to Graphs 224

Create a Column Graph 226

Create a Line Graph......................228

Create a Pie Graph 230

Edit Graph Data............................232

Change a Graph Type 233

Add Color to a Graph 234

Import Data for a Graph 236

AN INTRODUCTION TO GRAPHS

Illustrator lets you organize and display numeric information using a variety of graph styles.

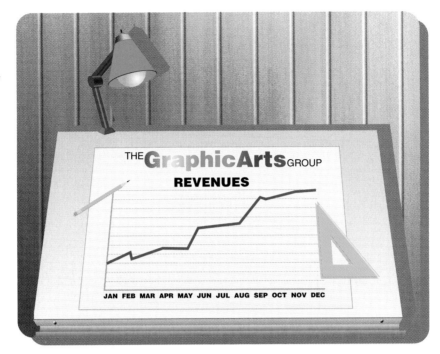

Column and Bar Graphs

Column and bar graphs offer an easy way to compare quantities. Column graphs display information with vertical rectangles that rest on the graph's x (bottom) axis, while bar graphs use horizontal rectangles that rest on the y (side) axis. You can customize your column and bar graphs by coloring the rectangles, or by replacing the rectangles with custom objects.

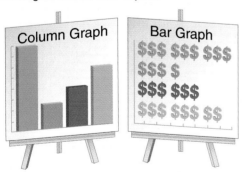

Line Graphs

You often use line graphs to compare quantities that change over time. Quantities are measured along the y (side) axis and time along the x (bottom) axis. You can color the lines of your line graphs to make them more attractive, or leave the lines off and display your data as unconnected points.

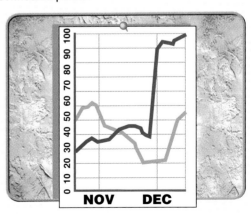

Pie Graphs

Pie graphs are convenient for displaying quantities that are components — or percentages — of a whole. In this type of graph, Illustrator represents each component as a wedge in a pie, with each wedge's size proportional to its quantity. You can display labels for the wedges in a separate legend, or on the wedges themselves.

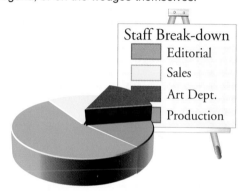

Other Graph Types

Illustrator also allows you to create *stacked column* and *bar graphs*, which let you add more information by subdividing a graph's rectangles; *area graphs*, which are similar to line graphs except that there is a solid area beneath the line; and *scatter graphs*, which let you display a set of x-y coordinate combinations.

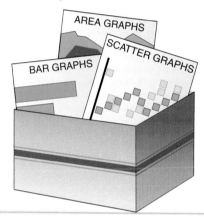

Specifying Graph Data

You type data for your Illustrator graph in a data dialog box. This box features rows and columns where you type the labels and values, which appear in your graph. After you create a graph, you can revisit the data dialog box to make edits or updates.

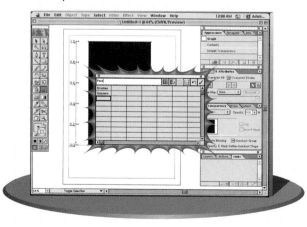

Importing Graph Data

Illustrator also allows you to import data for your graphs from text files. You can also copy and paste data from spreadsheet applications such as Microsoft Excel and Lotus 1-2-3. Because you may find entering data into Illustrator's data dialog box tedious, importing pre-existing data can really save you time.

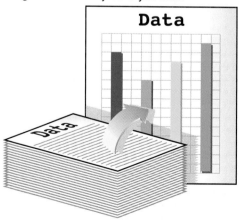

CREATE A COLUMN GRAPH

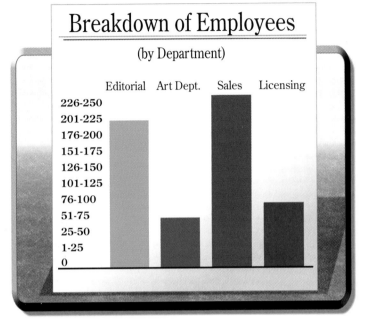

Breakdown of Employees

(by Department)

	Editorial	Art Dept.	Sales	Licensing
226-250				
201-225				
176-200				
151-175				
126-150				
101-125				
76-100				
51-75				
25-50				
1-25				
0				

You can compare several different quantities using a column graph. Displaying a table of data as a column graph can help your audience better understand it.

CREATE A COLUMN GRAPH

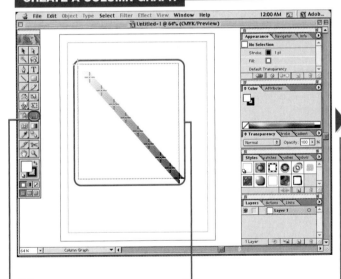

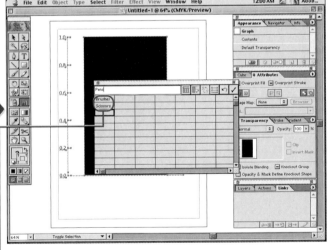

1 Click the Column Graph Tool ( ).

2 Click and drag a rectangle to define the area for your graph.

■ The data dialog box appears.

3 Type the labels for the graph in the first column.

■ These labels appear along the x (bottom) axis of the graph when you generate it.

■ To type data, click a cell and type data into the entry area.

How do I create a bar graph?

A bar graph is similar to a column graph, except that it features horizontal bars instead of vertical columns. You can create a bar graph by clicking the Bar Graph Tool (). You access the tool by clicking and holding . You can then perform the steps in this section, starting with step 2.

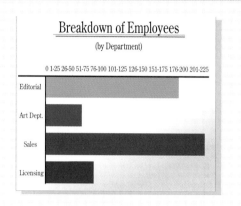

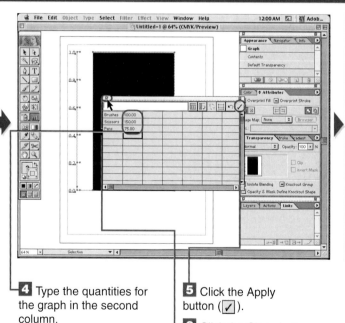

4 Type the quantities for the graph in the second column.

■ These quantities determine the height of the columns of the graph.

5 Click the Apply button ().

6 Click the Close button () for the data dialog box.

■ The column graph displays.

Note: To change the colors of the columns, see the section "Add Color to a Graph."

227

CREATE A LINE GRAPH

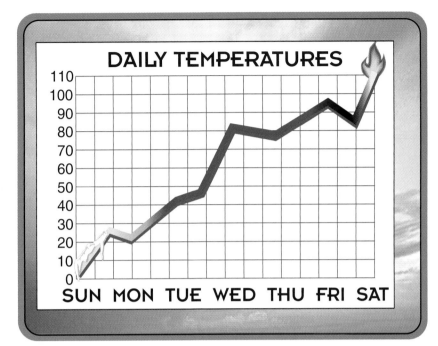

You can compare how quantities change over time using a line graph. This can help your audience visualize information trends.

CREATE A LINE GRAPH

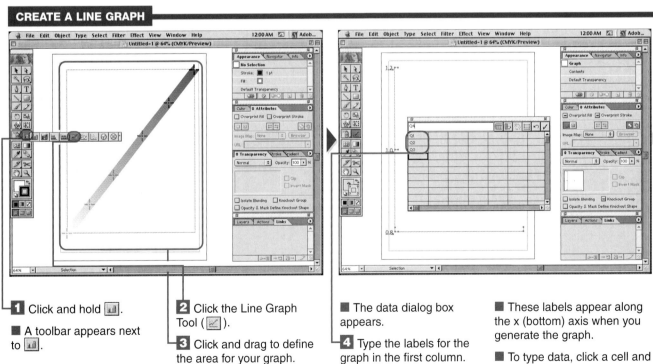

1 Click and hold 📊.

■ A toolbar appears next to 📊.

2 Click the Line Graph Tool (📈).

3 Click and drag to define the area for your graph.

■ The data dialog box appears.

4 Type the labels for the graph in the first column.

■ These labels appear along the x (bottom) axis when you generate the graph.

■ To type data, click a cell and type data into the entry area.

How do I display just the data points in a line graph without the line?

After creating your line graph, select the graph using the Selection Tool (). Click **Object**, **Graph**, and then **Type**. A dialog box appears allowing you to modify your graph. Deselect the **Connect Data Points** option (☑ changes to ☐). Click **OK** to apply the change.

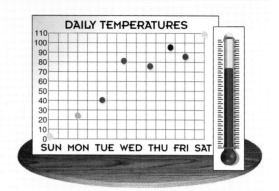

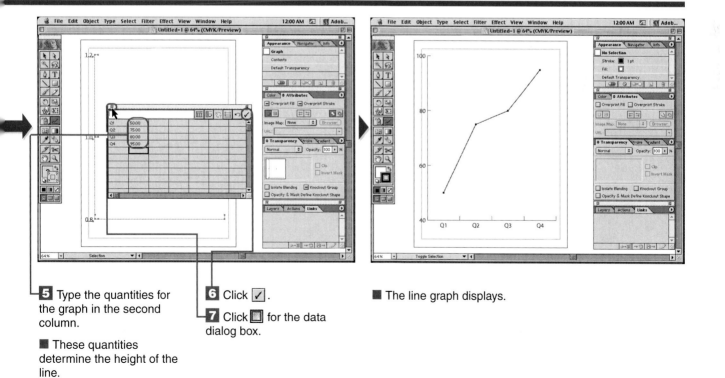

5 Type the quantities for the graph in the second column.

■ These quantities determine the height of the line.

6 Click ☑.

7 Click ▣ for the data dialog box.

■ The line graph displays.

CREATE A PIE GRAPH

You can compare
quantities that make up
a whole using a pie
graph. Pie graphs can
help an audience
visualize percentages.

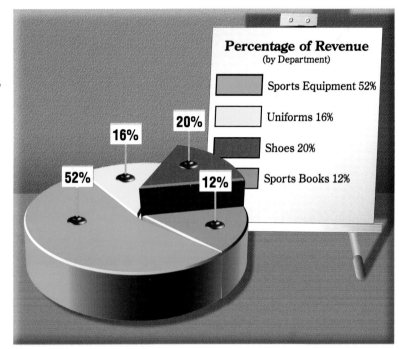

CREATE A PIE GRAPH

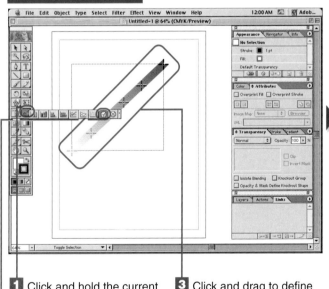

1 Click and hold the current graph tool.

2 Click the Pie Graph Tool (⊙).

3 Click and drag to define the area for your graph.

■ The data dialog box appears.

4 Type the labels for the graph in the first row.

■ These labels appear next to the pie graph as a legend.

■ To type data, click a cell and type data into the entry area.

How do I place labels on the pie wedges instead of in a legend?

After creating your line graph, select the graph using . Click **Object**, **Graph**, and then **Type**. The Graph Type dialog box appears allowing you to modify your graph. Click ▲ and then click **Legends in Wedges** in the Legend menu. Click **OK** to apply the change.

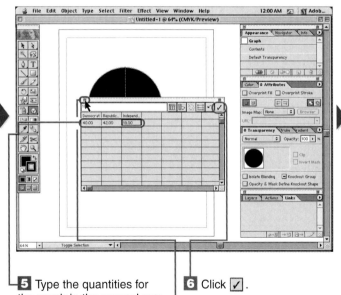

5 Type the quantities for the graph in the second row.

■ These quantities determine the size of the pie wedges.

6 Click ✓.

7 Click 🔲 for the data dialog box.

■ The pie graph displays.

Note: You can use positive or negative numbers for your pie graph values, but you cannot mix positive and negative numbers.

EDIT GRAPH DATA

You can make changes
to the data for a graph
to correct mistakes or
add more information.

EDIT AN EXISTING GRAPH

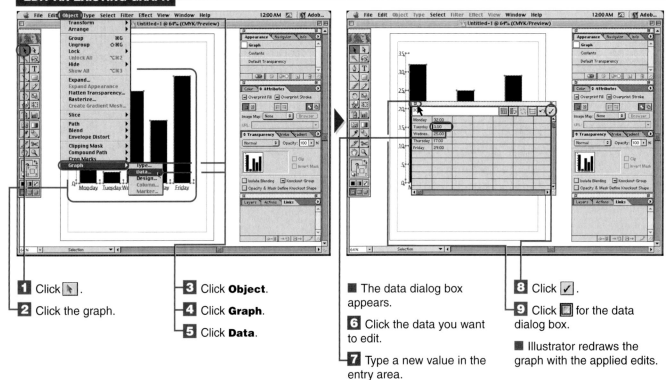

1 Click ▶.

2 Click the graph.

3 Click **Object**.

4 Click **Graph**.

5 Click **Data**.

■ The data dialog box
appears.

6 Click the data you want
to edit.

7 Type a new value in the
entry area.

8 Click ✓.

9 Click ▣ for the data
dialog box.

■ Illustrator redraws the
graph with the applied edits.

You can change the type
of graph to present your
data in a different
format.

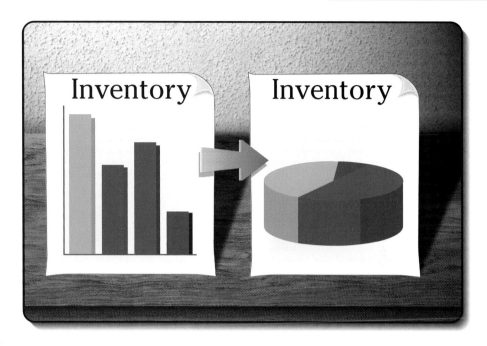

CHANGE A GRAPH TYPE

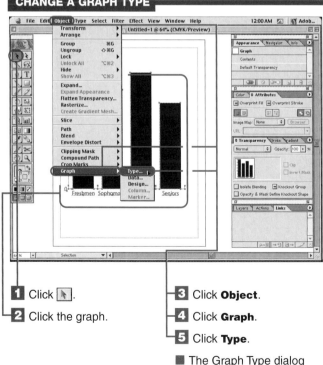

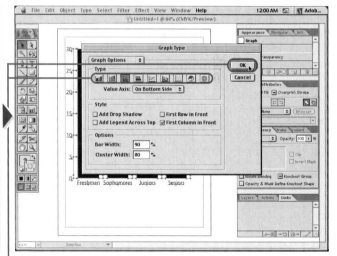

1 Click [pointer].

2 Click the graph.

3 Click **Object**.

4 Click **Graph**.

5 Click **Type**.

■ The Graph Type dialog
box appears.

6 Click an icon to select a
different type of graph.

7 Click **OK**.

■ The graph transforms into
the new graph type.

*Note: Depending on the new type
selected, you may need to rearrange
your data or resize your graph to
produce a result that displays
correctly. See the earlier tasks in this
chapter for details.*

ADD COLOR TO A GRAPH

You can add color to a graph to distinguish its different parts or to emphasize critical data.

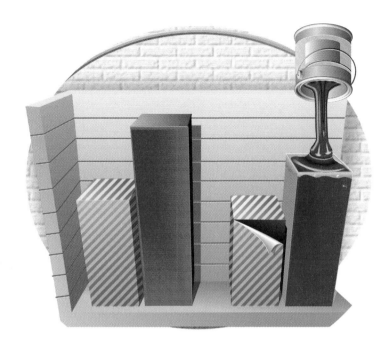

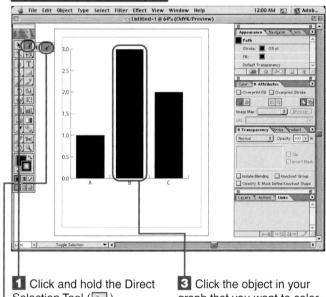

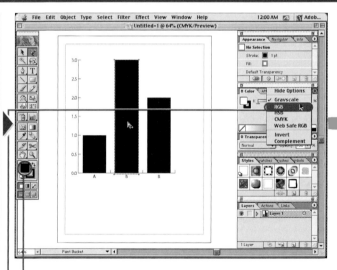

1 Click and hold the Direct Selection Tool ( ).

2 Click the Group Selection Tool ( ) from the Toolbar that appears.

3 Click the object in your graph that you want to color.

■ You can press **Shift** and then click another object if you want to select more than one object in the graph.

4 Click the Fill button ( ) in the Toolbox.

5 Click the **Colors** palette tab.

6 Click and click a color space.

Note: You can select Web Safe RGB to access colors that appear consistently across Web browser types. See Chapter 14 for details.

How do I add a drop shadow to my graph?

Click to select your graph using a selection tool. Click **Object**, **Graph**, and then **Type**. In the Graph Type dialog box, click the **Add Drop Shadow** check box (☐ changes to ☑). Click **OK** to apply the drop-shadow effect.

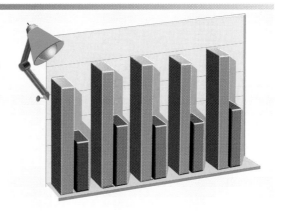

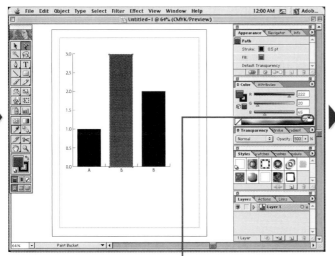

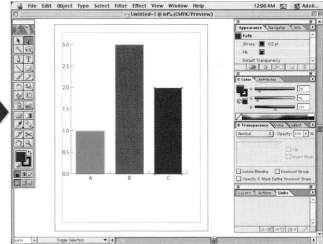

7 Place your cursor (➤) over the color ramp.

■ The ➤ becomes an eyedropper (✐).

8 Click a color.

■ You can also use the sliders to specify a color.

■ The color applies to the selected object in the graph.

9 You can repeat steps **3** through **8** to color other parts of your graph.

Note: See Chapter 7 for more information about coloring objects in Illustrator.

IMPORT DATA FOR A GRAPH

You can save having to type graph data by hand by importing data from another file.

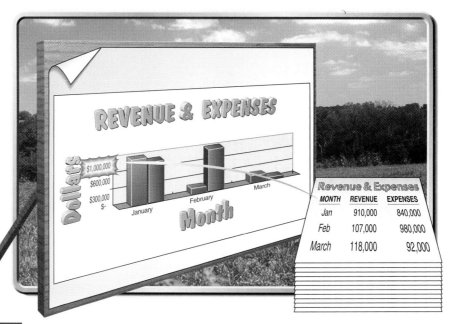

IMPORT DATA FOR A GRAPH

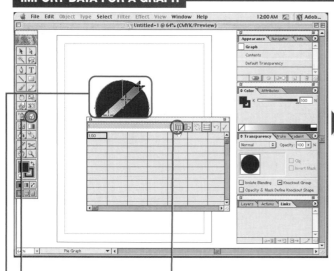

1 Select a graph tool.

Note: See the previous sections in this chapter for information on selecting tools for creating different types of graphs.

2 Click and drag to specify the area for the graph.

■ The data dialog box opens.

3 Click the Import Data button (🎛).

■ An Import Graph Data dialog box opens.

4 Click the folder containing the file with the data to import.

■ Illustrator can import data from text files, where values are separated by tabs, and rows are separated by line breaks.

5 Click the file.

6 Click **Import** or **Open**.

How do I import data from spreadsheet files?

You can import data from spreadsheets such as Microsoft Excel and Lotus 1-2-3 by first opening a file in the spreadsheet application. Then you can copy and paste the values from the spreadsheet into Illustrator's data dialog box.

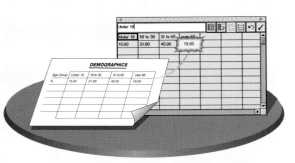

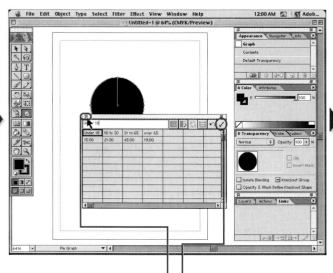

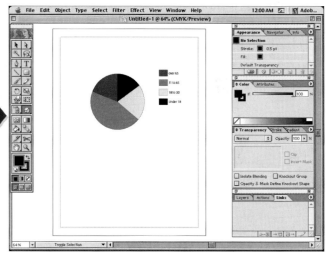

■ Illustrator imports the data from the file into the data dialog box.

■ You can import more data by clicking a data field and repeating steps **3** through **6**.

7 Click ✓.

8 Click ▣ for the data dialog box.

■ Illustrator creates the graph using the imported data.

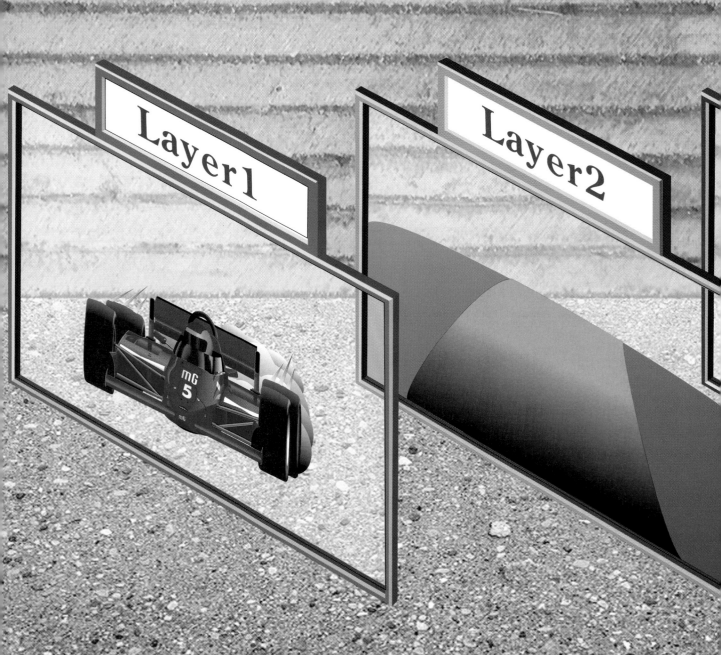

CHAPTER 11

Working with Layers

Layers let you separate elements of your Illustrator artwork so you can move and transform them independently of one another.

An Introduction to Layers 240

Create a New Layer 241

Delete a Layer 242

Hide a Layer 243

Lock a Layer 244

Rearrange Layers 245

Create a Sublayer 246

Move Objects Between Layers 248

Edit Layer Properties 250

Create a Template Layer 252

Merge Layers................................254

Flatten Artwork.............................255

Release Objects to Layers 256

Create a Clipping Mask
   with a Layer 258

AN INTRODUCTION TO LAYERS

You can create artwork in Illustrator that is made up of multiple layers, with each layer containing different objects. Layers let you easily manipulate some objects while leaving the other objects in your art alone.

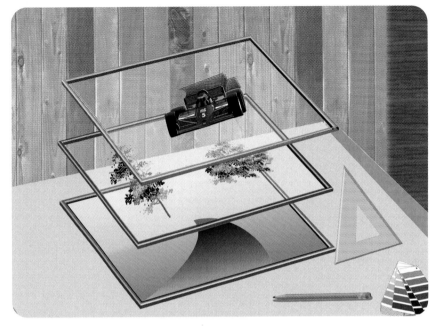

You can place objects in layers as an alternative to grouping objects. See Chapter 5 for more about grouping.

Layer Independence

Illustrator layers enable you to isolate as well as group different parts of your artwork. Each layer can include its own collection of shapes, paths, and applied effects that you can easily view and manipulate independently of the elements in other layers. You can also create a special type of layer that you can use as a template for creating art.

Using the Layers Palette

You can create, delete, and hide layers in your image using the Layers palette. The palette also lets you combine layers, or rearrange how they stack in your artwork. You can even organize layers in a nested fashion with the Layers palette by creating sublayers that exist within other layers.

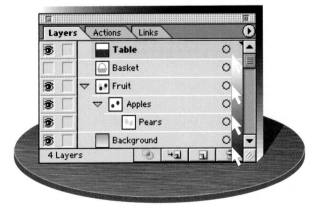

CREATE A NEW LAYER

You can create separate layers to keep elements in your artwork independent from one another, or to group certain elements together.

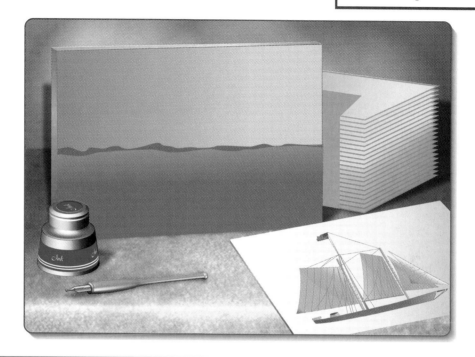

CREATE A NEW LAYER

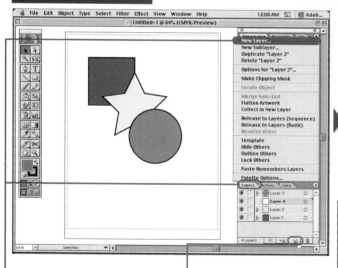

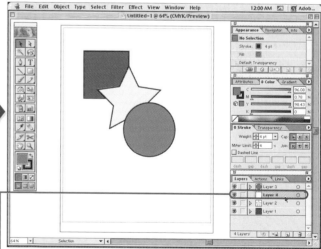

1 Click the **Layers** palette tab.

2 If your document already has more than one layer, select the layer below where you want to create the new layer.

3 Click the Create New Layer button ( ).

■ You can also click ▶ from the Layers palette and click **New Layer**.

■ Illustrator creates and selects a new layer.

■ Illustrator adds any newly created art to the selected layer.

DELETE A LAYER

You can delete a layer when you no longer have a need for the elements in it.

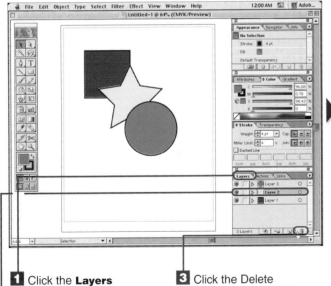

1 Click the **Layers** palette tab.

2 Click a layer.

3 Click the Delete Selection button ( ).

■ You can also click ▶ from the Layers palette and click **Delete**.

■ If the selected layer contains artwork, Illustrator prompts you to confirm that you want to delete it.

■ Illustrator deletes the selected layer.

■ You can undo the deletion by clicking **Edit**, and then **Undo Deletion**.

Note: To hide a layer without deleting it, see the section "Hide a Layer."

You can hide a layer to
temporarily remove
elements in that layer
from view or to keep
elements from printing.

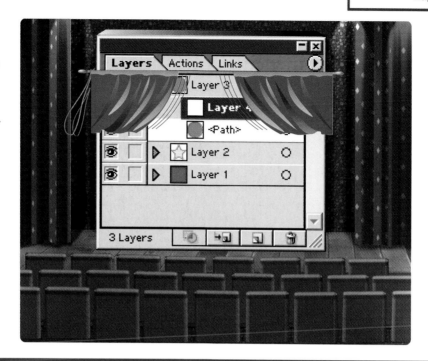

HIDE A LAYER

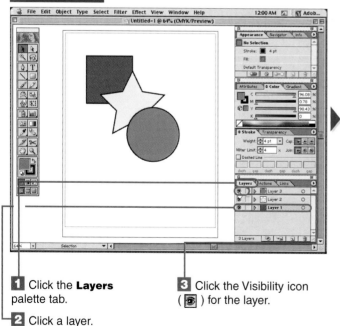

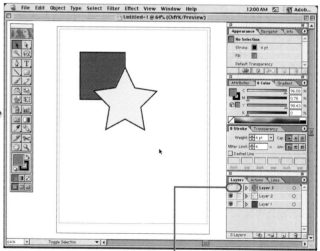

1 Click the **Layers** palette tab.

2 Click a layer.

3 Click the Visibility icon (👁) for the layer.

■ Illustrator hides the layer and does not display the elements in that layer.

■ You can click the blank area to make the layer visible again and the 👁 reappears.

Note: To remove a layer permanently, see the section "Delete a Layer."

LOCK A LAYER

You can lock a layer to keep yourself or others from selecting or editing artwork on that layer. Locking a layer protects finished elements from accidental changes or deletions.

LOCK A LAYER

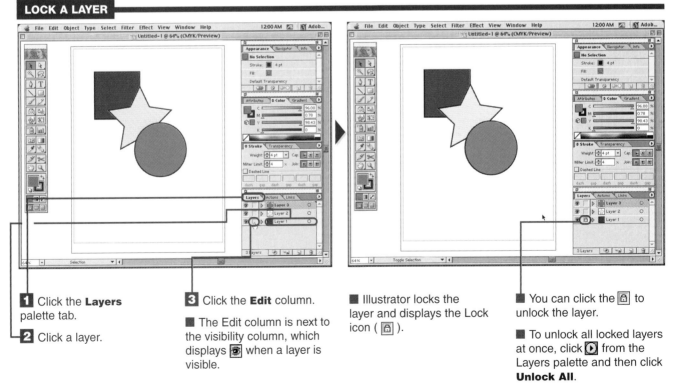

1 Click the **Layers** palette tab.

2 Click a layer.

3 Click the **Edit** column.

■ The Edit column is next to the visibility column, which displays 👁 when a layer is visible.

■ Illustrator locks the layer and displays the Lock icon (🔒).

■ You can click the 🔒 to unlock the layer.

■ To unlock all locked layers at once, click ▶ from the Layers palette and then click **Unlock All**.

REARRANGE LAYERS

You can rearrange how layers stack to modify how elements in your artwork overlap.

REARRANGE LAYERS

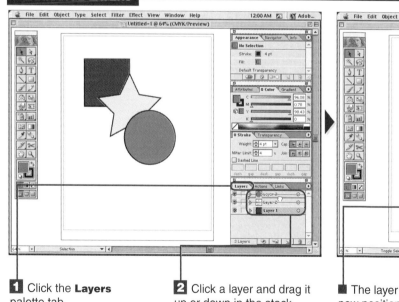

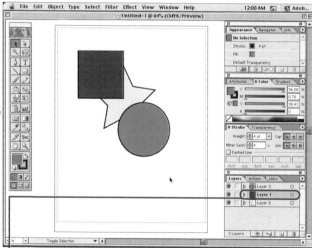

1 Click the **Layers** palette tab.

2 Click a layer and drag it up or down in the stack.

■ The layer assumes its new position in the stack.

■ Rearranging your layers has no effect on their attributes, such as whether they are hidden or locked.

CREATE A SUBLAYER

You can create *sublayers* that nest inside other layers. Sublayers enable you to arrange elements in your artwork in complex ways.

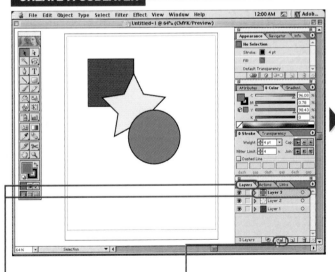

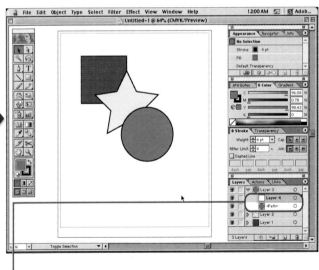

CREATE A NEW SUBLAYER

1 Click the **Layers** palette tab.

2 Click the layer inside which you want to add a sublayer.

3 Click the Create New Sublayer button ( ).

■ You can also click ▶ from the Layers palette and click **New Sublayer**.

■ A new sublayer appears.

■ You can create sublayers inside of other sublayers.

TY TEACH YOURSELF

What happens to a sublayer if the layer enclosing it is hidden or locked?

The sublayer also is hidden or locked. A sublayer inherits these characteristics from the layer that encloses it.

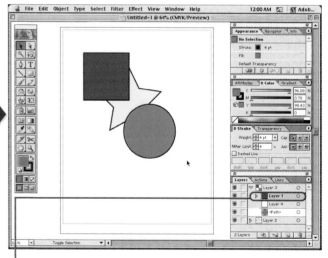

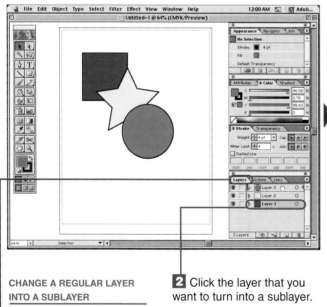

CHANGE A REGULAR LAYER INTO A SUBLAYER

1 Click the **Layers** palette tab.

2 Click the layer that you want to turn into a sublayer.

3 Drag the layer onto a second layer.

■ The first layer becomes a sublayer inside the second layer.

■ You can click and drag the layer to rearrange the sublayer with any existing objects of the enclosing layer.

MOVE OBJECTS BETWEEN LAYERS

You can cut — or copy — and then paste objects between layers. This lets you rearrange the hierarchy of your artwork.

MOVE OBJECTS BETWEEN LAYERS

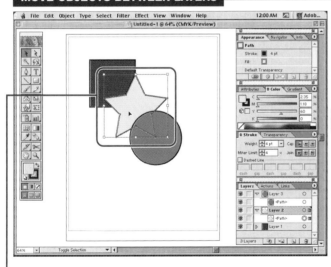

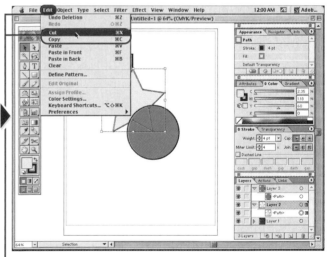

1 Click the object you want to move on the artboard.

2 Click **Edit**.

3 Click **Cut** or **Copy**.

■ The keyboard shortcut for Cut is ⌘+X or Ctrl+X. The keyboard shortcut for Copy is ⌘+C or Ctrl+C.

Does Illustrator offer a shortcut for moving objects between layers?

Yes. You can click and drag objects from one layer to another in the Layers palette, just as you can click and drag to rearrange the order of layers. See the section "Rearrange Layers" for more information.

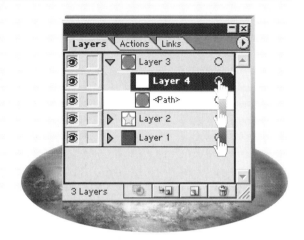

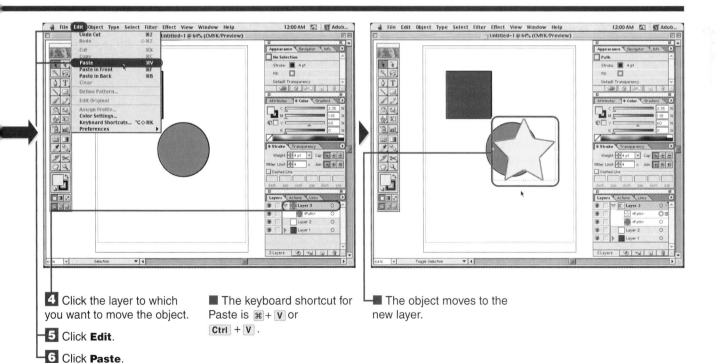

4 Click the layer to which you want to move the object.

5 Click **Edit**.

6 Click **Paste**.

■ The keyboard shortcut for Paste is ⌘ + **V** or **Ctrl** + **V** .

■ The object moves to the new layer.

EDIT LAYER PROPERTIES

You can access a variety of layer settings — including a layer's name, its color, and its visibility — in the Layer Options dialog box.

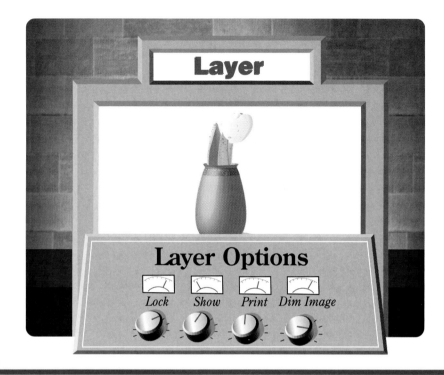

EDIT LAYER PROPERTIES

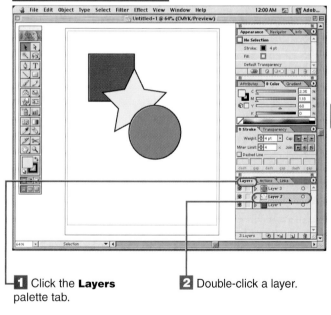

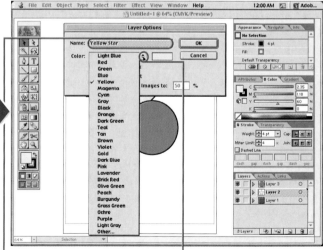

1 Click the **Layers** palette tab.

2 Double-click a layer.

■ The Layer Options dialog box opens.

3 Type a new name for the layer.

4 Click ⬍ or ⬇ and click a selection color.

■ Illustrator highlights any selected objects from the layer with this color.

Why would I want to dim my bitmap images?

Dimming your images can make tracing them with drawing tools easier. Images dimmed using the Layer Options dialog box do not dim when you print the artwork.

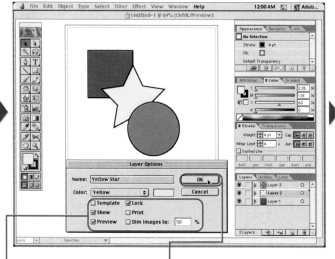

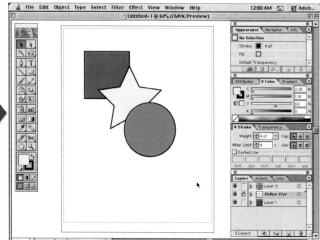

5 Click to specify other layer options (☐ changes to ☑).

■ You can specify whether to display the layer when you print your artwork.

■ You can specify that bitmap images in your layer be dimmed.

6 Click **OK**.

■ The settings take effect in the layer.

CREATE A TEMPLATE LAYER

You can define a layer
as a template that you
can then use as a guide
for creating artwork.

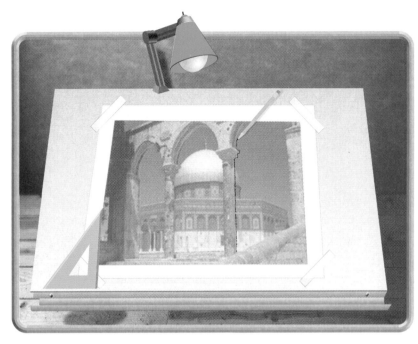

You typically
place a
template layer
under other
layers. The
template layer
contains a
dimmed bitmap
image.

CREATE A TEMPLATE LAYER

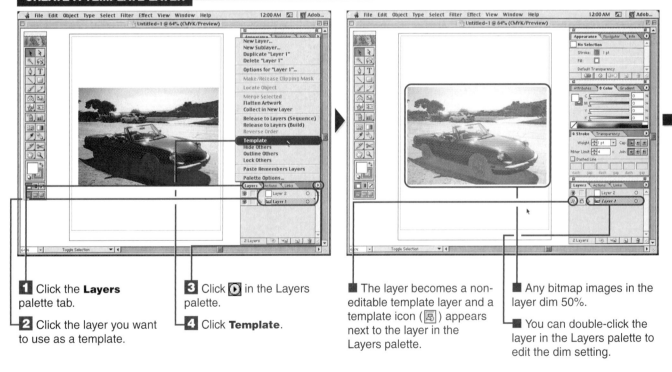

1 Click the **Layers**
palette tab.

2 Click the layer you want
to use as a template.

3 Click ▶ in the Layers
palette.

4 Click **Template**.

■ The layer becomes a non-
editable template layer and a
template icon (▤) appears
next to the layer in the
Layers palette.

■ Any bitmap images in the
layer dim 50%.

■ You can double-click the
layer in the Layers palette to
edit the dim setting.

I cannot select objects in my template layer. Why?

By default, a template layer locks when you create it, so you cannot select or edit objects in it. This is usually useful, because you probably want to make your modifications in other layers and keep the template layer fixed. If you need to edit elements in the template layer, you can unlock the layer in the Layers palette. See the section "Lock a Layer" for more information.

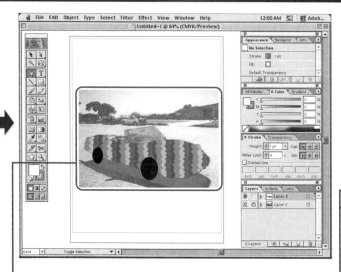

5 Create your artwork with drawing tools in one or more layers on top of the template layer.

Note: You can learn how to create artwork in Chapters 1 through 9.

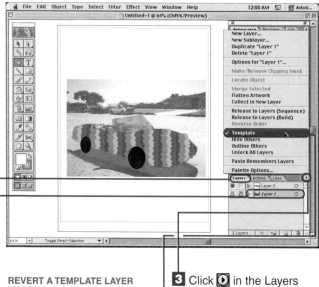

REVERT A TEMPLATE LAYER

1 Click the **Layers** palette tab.

2 Click the template layer you want to change back to a normal layer.

3 Click ▶ in the Layers palette.

4 Click **Template** to revert the layer.

■ The dimmed image in the layer reverts.

MERGE LAYERS

You can merge layers to combine elements into a single layer. Merging layers can also save memory and enable you to work faster, because more memory becomes available for other tasks.

MERGE LAYERS

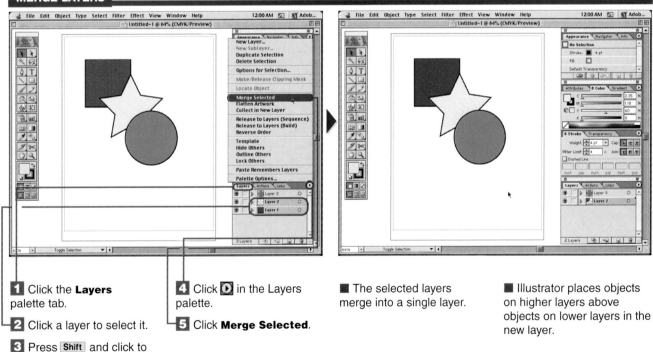

1 Click the **Layers** palette tab.

2 Click a layer to select it.

3 Press **Shift** and click to select one or more other layers.

4 Click ▶ in the Layers palette.

5 Click **Merge Selected**.

■ The selected layers merge into a single layer.

■ Illustrator places objects on higher layers above objects on lower layers in the new layer.

254

You can merge all a picture's layers into one layer through a process called *flattening*. You may find this useful if you no longer need to work with elements in your layers individually. Flattening can also save memory and enable you to work faster, because more memory becomes available for other tasks.

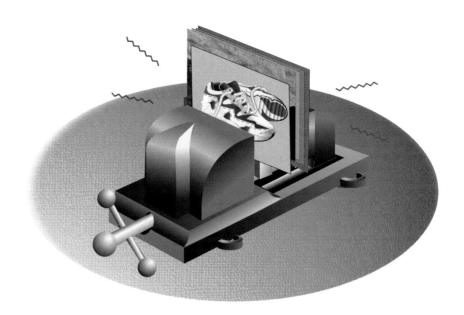

FLATTEN ARTWORK

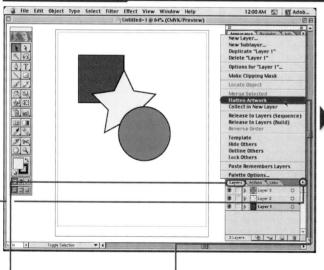

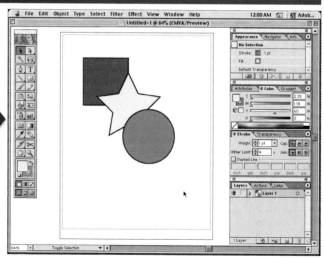

1 Click the **Layers** palette tab.

2 Click ▶ to open the Layers palette menu.

3 Click **Flatten Artwork**.

■ If any of the layers are hidden prior to flattening, Illustrator asks whether to keep or discard the hidden artwork.

■ The layers become a single layer. The new layer takes the name of the lowest layer in the original set.

■ In the new layer, objects on higher layers appear above objects on lower layers.

RELEASE OBJECTS TO LAYERS

You can place the objects held by a single layer into their own individual layers. You can find this useful if you plan to use the objects as frames in an animation. Most animation programs can automatically convert an image's layers into animation frames.

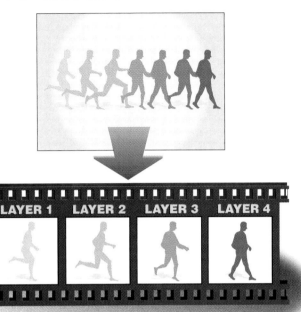

RELEASE OBJECTS TO LAYERS

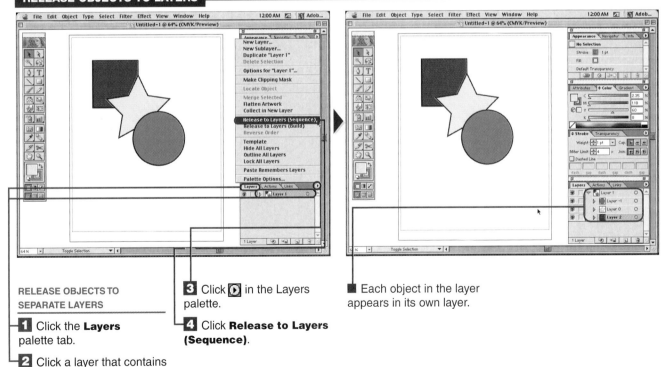

RELEASE OBJECTS TO SEPARATE LAYERS

1 Click the **Layers** palette tab.

2 Click a layer that contains several objects.

3 Click 〇 in the Layers palette.

4 Click **Release to Layers (Sequence)**.

■ Each object in the layer appears in its own layer.

256

How can I create Web animations using my Illustrator art?

Illustrator lets you turn your layered art into a simple Flash animation. See Chapter 14 for details. To build a GIF animation — the most popular type of animation found on the Web — you can use Adobe ImageReady or Macromedia Fireworks. To use your Illustrator files in these applications, save them as Photoshop (PSD) files.

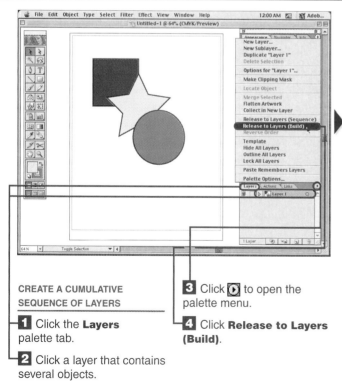

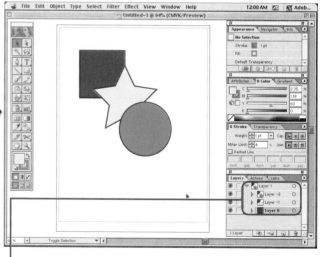

CREATE A CUMULATIVE SEQUENCE OF LAYERS

1 Click the **Layers** palette tab.

2 Click a layer that contains several objects.

3 Click ⊙ to open the palette menu.

4 Click **Release to Layers (Build)**.

■ Illustrator releases a cumulative sequence of objects into layers, with each layer containing an additional object compared to the layer before it.

CREATE A CLIPPING MASK WITH A LAYER

You can specify that the top-level object in a layer serve as a clipping mask. Only objects, or parts of objects, that overlap the top layer show through. This enables you to place an opaque border around a part of your art.

CREATE A CLIPPING MASK WITH A LAYER

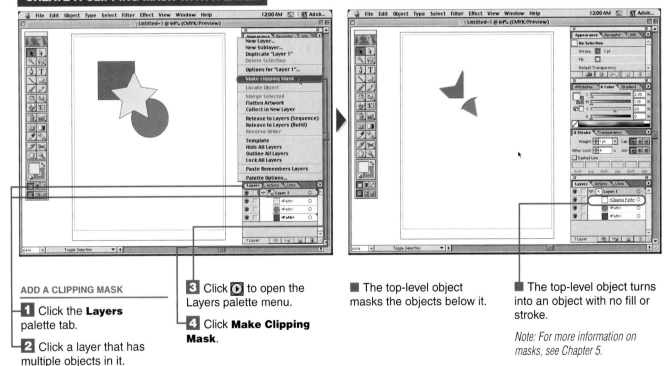

ADD A CLIPPING MASK

1 Click the **Layers** palette tab.

2 Click a layer that has multiple objects in it.

3 Click ▶ to open the Layers palette menu.

4 Click **Make Clipping Mask**.

■ The top-level object masks the objects below it.

■ The top-level object turns into an object with no fill or stroke.

Note: For more information on masks, see Chapter 5.

258

**How does my clipping mask affect
objects in layers beneath it?**

A clipping mask does not affect
layers beneath it unless those
layers happen to be sublayers of
the clipping mask's layer. For
more information on sublayers,
see the section "Create a
Sublayer."

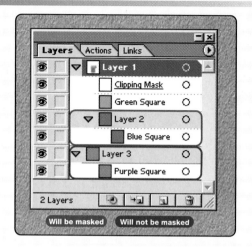

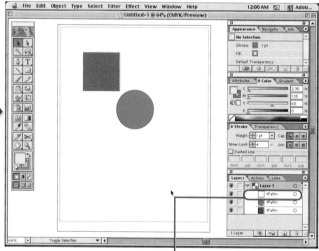

REMOVE A CLIPPING MASK

1 Click a layer that has a
clipping mask.

2 Click ▶ in the Layers
palette.

3 Click **Release Clipping
Mask**.

■ The objects below the
clipping mask release from
the mask.

■ The top-level object still
exists, but it has no fill or
stroke, so it is invisible.

*Note: For details on how to fill or
add a stroke to an object, see
Chapter 7.*

Working with Bitmap Images

For more flexibility when creating your art, you can bring bitmap images created in other applications into your Illustrator projects. You can also convert elements in your art to bitmap form, which lets you apply certain filters to them.

Understanding Images 262

Place an Image 264

Transform an Image 265

Trace an Image 266

Rasterize an Object 268

Copy an Image from Photoshop 270

UNDERSTANDING IMAGES

You can import pixel-based, or bitmap, images into Illustrator and edit them, or combine them with Illustrator objects. You can also convert vector-based Illustrator objects to bitmap images.

Vector-Based Art

Most of Illustrator's tools focus on creating and manipulating vector-based objects. *Vector-based objects* consist of mathematically defined outlines. Because of this mathematical definition, you can easily reshape and scale vector-based objects without loss in quality. Paths that you create with the Pen tool and shapes you create with the object tools are examples of vector-based art. For more on the Pen tool, see Chapter 3. To learn more about the object tools, see Chapters 5 and 6.

Bitmap Images

In contrast, photo-editing applications such as Photoshop work with bitmap images. *Bitmap images* consist of tiny, solid color squares known as *pixels*, which is short for "picture elements." Because they are made up of pixels, bitmap images are very efficient at representing photographic art. However, scaling them results in some loss of quality, because the scaling process requires the addition and subtraction of pixels.

Bitmap Images in Illustrator

You can place bitmap images into Illustrator alongside vector-based objects, and manipulate the images in many ways. You can use the transform tools to stretch or reflect your images. You can use the Auto Trace tool to outline the edges in images and then apply a stroke to the edges. You can also apply filters and effects to images. For more on transforming and tracing, see the sections "Transform an Image" and "Trace an Image."

Applying Filters

One way to radically transform images in Illustrator is with filters, which rearrange and recolor the pixels of an image. Filters, by nature, are designed to work with bitmap images. Most of the filters available in Illustrator are plug-ins from Adobe Photoshop. You can access filters, which are covered in Chapter 9, under the Filter menu.

Applying Effects

You can also alter your images in Illustrator with effects. Effects are similar to filters, except that you can remove or edit effects after you apply them. Some useful effects that you can apply on bitmap images allow you to feather the edge of an image, or to warp an image in various ways. You can access effects, which are covered in Chapter 9, under the Effect menu.

Converting to Bitmap

Sometimes you want to convert vector-based objects in your art to bitmap images. You can do this through the process called *rasterization*, which converts vector information into pixels. Sometimes you need to rasterize your art before you apply certain filter effects. You can also save your finished Illustrator artwork in a bitmap format such as GIF or JPEG for use on the Web. See the section "Rasterize an Object" for more about rasterization. See Chapter 14 for more on saving artwork in bitmap format.

PLACE AN IMAGE

You can use the Place command to import images and other files into the Illustrator workspace. This lets you use art from image editing programs in your Illustrator projects.

PLACE AN IMAGE

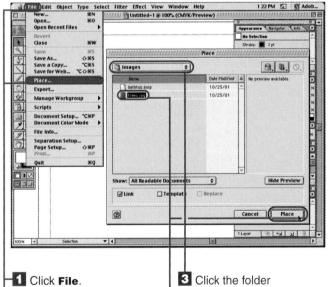

1 Click **File**.

2 Click **Place**.

■ The Place dialog box appears.

3 Click the folder containing the image.

4 Click the image filename.

5 Click **Place**.

■ Illustrator places the image on the artboard.

■ You can click to select the image and apply commands to it.

You can use
the transform
commands to
move, reflect,
or distort
images that
you have
previously
placed in your
artwork.

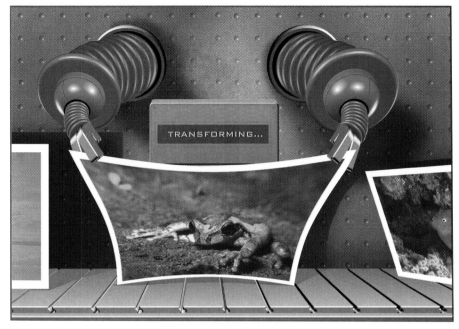

To learn how to
place images in
your artwork,
see the section
"Place an Image."

TRANSFORM AN IMAGE

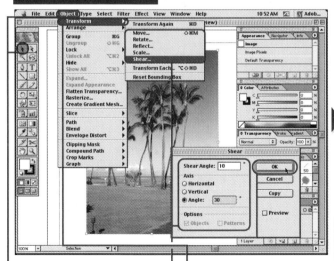

1 Click the Selection tool
(⬚).

■ You can also press **V** to
quickly select ⬚.

2 Click an image.

3 Click **Object**.

4 Click **Transform**.

5 Click a transform
command.

6 Select your
transformation settings from
the dialog box that appears.

7 Click **OK**.

■ The image is transformed.

■ To revert the
transformation, click **Edit**
and then **Undo**.

■ You can also apply filters
and effects to modify your
images.

*Note: See Chapter 9 for more
information on filters and effects.*

TRACE AN IMAGE

You can use the Auto Trace tool to automatically add a path around edges in an image. You may find this easier than tracing an object by hand with the Pen tool.

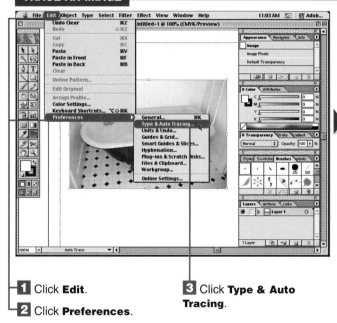

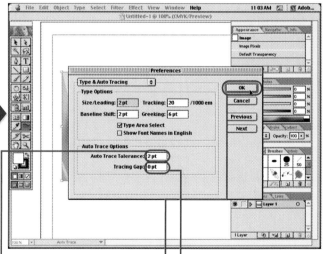

1 Click **Edit**.

2 Click **Preferences**.

3 Click **Type & Auto Tracing**.

■ The Preferences dialog box appears.

4 Type an Auto Trace Tolerance in points between 1 and 10 to specify the smoothness of the trace.

5 Type a Tracing Gap between 0 and 2, to allow the tool to trace over whitespace gaps along an edge.

6 Click **OK**.

How do I improve my tracing with the Auto Trace tool?

Try adjusting the Tolerance and Tracing Gap preferences for the tool. Or try clicking inside or outside the object you are trying to trace. If you still have problems, you may have to trace the edge by hand with the Pen tool — which you may find slower, but more precise.

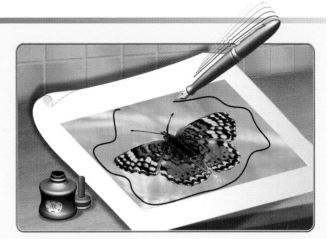

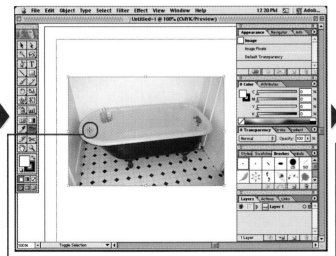

7 Click near an edge in an image.

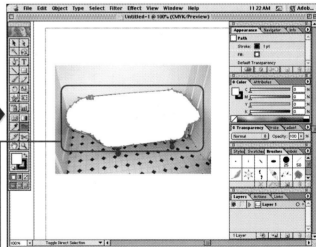

■ The tool attempts to trace the edge inside the image and creates a path with the current fill and stroke settings.

You can rasterize a
vector-based object
in Illustrator to turn
it into a bitmap, or
pixel-based, image.
Certain filters can
only be applied to
bitmap content.

After you rasterize
an image, you can
no longer edit its fill,
stroke, and other
attributes.

RASTERIZE AN OBJECT

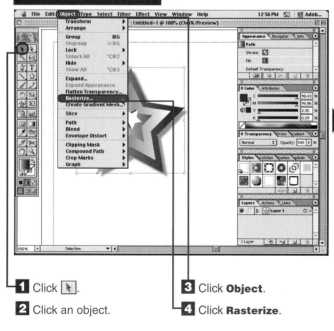

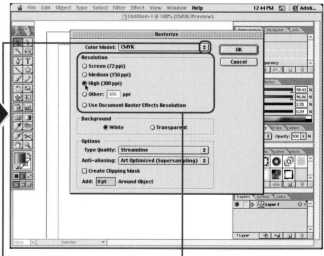

1 Click ▶.

2 Click an object.

3 Click **Object**.

4 Click **Rasterize**.

■ The Rasterize dialog box
appears.

5 Click ◆ or ▾ and click a
color mode.

*Note: For more information on color
modes, see Chapter 13.*

6 Click a resolution (○
changes to ◉).

■ Use a higher resolution if
you want to print the art on a
higher-resolution printer.

How can I rasterize an object but still edit its fill, stroke, and other attributes?

You can use the Rasterize effect. To do so, select the object and click Effect and then Rasterize. With the Rasterize effect, the object looks pixelated, but you can still edit it. For more information about effects, see Chapter 9.

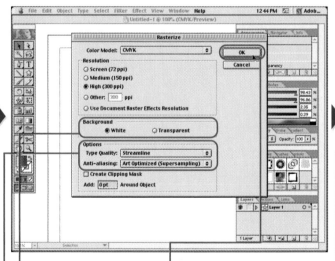

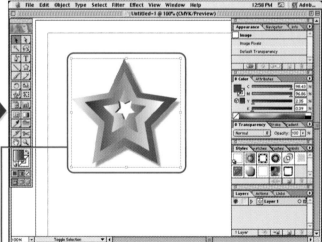

7 Click an option to specify how to display background areas of the object (○ changes to ◉).

■ If you rasterize type, you can specify the quality and anti-aliasing by clicking ▣ or ▾ and clicking appropriate settings.

■ Anti-aliasing reduces the appearance of jagged edges on rasterized objects.

8 Click **OK**.

■ Illustrator converts the object into pixels.

COPY AN IMAGE FROM PHOTOSHOP

You can copy an image to Illustrator directly from Photoshop. This is an alternative to placing an image into Illustrator from a file, a method you may find convenient if you have both applications running at the same time.

For more on placing a file, see the section "Place an Image."

COPY AN IMAGE FROM PHOTOSHOP

1 Open Photoshop.

2 Open an image.

3 Select all or part of the image with a selection tool.

Note: See the program instructions to open Photoshop and select an image.

4 Click **Edit**.

5 Click **Copy**.

■ The shortcut for Copy is ⌘ + **C** or **Ctrl** + **C**.

■ The selected image copies to the clipboard.

Can I copy art from Illustrator to Photoshop?

You can copy art from Illustrator to Photoshop using the clipboard as well. Just reverse the steps below.

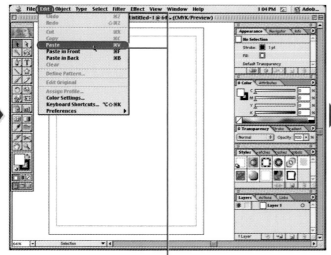

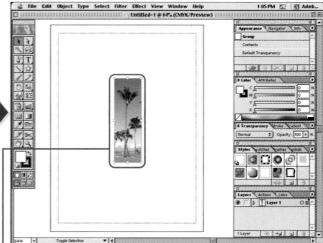

6 Switch to Illustrator.

Note: See Chapter 1 for more on starting Illustrator and opening a document.

7 If you are working with multiple layers, click the layer to which you want to paste the image.

8 Click **Edit**.

9 Click **Paste**.

■ The copied selection pastes from the clipboard to your Illustrator document.

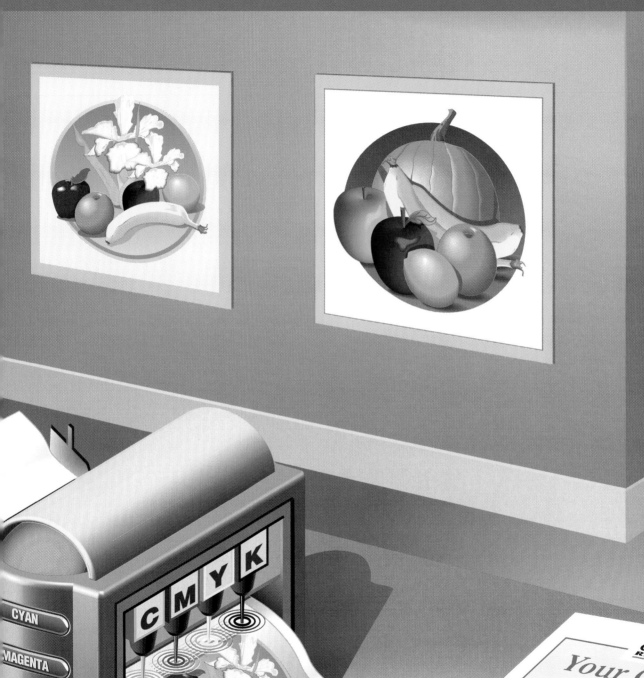

CHAPTER 13

Preparing Files for Printing

Illustrator offers a variety of tools that enable you to produce high quality printed art on many different types of printers, including high-end offset printing presses.

Understanding Printing 274

Understanding Printing Separations ..275

Using Process Color 276

Using Spot Color 278

Trap Colors 280

Using Knockouts...........................282

Create Crop Marks 284

Change Color Modes 285

Print Artwork on a PC 286

Print Artwork on a Mac...................288

UNDERSTANDING PRINTING

You can print your Illustrator art directly from your computer using an inkjet, dye-sublimation, laser, or other printer. You can also prepare your art for an offset printing press by creating color separations.

Printing in Black and White

Black-and-white laser printers can print your color art as shades of gray using a process known as *halftoning*. Halftoned art consists of patterns of tiny, evenly spaced dots, with larger dots generating darker grays and smaller dots generating lighter grays. Newspapers use this process to print photographs.

Color Printing

If you want to print in color from your computer, there are a variety of different computer printers you can buy — from low-cost inkjet printers to high-end dye-sublimation printers. You can also have your color art reproduced on an offset printer, which requires that you first *separate* the colors in your art into component inks.

CMYK and Printing

Color printers typically reproduce art by combining four different inks: cyan (C), magenta (M), yellow (Y), and black (K). Inkjet printers squirt these colors in varying amounts from ink cartridges. In offset printing, the printer applies the four colors one at a time on the page from separate printing plates. Colors in your Illustrator art that you create by combining CMYK inks are known as *process colors*.

Illustrator includes a number of useful features that allow you to easily and accurately produce CMYK color separations from your artwork. See the application's help documentation for specific information. You can use these separations to create the printing plates that reproduce your color art on an offset printer. You need access to a PostScript-capable printer to create separations in Illustrator.

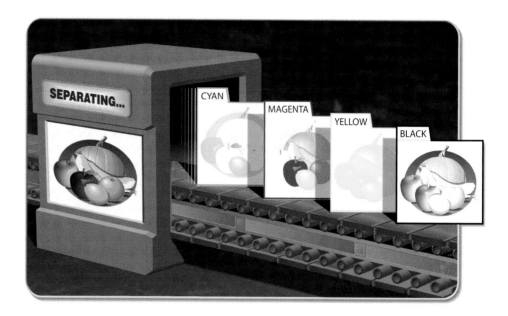

Spot Colors

You can also reproduce a color on a page using an ink of the same color instead of mixing CMYK colors. For example, to create a yellowish green color on a poster, you can apply yellowish green ink to poster paper. Colors reproduced this way in offset printing are known as *spot colors*. In Illustrator, you can create your color art using spot colors, process colors, or a mix of the two.

Trapping Colors

One challenge when creating color art on an offset printer involves lining up the colors you apply with different plates. If the printing process is off even slightly, it can result in extra space where colors meet. *Trapping* is the process of spreading colors slightly at their edge to avoid this space.

USING PROCESS COLOR

You generate *process* colors by combining the standard process inks: cyan, magenta, yellow, and black — CMYK. You can use process colors in your artwork, and then reproduce the colors on an offset printer by creating separations. See the application's help documentation for specific information concerning separations.

USING PROCESS COLOR

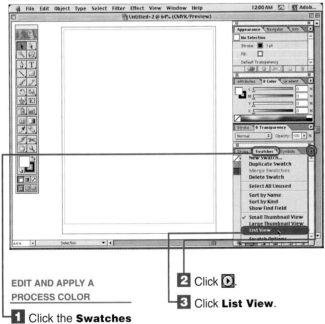

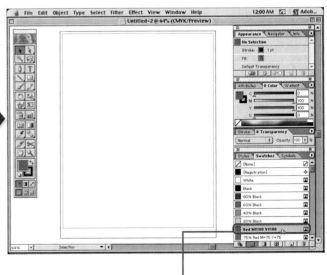

EDIT AND APPLY A PROCESS COLOR

1 Click the **Swatches** palette tab.

2 Click ▣.

3 Click **List View**.

■ Illustrator lists the process colors designating them with the Process Color icon (▣).

4 Double-click a process color.

276

How do the four CMYK colors combine to create process colors?

Each color — cyan, magenta, yellow, and black — prints as a separate pattern of tiny dots. Because the patterns are angled relative to one another, they appear to the eye as a single process color. Combining these four colors can produce most, but not all, of the colors in the visible spectrum.

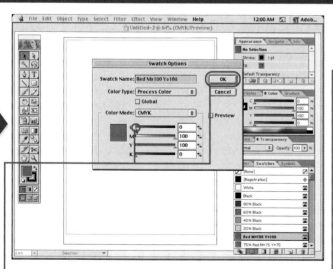

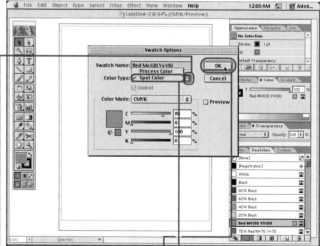

■ The process color settings display in the Swatch Options dialog box.

5 Click and drag the sliders (△) to edit the process color.

6 Click **OK**.

■ Illustrator saves the edited process color.

7 Apply the process color.

Note: See Chapter 7 for more information on applying colors.

CONVERT PROCESS COLOR TO SPOT COLOR

1 Perform steps **1** through **4** on the previous page.

2 Click ⬦ or ▾ in the Color Type box.

3 Click **Spot Color**.

4 Click **OK**.

■ The process color converts to a spot color and Illustrator designates it with a Spot Color icon (⬛).

USING SPOT COLOR

You can select spot colors from Illustrator's predefined color libraries to use in your artwork. Spot colors do not separate into cyan, magenta, yellow, and black during the offset printing process. They print with an ink of the same color.

USING SPOT COLOR

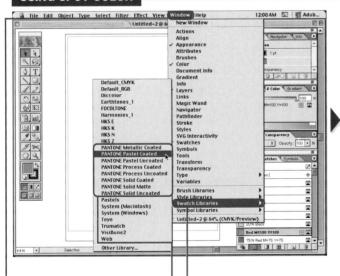

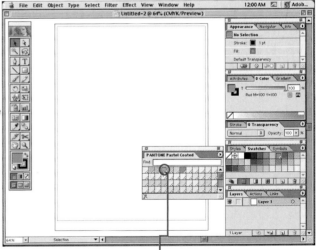

CHOOSE A SPOT COLOR FROM A LIBRARY

1 Click **Window**.

2 Click **Swatch Libraries**.

3 Click a PANTONE swatch library.

■ The library of swatches opens in a palette.

■ Illustrator designates spot colors with ☐.

4 Click a swatch.

Why are spot colors useful?

Illustrator cannot reproduce all colors in the spectrum using CMYK inks. For this reason, you may find spot colors useful when you want an exact color that lies outside the CMYK gamut. You can also use spot color in a printing job that requires fewer than four inks. For example, you may find it more efficient to use two spot colors instead of four CMYK colors for a simple printing job.

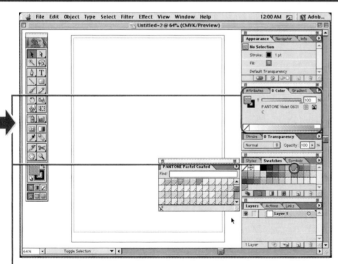

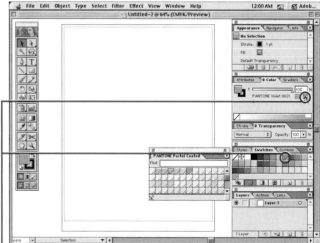

■ Information about the swatch appears in the Color palette.

■ The swatch copies to the main Swatches palette.

5 Apply the spot color.

Note: See Chapter 7 for more information on applying colors.

CONVERT SPOT COLOR TO PROCESS COLOR

1 Click a spot color swatch.

2 Click ▨.

■ The spot color converts to a similar process color that Illustrator represents with CMYK inks.

TRAP COLORS

You can use the Trap command to specify that colors in your art overlap slightly. This compensates for misalignment and eliminates extra white space when the colors print. You may find trapping useful when you intend to print your art on an offset printer.

The Trap command works only with CMYK documents.

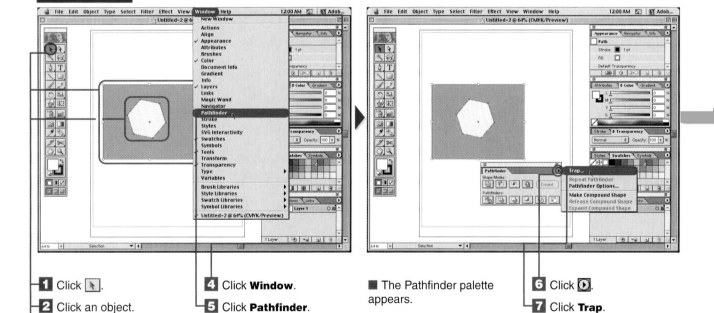

1 Click ▶.

2 Click an object.

3 Click a second object that has a common edge with the first.

4 Click **Window**.

5 Click **Pathfinder**.

■ The Pathfinder palette appears.

6 Click ▶.

7 Click **Trap**.

How much trap do I need?

This depends on the colors you are using, the type of printing press, and other factors. It is best to consult the commercial printer who will print the artwork about required trap settings.

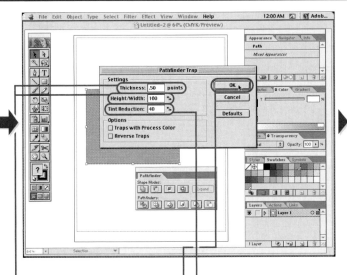

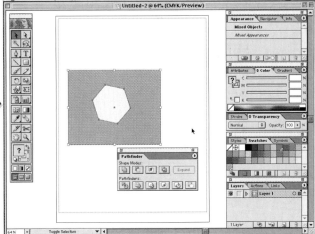

■ The Pathfinder Trap dialog box appears.

8 Type a thickness to specify the amount of overlap.

■ You can type a Height/Width value different from 100% if you want the thickness to vary.

■ You can type a Tint Reduction value of less than 100% to lighten the overlapping color.

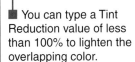

9 Click **OK**.

■ Illustrator traps the art so that lighter colors overlap the darker colors at the edges of the selected objects.

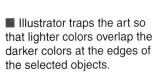

USING KNOCKOUTS

When you have a group of overlapping, transparent objects, you can specify that the top objects "knock out" those below them. The colors in the areas that overlap do not print. You can use knockouts to create interesting layered effects in your art.

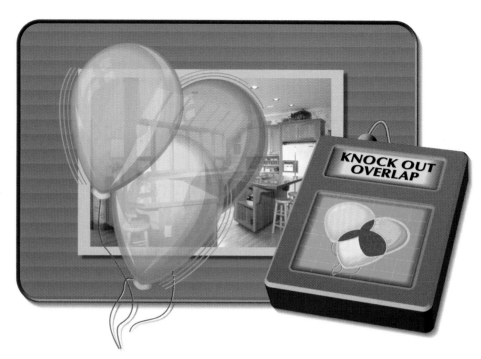

USING KNOCKOUTS

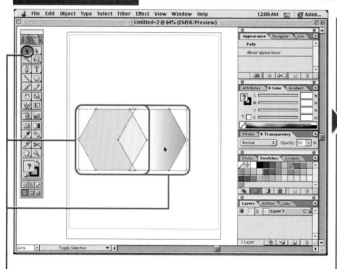

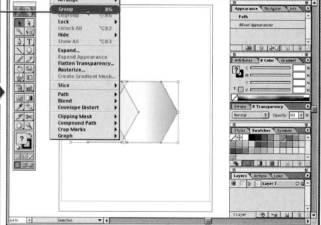

1 Click [pointer].

2 Click an object.

3 Press **Shift** and click a second, overlapping object.

■ The knockout effect works only on objects where Opacity is less than 100%.

4 Click **Object**.

5 Click **Group**.

■ A knockout affects only objects in a group. Objects not in the group are unaffected.

**What does it mean when
Illustrator has the Knockout
Group option checked and
grayed-out?**

This so-called neutral option lets
the knockout behavior of an
enclosing group override that of
interior groups. You do not have
to worry about this option unless
your artwork has groups within
groups.

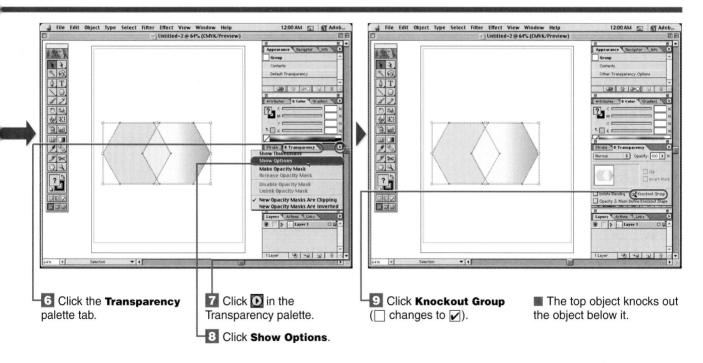

6 Click the **Transparency**
palette tab.

7 Click ▶ in the
Transparency palette.

8 Click **Show Options**.

9 Click **Knockout Group**
(☐ changes to ☑).

■ The top object knocks out
the object below it.

CREATE CROP MARKS

You can set crop marks around the edges of your art to mark how you want the artwork to trim after printing.

CREATE CROP MARKS

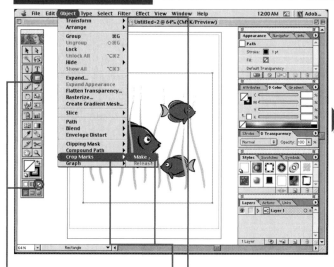

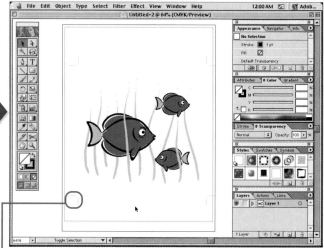

1 Click the Rectangle tool (🔲).

2 Click and drag to define how you want the art to trim.

3 Click 🔲 to make the fill for the rectangle transparent.

4 Click **Object**.

5 Click **Crop Marks**.

6 Click **Make**.

■ Illustrator applies crop marks ⌐ at the corners of the rectangle.

■ To remove the crop marks, click **Object**, **Crop Marks**, and then **Release**.

CHANGE COLOR MODES

You can convert your Illustrator document between CMYK and RGB color modes.

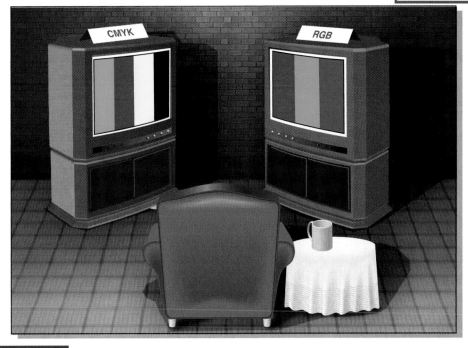

You can only use certain print-specific features, such as trapping, in the CMYK color mode. See the section "Trap Colors" for more information.

CHANGE COLOR MODES

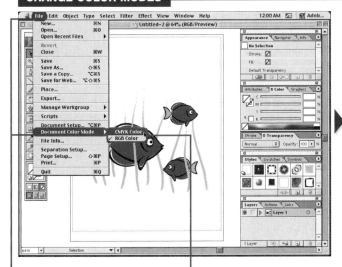

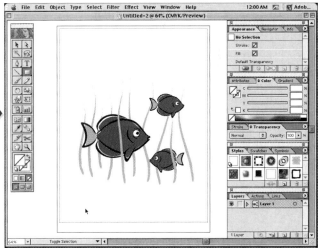

■1 Click **File**.

■2 Click **Document Color Mode**.

■3 Click a color mode.

Note: To learn about which color mode is correct for your situation, or to create a color, see Chapter 7.

■ The document changes to the selected color mode.

PRINT ARTWORK ON A PC

You can print your art on a printer attached to your PC or on your network to create a hardcopy version of your work.

PRINT ARTWORK ON A PC

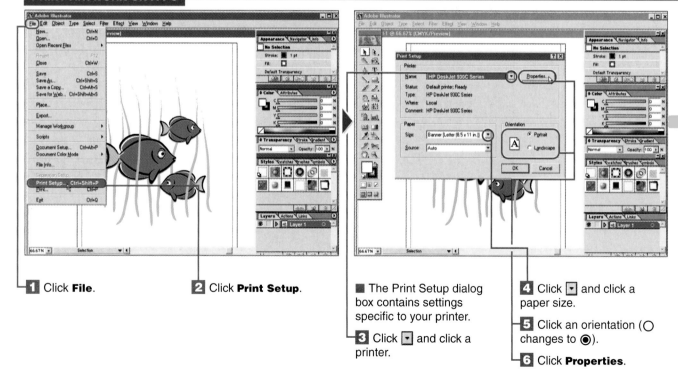

1 Click **File**.

2 Click **Print Setup**.

■ The Print Setup dialog box contains settings specific to your printer.

3 Click ▾ and click a printer.

4 Click ▾ and click a paper size.

5 Click an orientation (○ changes to ●).

6 Click **Properties**.

How do I keep objects in my artwork from printing?

You can move an object to its own layer and then hide the layer to keep the object from printing. See Chapter 11 for more information. To have the object visible onscreen but not in the printed document, double-click the object's layer to open the Layers Options dialog box and then deselect the **Print** option.

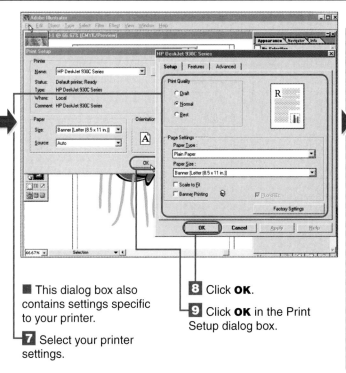

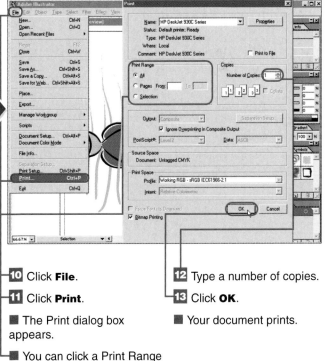

■ This dialog box also contains settings specific to your printer.

7 Select your printer settings.

8 Click **OK**.

9 Click **OK** in the Print Setup dialog box.

10 Click **File**.

11 Click **Print**.

■ The Print dialog box appears.

■ You can click a Print Range option (○ changes to ◉).

12 Type a number of copies.

13 Click **OK**.

■ Your document prints.

PRINT ARTWORK ON A MAC

You can print your art on a printer attached to your Mac or on your network to create a hardcopy version of your work.

PRINT ARTWORK ON A MAC

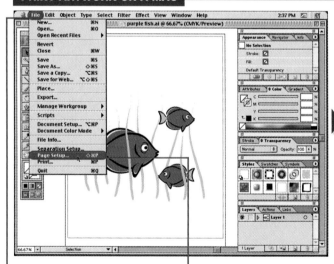

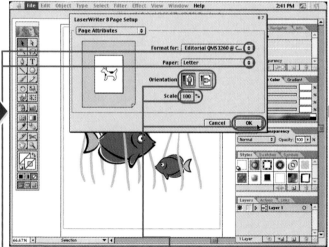

1 Click **File**.

2 Click **Page Setup**.

■ The Page Setup dialog box contains settings specific to your printer.

3 Click ◆ and click a printer.

4 Click ◆ and click a paper size.

5 Click an orientation (◻ or ◻).

■ You can type a scale value to increase or decrease the size of the illustration on the page.

6 Click **OK**.

What does the PostScript printer description (PPD) file do?

The file contains important information about your printer, including its resolution, available page sizes, and halftone settings. The file determines what values you can select in the Separation Setup dialog box.

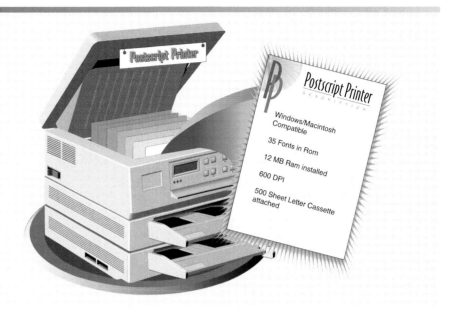

Postscript Printer

Windows/Macintosh Compatible

35 Fonts in Rom

12 MB Ram installed

600 DPI

500 Sheet Letter Cassette attached

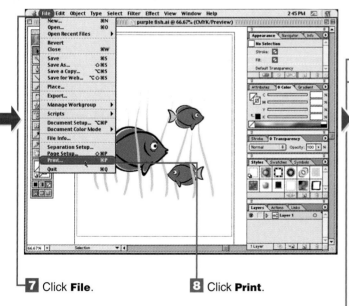

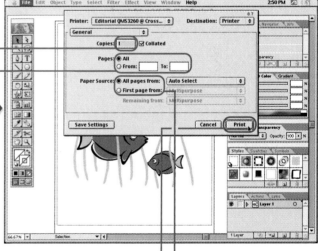

7 Click **File**.

8 Click **Print**.

■ The print dialog box appears.

9 Type a number of copies.

10 Click to print all pages or a specific range (○ changes to ●).

■ You can select a paper source (○ changes to ●).

11 Click **Print**.

■ Your document prints.

CHAPTER 14

Creating Art for the Web

You can make professional-looking images for your personal or corporate Web site using Illustrator's tools. In this chapter, you learn how to pick Web-Safe Colors, create and export slices, build buttons and animations, and more.

Understanding Web Art 292

Select a Web-Safe Color 294

Work in Pixel Preview Mode 295

Save a GIF Image for the Web 296

Save a JPEG Image for the Web 298

Make a Button 300

Slice Artwork 302

Export Sliced Artwork 304

Export a Flash Animation 306

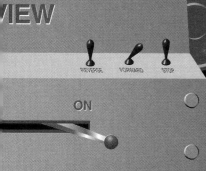

UNDERSTANDING WEB ART

You can create art in Illustrator and then save it in various formats for display on the Web.

Web Art Basics

Creating art for the Web involves special challenges. Because people view Web pages by connecting to remote servers around the world, Web images need to have small file sizes so that pages download quickly. For fast downloads, the majority of Web graphics are saved in one of two compressed file formats: GIF or JPEG.

GIF Images

GIF is the file format you want to use when saving flat-color illustrations for your Web pages. GIF supports only 256 or fewer colors, so it is less appropriate for photographic images. The GIF format supports transparency. See the section "Save a GIF Image for the Web" for details.

JPEG Images

You want to use the JPEG format when saving photographic or other continuous-tone art for the Web. With the JPEG format, you can control the amount of compression applied to the image to balance file size with image quality. JPEG does not support transparency. See the section "Save a JPEG Image for the Web" for more information.

Web-Safe Colors

If you view a Web page on a monitor that supports only 256 colors, you just see the Web-safe colors. Colors on the page that are not Web-safe are converted to ones that are, which can degrade the quality of the images on the page. Monitors set to greater than 256 colors do not have this problem. Choosing Web-safe colors when creating Web art helps ensure that all viewers see your art as you intended. For information on Web-safe colors, see the section "Select a Web-Safe Color."

Slicing Artwork

Web pages often consist of many different images — such as buttons, logo art, and illustrations — each of which is optimized differently. You can create these multi-image pages as a single Illustrator document, and then slice the document to create and optimize the images. For more information, see the section "Slice Artwork."

Flash Content

Another popular type of Web content is Flash multimedia, which can feature motion, sound, and interactivity. You can use Illustrator to create a simple Flash animation, with no sound or interactivity, by building the animated frames as separate layers and then exporting the layers in the Flash file format.

SELECT A WEB-SAFE COLOR

You can configure your Color palette so that you can select only Web-safe colors. This helps ensure that everyone sees your Web images as you intended.

There are 216 colors that are considered *Web-safe*. They display consistently across different Web browsers, operating systems, and monitor settings.

SELECT A WEB-SAFE COLOR

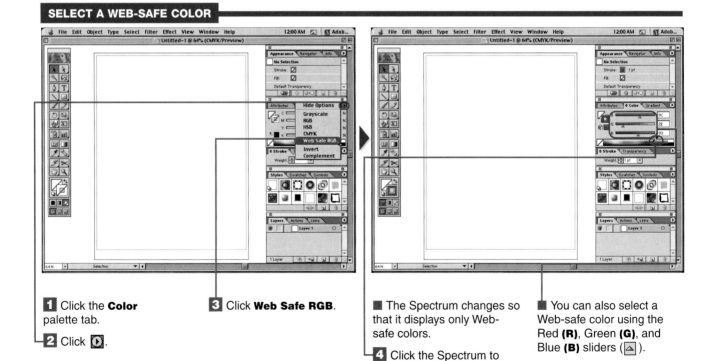

1 Click the **Color** palette tab.

2 Click ⬕.

3 Click **Web Safe RGB**.

■ The Spectrum changes so that it displays only Web-safe colors.

4 Click the Spectrum to select a color.

■ You can also select a Web-safe color using the Red **(R)**, Green **(G)**, and Blue **(B)** sliders (△).

You can preview how
your art appears on the
Web as a GIF or JPEG
image by using Pixel
Preview Mode.

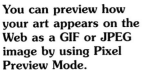

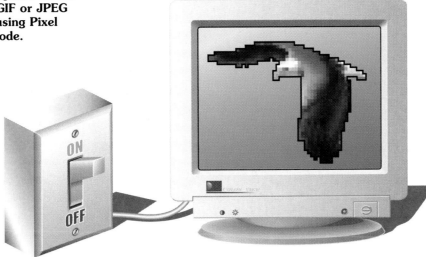

The vector-based
objects that you work
with in Illustrator must
be converted — or
rasterized — into pixels
if you want to display the
objects on the Web. For
more information on
rasterization, see
Chapter 12.

WORK IN PIXEL PREVIEW MODE

1 Click **View**.

2 Click **Pixel Preview**.

■ You art displays as it
would as a Web image, in
rasterized form.

■ You can zoom in with the
Zoom tool (🔍) to see the
pixelated effects.

■ In Pixel Preview, Illustrator
has not rasterized your art
permanently.

■ You can switch your art
back to its original state by
clicking **View** and then **Pixel
Preview** again.

SAVE A GIF IMAGE FOR THE WEB

You can optimize your artwork and save it in the *GIF (Graphics Interchange Format)* file format for display on the Web. The GIF format is best for flat-color art, and helps ensure that the art downloads quickly.

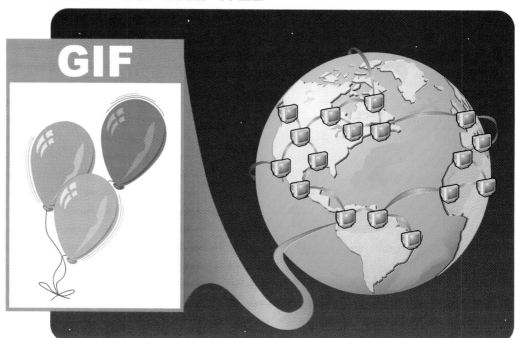

SAVE A GIF IMAGE FOR THE WEB

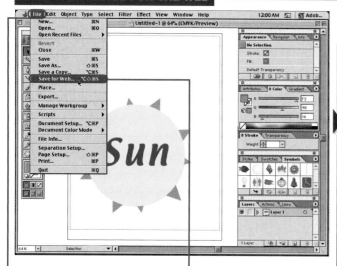

1 Click **File**.

2 Click **Save for Web**.

■ The Save for Web dialog box appears.

3 Click the **2-Up** tab to view the original and optimized versions of your art side by side.

■ Illustrator displays a file size and estimated download time.

4 Click ▲ or ▼ .

5 Click **GIF**.

What is PNG?

PNG is a file-format alternative to
GIF and JPEG that newer Web
browsers — Microsoft Internet
Explorer and Netscape Navigator
versions 4 and greater — support.
Many older browsers in use do not
support PNG. Like GIF, PNG
excels at saving flat-color art. To
save a PNG file, select **PNG-8**
(8-bit) or **PNG-24** (24-bit) from the
Save for Web file-type dialog box.

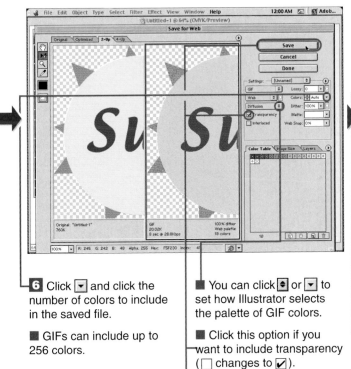

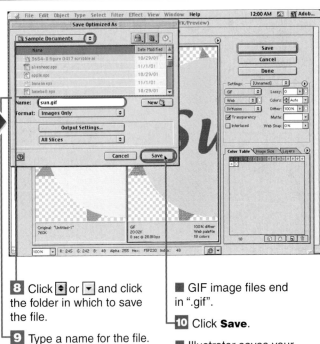

6 Click ▾ and click the
number of colors to include
in the saved file.

■ GIFs can include up to
256 colors.

■ You can click ⬍ or ▾ to
set how Illustrator selects
the palette of GIF colors.

■ Click this option if you
want to include transparency
(☐ changes to ☑).

7 Click **Save**.

8 Click ⬍ or ▾ and click
the folder in which to save
the file.

9 Type a name for the file.

■ GIF image files end
in ".gif".

10 Click **Save**.

■ Illustrator saves your
image in GIF format.

SAVE A JPEG IMAGE FOR THE WEB

You can optimize your artwork and save it in the JPEG file format for display on the Web. The *JPEG* — or *Joint Photographic Experts Group* — format is best for photographic and other continuous-tone art, and helps ensure that the art downloads quickly.

SAVE A JPEG IMAGE FOR THE WEB

1 Click **File**.

2 Click **Save for Web**.

■ The Save for Web dialog box appears.

3 Click the **2-Up** tab to view the original and optimized versions of your art side by side.

■ File size and download time display here.

4 Click ▲ or ▼.

5 Click **JPEG**.

298

What quality setting should I use for my JPEG files?

It depends on your needs. Low quality produces smaller files sizes — which download quickly — but also introduces blurriness and pixel artifacts to your art. High quality produces larger file sizes but also results in images that are more faithful to the original. Which setting you choose depends on how much you want to sacrifice quality for download speed.

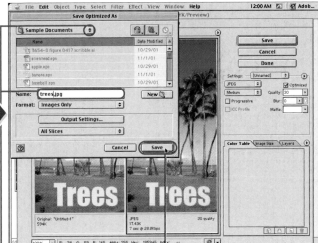

6 Type an image quality between 0 and 100.

7 Click 🔺 or 🔻 and click a color with which to matte any transparency in your original image.

■ Unlike GIFs, you cannot save JPEGs with transparency.

8 Click **Save**.

■ The Save Optimized As dialog box appears.

9 Click 🔺 or 🔻 and click the folder in which to save the file.

10 Type a name for the file.

■ JPEG image files end in ".jpeg" or ".jpg".

11 Click **Save**.

■ Illustrator saves your image in JPEG format.

MAKE A BUTTON

You can create a custom button for your Web page using the shape, text, and effects tools. Buttons offer users a visually appealing way to navigate your Web site.

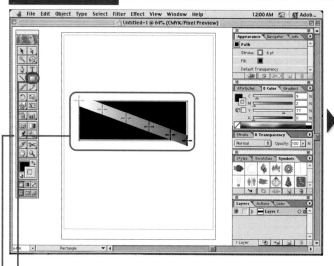

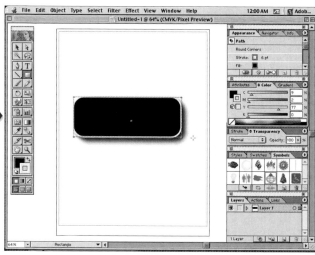

1 Click a shape tool.

2 Click and drag on the Artboard to create your button shape.

3 Color and stroke your shape using the fill and stroke commands.

Note: To create a shape, see Chapter 5. To color your shape, see Chapter 7.

4 With the button object selected, apply effects from the Effects menu.

■ In this example, two Stylize effects are added: **Drop Shadow** and **Rounded Corners**.

Note: To select an object, see Chapter 2. For more information about effects, see Chapter 9.

Should I save my buttons in the GIF or JPEG file format?

That depends on what your buttons look like. GIF is best for buttons that contain mostly flat colors. If your buttons have continuous tone features such as gradients or are based on photographs, you probably want to save them as JPEG.

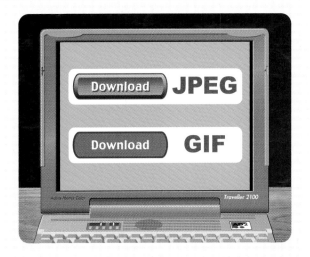

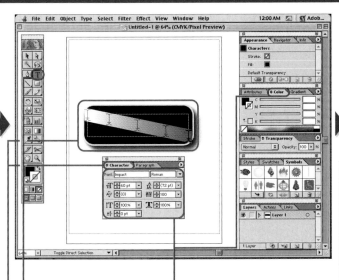

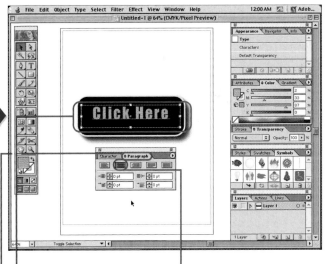

5 Press T to select the Type tool.

6 Click and drag over the button object to create a text box.

7 Click the **Character** palette tab.

■ To open the Character palette, you can press ⌘+T or Ctrl + T.

8 Specify the character attributes.

Note: See Chapter 7 for more information.

9 Define a type color with the Color palette.

10 Type a label for the button.

Note: See Chapter 8 for more information.

11 Click the **Paragraph** palette tab.

12 Click an alignment option for your label.

13 Save your button.

Note: See "Save a GIF Image for the Web" or "Save a JPEG Image for the Web" to save the button.

■ Your button is ready to place on the Web.

SLICE ARTWORK

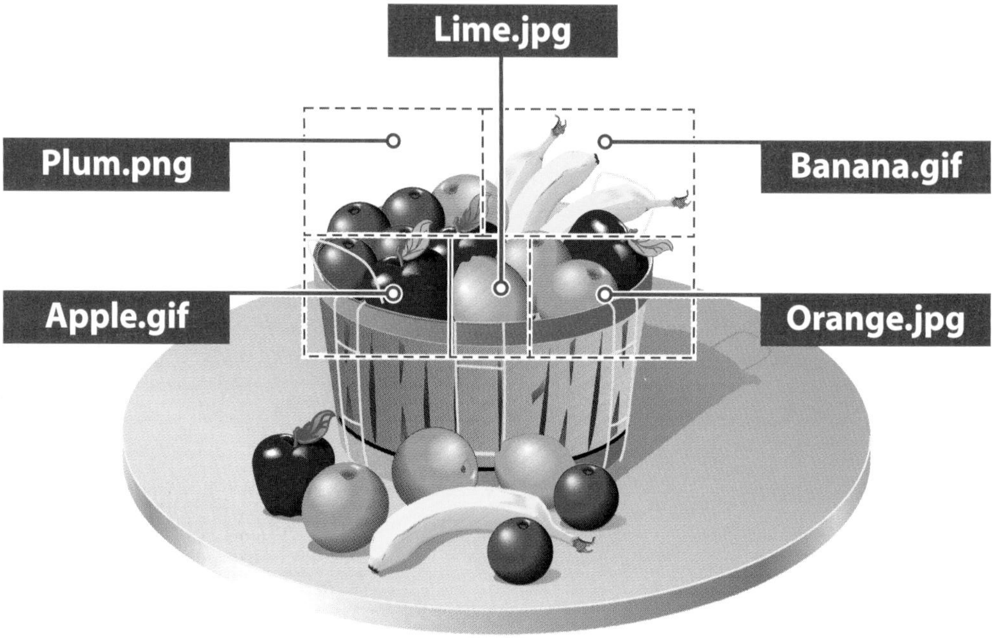
Lime.jpg
Plum.png
Banana.gif
Apple.gif
Orange.jpg

You can divide your artwork into different slices, which you can later save as separate image files. Slices can help you create complex Web content that downloads fast.

To use sliced artwork on the Web, you need to export the different slices as separate image files. See the section "Export Sliced Artwork" for more information.

SLICE ARTWORK

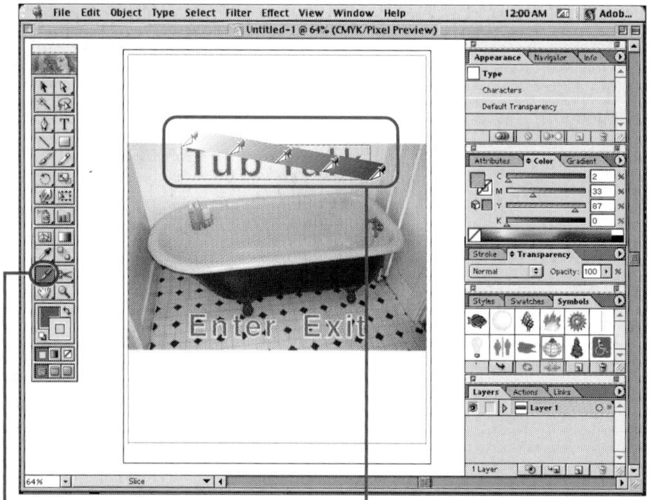
File Edit Object Type Select Filter Effect View Window Help
Untitled-1 @ 64% (CMYK/Pixel Preview)
Tub Talk
Enter Exit

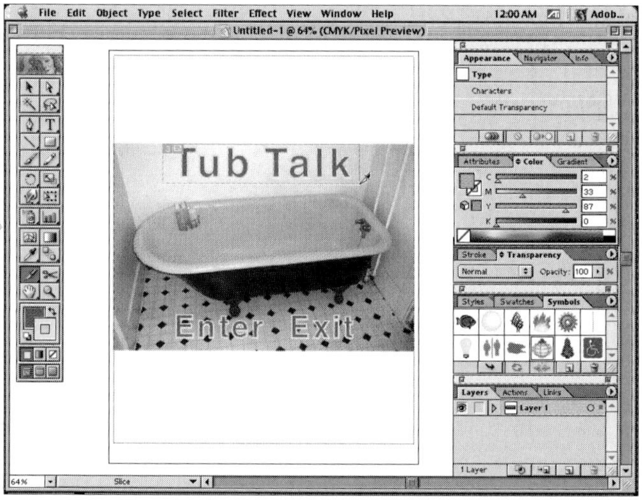
File Edit Object Type Select Filter Effect View Window Help
Untitled-1 @ 64% (CMYK/Pixel Preview)
Tub Talk
Enter Exit

CREATE A SLICE

1 Click the Slice Tool ( ).

2 Click and drag to define a slice.

■ Illustrator generates a rectangular slice over your artwork and automatically generates other slices to define the rest of your art.

■ You can click and drag to define another slice.

What optional settings can I define for my slices?

The Slice Options dialog box allows you to assign a link URL to a slice, specify that a slice not be an image, and other options. Open it by selecting a slice and clicking **Object**, **Slice**, then **Slice Options**.

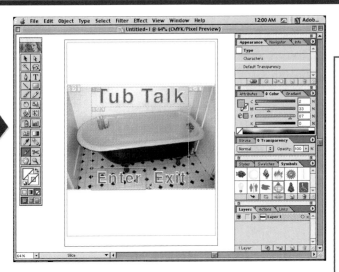

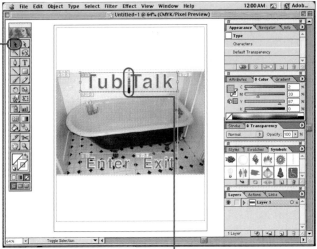

■ Another slice is defined.

■ The other slices change shape to accommodate the new slice.

■ You can hide the slices by clicking **View** and then **Hide Slices**.

Note: To export your sliced artwork as Web images, see the section "Export Sliced Artwork."

EDIT SLICES

1 Click ▶.

2 Click the edge of a slice to select it.

3 Click and drag a handle to change the size of a slice.

■ The slice changes size.

■ You can press `Delete` to delete a selected slice.

EXPORT SLICED ARTWORK

You can optimize each of the slices in your artwork independently of one another, and then save the slices as separate image files. Illustrator also creates an HTML file that allows you to publish your art as a Web page.

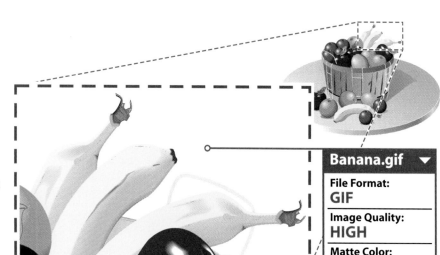

Banana.gif ▼

File Format:
GIF

Image Quality:
HIGH

Matte Color:
WHITE

You can publish your artwork on the Web using a Web editing program such as Adobe Go Live, Macromedia Dreamweaver or Microsoft FrontPage.

EXPORT SLICED ARTWORK

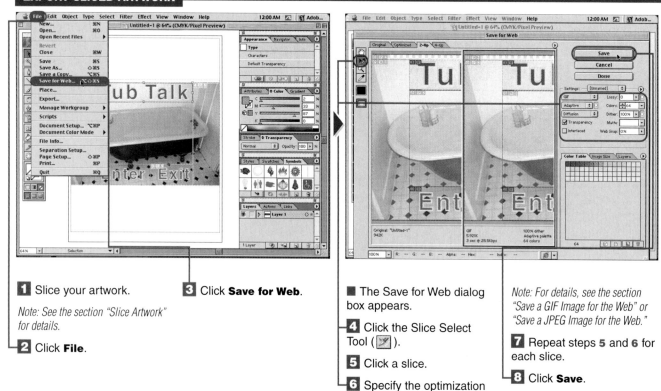

1 Slice your artwork.

Note: See the section "Slice Artwork" for details.

2 Click **File**.

3 Click **Save for Web**.

■ The Save for Web dialog box appears.

4 Click the Slice Select Tool (⬚).

5 Click a slice.

6 Specify the optimization settings for the slice.

Note: For details, see the section "Save a GIF Image for the Web" or "Save a JPEG Image for the Web."

7 Repeat steps **5** and **6** for each slice.

8 Click **Save**.

What if I want to export my sliced artwork as a Web page, but also want the option of editing the artwork later?

You can save your sliced artwork as an Illustrator file. The saved file contains your artwork with all the current slice information included. You can edit this file later, and use the edited version to create revised versions of your Web page.

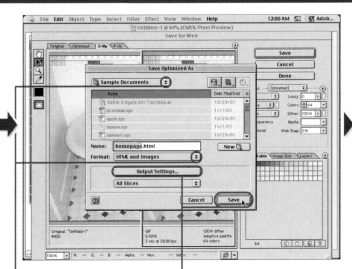

■ The Save Optimized As dialog box appears.

9 Click ⬍ or ▼ and click a folder in which to save your files.

10 Click ⬍ or ▼ and select how you want to save your slices.

■ You can save your slices as images and an HTML file to generate a Web page.

■ You can click **Output Settings** to specify how Illustrator names files and writes the HTML.

11 Click **Save**.

■ Illustrator saves the sliced artwork.

■ Saving your slices as images and HTML gives you a Web page that you can publish.

EXPORT A FLASH ANIMATION

You can export a multi-layered Illustrator document as a Flash animation. Each layer in the document turns into a frame in the animation.

EXPORT A FLASH ANIMATION

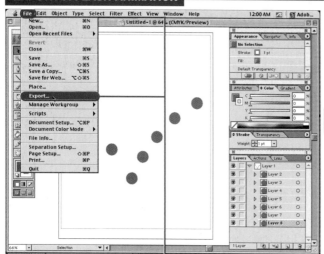

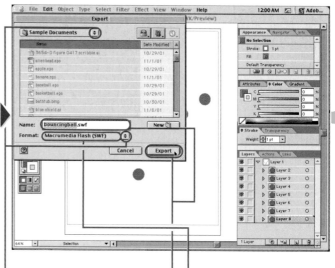

1 Create a multilayered Illustrator document.

■ Each layer should include art for one frame in your animation.

Note: See Chapter 11 for details about creating layers.

2 Click **File**.

3 Click **Export**.

■ The Export dialog box appears.

4 Click ▲ or ▼ and click a folder in which to save your animation.

5 Click ▲ or ▼ .

6 Click the **Macromedia Flash** file type.

7 Type a name for your animation ending with the extension ".swf".

8 Click **Export** or **Save**.

What are the advantages of using Flash for animations?

Flash animations are vector-based, which makes them particularly suited for Illustrator-based animations. Many Web browsers also come with Flash capability built-in, which means many Web users can view Flash animations.

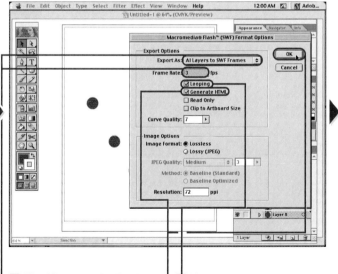

■ The Macromedia Flash (SWF) Format Options dialog box appears.

9 Click ⬦ or ⬇ and click AI Layers to SWF Frames.

10 Type a frame rate (animation speed).

■ You can click **Looping** to create an animation that repeats (☐ changes to ☑).

11 Click **Generate HTML** to create a Web page that displays the animation.

12 Click **OK**.

■ Illustrator saves the artwork as a Flash animation.

■ You can view the animation by opening the SWF file in any Flash-capable Web browser.

SHORTCUT KEY QUICK REFERENCE

You can use the following shortcuts to quickly perform specific tasks. These shortcuts enable you to exclusively use the keyword.

SHORTCUT KEY QUICK REFERENCE

Macintosh Shortcut Key	Windows Shortcut Key	Function
⌘ + 0 or double-click 🖐	Ctrl + 0 or double-click 🖐	Fit page in window
⌘ + 1 or double-click 🔍	Ctrl + 1 or double-click 🔍	View at 100%
⌘ + 2	Ctrl + 2	Lock selected artwork
⌘ + 3	Ctrl + 3	Hide selected artwork
⌘ + A	Ctrl + A	Select All
⌘ + C	Ctrl + C	Copy selected objects
⌘ + G	Ctrl + G	Group selected artwork
⌘ + J	Ctrl + J	Join points
⌘ + K	Ctrl + K	Open the Preferences dialog box
⌘ + M	Ctrl + M	Open the Paragraph palette
⌘ + O	Ctrl + O	Open a file
⌘ + R	Ctrl + R	Show rulers
⌘ + T	Ctrl + T	Open the Character palette
⌘ + U	Ctrl + U	Show/Hide Smart Guides
⌘ + V	Ctrl + V	Paste objects
⌘ + W	Ctrl + W	Close a file
⌘ + X	Ctrl + X	Cut an object
⌘ + Y	Ctrl + Y	Changes to Outline View
⌘ + Z	Ctrl + Z	Undo a command
⌘ + +	Ctrl + +	Zoom in
⌘ + -	Ctrl + -	Zoom out
⌘ + "	Ctrl + "	Show the grid
⌘ +]	Ctrl +]	Move an object forward
⌘ + [	Ctrl + [	Move an object backward
⌘ + Shift + O	Ctrl + Shift + O	Convert outlines
⌘ + Shift + Z	Ctrl + Shift + Z	Redo a command
⌘ + any tool (except Selection tools)	Ctrl + any tool (except Selection tools)	Activate Selection tool last used (Selection, Direct Selection, or Group Selection)
⌘ + Tab	Ctrl + Tab	Toggle between Selection and Direct Selection (or between Selection and Group Selection)
⌘ + drag with ✎	Ctrl + drag with ✎	Connect path to end of another path (both paths must be selected)

Macintosh Shortcut Key	Windows Shortcut Key	Function
option + ⌘ + 2	Alt + Ctrl + 2	Unlock all artwork
option + ⌘ + 3	Alt + Ctrl + 3	Show all hidden artwork
option + ⌘ + Y	Alt + Ctrl + Y	Changes to Pixel Preview
Shift + click with [eyedropper]	Shift + click with [eyedropper]	Sample specific color from gradient
option + drag with [pen] or [pencil]	Alt + drag with [pen] or [pencil]	Create closed path while drawing
option + [pencil] tool	Alt + [pencil]	Toggle between [pencil] and [smooth]
option + → or ←	Alt + → or ←	Increase or decrease Tracking/Kerning
option + ⌘ + Spacebar	Alt + Ctrl + Spacebar	Change any tool into [zoom]
Shift + X	Shift + X	Swap Stroke and Fill colors of an object
Shift + ⌘ + G	Shift + Ctrl + G	Ungroup selected artwork
Shift + option + click with [eyedropper]	Shift + Alt + click with [eyedropper]	Add appearance of other object to Appearance palette of currently selected artwork
Shift + F11	Shift + F11	Open the Symbols palette
Shift + click with any Selection tool	Shift + click with any Selection tool	Add to or subtract from selection
Shift + press any arrow key	Shift + press any arrow key	Move selection in 10-point increments
Shift + drag with any Selection tool	Shift + drag with any Selection tool	Constrain movement to 45-degree angles
Shift + ⌘ + A	Shift + Ctrl + A	Deselect All
Shift + ⌘ + J	Shift + Ctrl + J	Justify text
Shift + ⌘ + L, R, or C	Shift + Ctrl + L, R, or C	Align text to left, right, or center
Shift + ⌘ + Q	Shift + Ctrl + Q	Reset Tracking/Kerning to 0
Shift + ⌘ + X	Shift + Ctrl + X	Reset Horizontal Scaling to 100 percent
Shift + ⌘ + .	Shift + Ctrl + .	Increase font size
Shift + ⌘ + "	Shift + Ctrl + "	Decrease font size
Shift + option + ⌘ + 2	Shift + Alt + Ctrl + 2	Lock all unselected artwork
option + [paintbucket] or [eyedropper]	Alt + [paintbucket] or [eyedropper]	Toggle between the two tools
D	D	Set Stroke and Fill colors to black and white
Click + Spacebar + [pen]	Spacebar + [pen]	Move anchor point while drawing
Double-click word	Double-click word	Select entire word
Triple-click a word in the paragraph	Triple-click a word in the paragraph	Select entire paragraph
Spacebar (when not editing text)	Spacebar (when not editing text)	Change any tool into the Hand tool
Any arrow key	Any arrow key	Move selection in one-point increments

INDEX

Numbers and Symbols

45° angles, 49

A

actions, undo levels, 25
Add Anchor Point tool, 74, 79, 84
Add Anchor Points command, 74
Add Arrowheads effect, 205
Adobe Illustrator Startup_CMYK.ai file, 25
Adobe Illustrator Startup_RGB.ai file, 25
Adobe Online, 19
Adobe Online command, 19
Adobe PageMaker, 7
.AI file extension, 14
AI (Adobe Illustrator) format, 14–15
align
    objects, 116
    paragraphs, 186–187
Align command, 116
Align palette, 116–117
anchor points, 46
    average, 86–87
    control handles, 47
    convert type, 76–81
    delete, 61
    excess, 82–83
    location of tools, 79
    number added by Anchor Point tool, 75
    remove, 75
    remove stray, 84–85
    reshape curves, 59
    types, 77
animation, 257, 306–307
anti-alias, 269
appearance attributes, 212–213
Appearance palette, 8, 201
    Delete Selected Item button, 207
    edit styles, 213
    Redefine Style, 213
    Reduce to Basic Appearance, 207
    view appearance attributes, 212–213
Appearance palette tab, 212
Arc Segment Tool Options dialog box, 53
Arc tool, 52–53
arcs, 52–53
area graphs, 225
area type, 181
Area Type tool, 181
Arrange command, 118, 193, 195
arrowheads, 205
art brushes, 164–165
artwork
    dimensions, 23
    edit symbols, 142
    export sliced, 304–305
    flatten, 255
    halftone, 274
    insert symbols, 140
    Paint as a pointillist, 210–211
    Print with a Macintosh, 288–289
    Print with a PC, 286–287
    scatter copies of, 162–163
    slice, 293, 302–303
    vector-based, 262
Auto Trace tool, 83, 263, 266, 267
Average command, 86, 87
    ⌘ + option + J keyboard shortcut, 86
    Ctrl + Alt + J keyboard shortcut, 86
Average dialog box, 86–87

B

Bar Graph tool, 227
bar graphs, 224–225, 227
Bézier curves, 46, 56–57
bitmap images, 6
    convert to, 263
    dim, 251, 252
    Illustrator, 263
    scale, 262
black-and-white laser printers, 274
black-and-white printing, 274
blend
    color, 149
    layers, 175
Blend command, 219
Blend Options dialog box, 218
Blend tool, 218
blends, 218–219
Bloat effect, 135
Blocks command, 193
blurred offset shadow, 205
bounding box, 36, 37, 39, 113
brightness, 149
Bring Forward command, 118
    ⌘ +] keyboard shortcut, 118
    Ctrl +] keyboard shortcut, 118
Bring to Front command, 118
    ⌘ + Shift +] keyboard shortcut, 118
    Ctrl + Shift +] keyboard shortcut, 118
Brush Libraries command, 165
brushes
    predefined, 165
    styles, 158
Brushes palette, 149, 163
Brushes palette tab, 158–160, 162, 164
bulge image out from points, 135
buttons on Web pages, 300–301

C

Calligraphic Brush Options dialog box, 160
calligraphic brushes
    angle of, 160
    brush style, 158–159
    customize, 160–161
    diameter, 160
    even-width lines, 158
    random, 161
    roundness, 160
    variable-width lines, 159
center-align text, 186
Change Case command, 188
Change Case dialog box, 188
Character command, 184
Character palette, 184
    ⌘ + T keyboard shortcut, 184, 301
    Ctrl + T keyboard shortcut, 184, 301
Character palette tab, 301
Check Spelling command, 190
Check Spelling dialog box, 190
circles, 100–101
Clean Up command, 85
Clean Up dialog box, 85
Clean Up tool, 85
clip mask, 258–259
clockwise spirals, 105
Close command, 17
close documents, 17
Close File
    ⌘ + W keyboard shortcut, 17
    Ctrl + W keyboard shortcut, 17

closed paths, 46
  curves, 62
  open, 64–65
  straight lines, 62
CMYK color mode, 25, 285
  custom, 150–151
  save, 151
CMYK color separations, 275
CMYK color space, 148
CMYK colors, print, 150
CMYK inks, 274
color modes, change, 285
Color palette, 8, 149, 159, 279
  custom RGB color, 152
  edit color, 155
  Fill box, 153
  Swatches palette tab, 153
  Web-safe colors, 152
Color palette tab, 158, 220, 234
  custom CMYK color, 150–151
  RGB, 152
  Spectrum, 150
  Web Safe RGB, 152, 294
Color Picker dialog box, 153
color separations, 275
color spaces
  CMYK, 148
  RGB, 149
color swatches
  display, 156
  name, 151
  remove, 156
  save, 151
colors
  apply, 149, 173
  blend, 149
  brightness, 149
  color spaces, 148
  custom, 148, 153
  edit, 155
  eminate inward or outward, 205
  fills, 149, 154
  gradients, 149
  graphs, 234–235
  hue, 149
  images, 6
  manage, 151
  mesh, 220
  multicolor patterns, 149
  opacity, 149
  predefined, 155
  print, 274
  process, 276–277
  remove, 154
  saturation, 155
  save, 172
  separate, 274
  spot, 275, 278–279
  strokes, 149
  trap, 275, 280–281
  Web-safe, 293, 294
Colors command, 155
Column Graph tool, 226
column graphs, 224, 226–227
combination corner points, 47, 77
  convert smooth point to, 76
commands
  keyboard activation, 9
  undo and redo, 42–43

complex mesh, 221
composite images, 5
Compound Path command, 94
compound paths, 46, 94–95
constrained spirals, 105
continuous straight lines, 55
control handles, 47, 58
convert
  anchor point type, 76–81
  type to outlines, 196–197
Convert Anchor Point tool, 77–80
Convert to Outlines
  ⌘ + Shift + O keyboard shortcut, 196
  Ctrl + Shift + O keyboard shortcut, 196
copy
  attributes between objects, 173
  image from Illustrator, 271
  image from Photoshop, 270–271
  text, 192
copy and paste
  from menus, 40
  with mouse, 41
  objects, 40–41
Copy command, 40, 192, 248, 270
  ⌘ + C keyboard shortcut, 40, 248, 270
  Ctrl + C keyboard shortcut, 40, 248, 270
corner points, 47
counterclockwise spirals, 105
Create Gradient Mesh command, 221
Create Outlines command, 196, 197
crop marks, 284
Crop Marks command, 284
crosshatch, 208–209
Crystallize effect, 135
cumulative sequence of layers, 257
curly quotes (' or "), 189
curved corner points, 47
  convert smooth point to, 77
  convert straight corner point to, 81
  convert to smooth point, 79
  convert to straight corner point, 80
curves, 52–53, 56–57
  closed path, 62
  reshape, 58–59
  undo reshape, 59
custom CMYK color, 150–151
custom color, 148, 153
custom RGB color, 152–153
customize
  art brushes, 165
  calligraphic brush, 160–161
  Illustrator, 24–25
  patterns, 171
  scatter brush, 163
  strokes, 157
  transitions between gradients, 169
Cut command, 248
  ⌘ + X keyboard shortcut, 248
  ⌘ + X keyboard shortcut, 248
cut objects, 122–123

D

darkening effect, 175
Data command, 232
data dialog box, 226–227
Define Pattern command, 171

delete
  anchor points, 61
  appearance attributes, 213
  effects, 207
  layers, 242
  part of path, 67
  paths, 66
  styles, 215
  symbols, 141
Delete Anchor Point, 79
Deselect command, 156
deselect objects, 37
Direct Selection tool, 38–39, 58–59, 66–67, 74–75, 193, 234
distort
  image around points, 135
  objects, 130–131
  outlines, 202–203
Distort & Transform command, 202
distortion effects, 126
distribute objects, 116
dock palettes, 31
Document Color Mode command, 210, 285
Document Settings
  ⌘ + Alt + P keyboard shortcut, 22
  option + ⌘ + P keyboard shortcut, 22
Document Setup command, 22
Document Setup dialog box, 22–23
document window, 8, 29
documentation, 18–19
documents
  change settings, 22–23
  close, 17
  measurement units, 23
  name, 13, 14
  new, 12–13, 23
  open, 16
  save, 14–15
  start Illustrator with, 11
downloadable fonts, 185
draw images, 4
Drop Shadow effect, 205, 300
drop shadows, 235
dye-sublimation printers, 274

E

edit
  color, 155
  draw, 4
  effects, 206–207
  graph data, 232
  layer properties, 250–251
  predefined gradients, 169
  process color, 276–277
  slices, 303
  styles, 213
  symbols, 142
effects, 126
  apply, 200
  delete, 207
  edit, 206–207
  filters as, 201
  images, 263
  symbols, 144–145
Ellipse tool, 100
ellipses, 100–101
em dash (—), 189
empty text paths, 85
Envelope Distort command, 132
Envelope Distort tool, 132–133
envelopes, 132–133
.EPS extension, 15

EPS (Encapsulated PostScript) format, 14–15
Erase Tool, 68–69
erase parts of paths, 68–69
evenly distribute objects, 117
even-width lines, 158
exact line segments, 49
Excel, import data from, 237
Export command, 306
Export dialog box, 306
export sliced artwork, 304–305
extend open path, 74
Eyedropper tool, 172

F

Feather command, 204
Feather effect, 204–205
fidelity, 51
figure eight, 57
files, save in different formats, 15
Fill style, 214
fills
  color, 149, 154
  gradients, 166
  patterns, 170–171
  predefined colors, 155
  remove color, 154
filters, 7, 200
  as effect, 201
  images, 263
  vector-based, 208
Fireworks, 257
first-line indents, 187
Flag command, 128
Flag effect, 129
Flare tool, 136–137
Flare Tool Options dialog box, 137
flares, 136–137
Flash animation, 257, 306–307
Flash multimedia, 293
flatten artwork, 255
font libraries, 185
fonts, 178
  change, 184–185
  downloadable, 185
  find, 185
  PostScript, 179
  raster, 179
  resize, 184–185
  TrueType, 179
  vector, 179
force perspective, 114
Free Transform tool, 130
freehand lines, 50–51

G

general preferences, 24
General units, 25
GIF animation, 257
GIF (Graphics Interchange Format) file, 296–297
GIF file format, 301
GIF images, 292
GoLive, 7
Gradient palette, 166, 168, 169
Gradient palette tab, 166, 168
Gradient tool, 166
gradients
  customize transitions between, 169
  linear, 166
  multicolor, 168–169

predefined, 167
radial, 166
start and end color, 167
two-color, 166–167
Graph command, 229, 231–233, 235
Graph Type dialog box, 231, 233, 235
graphs
area, 225
bar, 224, 225, 227
change type, 233
color, 234–235
column, 224, 226–227
data, 225
data dialog box, 226–227, 232
drop shadow, 235
edit data, 232
import data, 225, 236–237
line, 224, 228–229
modify, 229
pie, 225, 230–231
scatter, 225
spreadsheet data, 237
stacked column, 225
Grid
⌘ + " keyboard shortcut, 29
⌘ + " keyboard shortcut, 29
grids, 106–107
change measurements, 29
settings, 107
Group command, 120, 282
⌘ + G keyboard shortcut, 120
⌘ + G keyboard shortcut, 120
group objects
from different layers, 120
knockouts, 282
Group Selection tool, 87, 94, 234
grouped objects, rotate, 110
Guides & Grid command, 29

H

halftone, 274
hanging indents, 187
Hatch Effects command, 208
Hatch Effects dialog box, 208–209
Hatch Effects filter, 208–209
help
Search link, 18
topics, 19
Help (F1) keyboard shortcut, 18
Hide Grid command, 29
hide layers, 243
Hide Rulers command, 28
Hide Slices command, 303
horizontal shear, 114
hue, 149

I

Illustrator
bitmap immages, 263
copy image from, 271
customize, 24–25
restore defaults, 25
start, 10–11
Illustrator 10 Bible, 95, 200
Illustrator files, save, 14
Illustrator Help command, 18
ImageReady, 257
images, 4
anti-alias, 269
bitmap, 262

change color modes, 285
color, 6
composite, 5
copy from Illustrator, 270
copy from Photoshop, 270–271
crop marks, 284
dim, 251–252
distort, 126
draw, 4
effects, 263
filters, 263
GIF, 292
halftone, 274
import, 264
JPEG, 292
knockouts, 282–283
magnify, 34–35
organize, 5
place, 264
printing-press-friendly, 7
rasterize, 268–269
share with other applications, 7
trace, 266–267
transform, 265
undo transformation, 265
use of, 5
vector-based, 262
warp, 132–133
Web-friendly, 7
zoom, 34–35
import
Excel data, 237
graph data, 225, 236–237
images, 264
Lotus 1-2-3 data, 237
Import Graph Data dialog box, 236
indent paragraphs, 187
inkjet printers, 274
Inner Glow effect, 205
intersecting paths, 92
invisible paths, 47

J

jagged outline, 202–203
Join command, 88, 89
⌘ + J keyboard shortcut, 88
⌘ + J keyboard shortcut, 88
Join dialog box, 89
joining points, 88–89
JPEG (Joint Photographic Experts Group) file format, 298–299, 301
JPEG images, 292

K

keyboard, navigate with, 9
Keyboard command, 30
keyboard shortcuts, 9
list, 30
Macintosh, 308–309
palettes, 30
PC, 308–309
polar grid appearance, 109
quick reference, 308–309
Knife tool, 65, 122, 123
knockouts, 282–283

L

laser printers, 274
Layer Options dialog box, 250–251

INDEX

layers, 5
    add artwork to, 241
    blend, 175
    change to sublayer, 247
    clip mask, 258–259
    creation of, 241
    cumulative sequence of, 257
    delete, 242
    edit properties, 250–251
    group objects from different, 120
    hide, 243
    independence of, 240, 241
    lock, 244
    merge, 254–255
    move objects between, 248–249
    overlap order, 118–119
    rearrange, 245
    release objects to, 256–257
    rename, 250
    revert from templates, 253
    sublayers, 246–250
    as templates, 240, 252–253
    undo deletion, 242
    unlock, 244
Layers Options dialog box, 287
Layers palette, 8, 240
    Delete, 242
    Flatten Artwork, 255
    Make Clipping Mask, 258
    Merge Selected, 254
    move objects between layers, 249
    New Layer, 241
    New Sublayer, 246
    Release Clipping Mask, 259
    Release to Layers (Sequence), 256
    Template, 252–253
    template icon, 252
    Unlock All, 244
Layers palette tab, 250, 252
    Create New Layer button, 241
    Create New Sublayer button, 246
    Delete Selection button, 242
    Edit column, 244
    Release to Layers (Build), 257
    Visibility icon, 243
left-align text, 187
Legends in Wedges command, 231
lightening effect, 175
Line Graph tool, 228
line graphs, 224, 228–229
Line Segment tool, 49, 104
line segments, 48
Line tool, 48–49
linear gradients, 166
lines
    even-width, 158
    not filling in curves of, 159
    reshape, 60–61
    smooth, 70–71
    variable-width, 159
link
    two end points with line segment, 89
    type blocks, 192–193
Link command, 193
Liquify tool, 134–135
liquify objects, 134–135
LiveMotion, 7
localized warping, 135
lock layers, 244

Lotus 1-2-3, import data from, 237
lowercase text, 188

M

Macintosh
    close palettes, 9
    keyboard shortcuts, 308–309
    print artwork, 288–289
    start Illustrator, 10
Macromedia Flash (SWF) Format Options dialog box, 307
magnify images, 34–35
main toolbox, 8
Make command, 94, 195, 284
Make With Warp command, 132
marquee box, 36, 37
measurement units, 23
menu bar, 8
menus
    copy and paste objects, 40
    keyboard activation, 9
    mouse activation, 9
merge layers, 254–255
mesh
    add or delete points, 221
    color, 220
    complex, 221
mesh object, 220
Mesh tool, 220–221
mixed-case text, 188
mouse
    copy and paste objects, 41
    navigate with, 9
    tool or menu activation, 9
move
    object backward, 119
    objects between layers, 248–249
    objects forward, 118
    symbols, 145
    tabs between palettes, 32
Move Backward
    ⌘ + [keyboard shortcut, 119
    Ctrl + [keyboard shortcut, 119
Move Objects Back command, 193, 195
Move Objects Forward command, 193, 195
Move to Back
    ⌘ + Shift + [keyboard shortcut, 119
    Ctrl + Shift + [keyboard shortcut, 119
multicolor
    gradients, 168–169
    patterns, 149

N

navigate
    with keyboard, 9
    with mouse, 9
    palettes, 9
    work area, 8–9
New command, 12
New Document
    ⌘ + N keyboard shortcut, 13
    Ctrl + N keyboard shortcut, 13
New Document dialog box, 12–13, 23
New Swatch dialog box, 171
New Symbol command, 138
non-uniform scaling, 112

O

Object command, 84
object effects, 126

objects
    align, 116
    blend, 175
    blurred offset shadow, 205
    bounding box, 36–37
    bulge out from point, 135
    change overlap order, 118–119
    color eminating inward or outward, 205
    color fills, 154
    copy and paste, 40–41
    copy attributes between, 173
    cut, 122–123
    deselect, 37
    distort, 130–131
    distort around point, 135
    distribute, 116
    evenly distribute, 117
    in front of text, 195
    group, 120
    jagged outline, 202–203
    keep from printing, 287
    liquify, 134–135
    move backward, 119
    move between layers, 248–249
    move forward, 118
    move with arrow keys, 24
    opacity, 174
    outline, 156–157
    rasterize, 210, 268–269
    reflect, 111, 130–131
    reorder, 193
    resize, 112–113
    reusable, 126
    reuse, 138–139
    revert to generic state, 207
    RGB color, 210
    rotate, 110, 130–131
    scale, 112–113, 130–131
    scalloped edges around, 135
    select in template layers, 253
    select part of, 38–39
    shard-like, 135
    shear, 114–115, 130–131
    soften edges, 204–205
    spin around point, 135
    stroke, 156–157
    three-dimensional, 220–221
    ungroup, 120
    view appearance attributes, 212–213
    warp, 128–129, 132–133
    wrap type around, 194–195
    wrinkles, 135
offset printing, 274
opacity, 174
open
    closed path, 64–65
    documents, 16
Open command, 16
Open dialog box, 16
Open File
    ⌘ + O keyboard shortcut, 16
    Ctrl + O keyboard shortcut, 16
open paths, 46
    close, 62–63
Open Recent Files command, 16
Options dialog box, 49
organize images, 5
Outer Glow effect, 205
Outline command, 26
Outline Mode and paths, 27, 47
outline objects, 156–157

Outline view, 26–27
outlines
    convert type to, 196–197
    distort, 202–203
    spell-check and, 191
overlap order, 118–119
overlapping paths or shapes, 90–91

P

Page Setup command, 288
Page Setup dialog box, 288
pages, 8
    display options, 23
    orientation, 23
    resize, 22
paint
    art brush, 164–165
    calligraphic brush, 158–161
    Scatter brush, 162–163
Paint Bucket tool, 173
Paintbrush tool, 158
paintbrushes, 149
palette options menu, 33
palettes
    active tab, 33
    change options, 32–33
    dock, 31
    double arrowhead not on tab, 33
    keyboard shortcuts, 30
    move tabs between, 32
    navigate, 9
    Option button, 33
    view, 30
PANTONE swatch library, 278
Paragraph command, 186
Paragraph palette, 186–187
    ⌘ + M keyboard shortcut, 186
    Ctrl + M keyboard shortcut, 186
Paragraph palette tab, 301
paragraphs
    align, 186–187
    indent, 187
Paste command, 40, 192, 249, 271
    ⌘ + V keyboard shortcut, 40, 249
    Ctrl + V keyboard shortcut, 40, 249
paste text, 192
pasteboard, 8
Path command, 74, 82, 85, 88–89
Pathfinder command, 90, 280
Pathfinder palette
    Add to Shape Area button, 90
    Exclude Shape Areas button, 93
    Intersect Shape Areas button, 92
    Shift + F9 keyboard shortcut, 90
    Subtract from Shape Area button, 91
    Trap, 280
Pathfinder Trap dialog box, 281
paths
    add, 67
    add segments, 67
    anchor points, 46, 47, 74
    area of two overlapping paths, 90–91
    average anchor points, 86–87
    Bézier curves, 46
    clean up stray anchor points, 84–85
    closed, 46
    compound, 46, 94–95
    convert anchor point type, 76–81
    delete, 66
    delete part of, 67

INDEX

paths (continued)
 erase parts of, 68–69
 fidelity, 51
 intersect, 92
 invisible, 47
 join points, 88–89
 open, 46
 Outline Mode, 27, 47
 Preview mode, 47
 remove anchor points, 75
 remove excess anchor points, 82–83
 remove intersecting areas, 93
 remove non-intersecting, 92
 remove non-overlapping area, 91
 return to original shape, 61
 rotate, 110
 segment, 64–65
 segments, 46
 select part of, 38–39
 smooth, 70–71
 smoothness, 51
 text above, 182
 text below, 183
 type along, 182–183
 type outlines, 179
 types, 46
 visible, 47
patterns
 apply, 170
 customize, 171
 multicolor, 149
 name, 171
 remove, 170
 as stroke, 171
.PDF extension, 15
PDF (Portable Document Format) format, 14–15
Pen & Ink command, 208, 209
Pen tool, 54–57, 61–62, 74, 79, 262
 erase paths drawn by, 69
 switch modes, 81
Pencil tool, 50–51, 83
perspective, force, 114
Photo Crosshatch command, 209
Photo Crosshatch filter, 209
photographs
 hatch effect, 209
 sharpen blurry, 211
photonegative effect, 175
Photoshop, 7, 270–271
Photoshop (PSD) files, 257
Pie Graph tool, 230
pie graphs, 225, 230–231
Pixel Preview, 26–27
 ⌘ + option + Y keyboard shortcut, 27
 Ctrl + Alt + Y keyboard shortcut, 27
Pixel Preview command, 295
Pixel Preview Mode, 295
Pixelate command, 211
pixels, 262
Place command, 264
Place dialog box, 264
place images, 264
Plug-ins folder, 201
PNG file-format, 297
point type, 180
Pointillize command, 211
Pointillize dialog box, 211
Pointillize filter, 210–211
points
 bulge image out from, 135
 distort image around, 135

 join, 88–89
 rotate objects around, 110
 spin object around, 135
Polar Grid Properties dialog box, 109
Polar Grid tool, 108–109
Polar Grid Tool Options dialog box, 108
polar grids, 108–109
Polygon dialog box, 102
Polygon tool, 102
PostScript fonts, 179
PostScript printer description file, 289
PostScript-capable printer, 275
precise cursors, 24
predefined
 brushes, 165
 colors, 155
 gradients, 167, 169
 styles, 215
preferences, 24–25
Preferences command, 24, 29, 71, 266
 ⌘ + K keyboard shortcut, 24
 Ctrl + K keyboard shortcut, 24
Preferences dialog box, 24, 29, 71, 266
Preview Mode, 26–27, 47
print
 artwork in Windows, 286–287
 black-and-white, 274
 CMYK colors, 150
 color, 274
 keep objects from, 287
 process colors, 274
 stray anchor points, 84
Print command, 287, 289
Print dialog box, 287, 289
Print Setup command, 286
Print Setup dialog box, 286–287
printers
 dye-sublimation, 274
 inkjet, 274
 PostScript-capable, 275
printing-press-friendly images, 7
process color
 apply, 276–277
 convert spot color to, 279
 convert to spot color, 277
 edit, 276–277
Process Color icon, 276
process colors, 274, 276–277
Pucker effect, 135

R

radial gradients, 166
raster fonts, 179
rasterization, 263
Rasterize command, 210, 268–269
Rasterize dialog box, 268
Rasterize effect, 269
rasterize images, 268–269
rearrange layers, 245
Rectangle tool, 98, 99, 136, 284
rectangles, 98–99
Rectangular Grid tool, 106
Rectangular Grid Tool Options dialog box, 106
rectangular grids, 106–107
Redo command, 43
 ⌘ + Shift + Z keyboard shortcut, 43
 Ctrl + Shift + Z keyboard shortcut, 43
redo commands, 42–43
Reflect command, 111
reflect objects, 111, 130–131

Reflect properties dialog box, 111
Refresh, 19
regular cursors, 24
regular polygons, 102
Release command, 219, 284
release objects to layers, 256–257
Remove Anchor Point tool, 75
rename layers, 250
reorder objects, 193
reshape
    curves, 58–59
    lines, 60–61
Reshape tool, 60–61
resize
    ellipses, 101
    fonts, 184–185
    objects, 112–113
    pages, 22
    rectangles, 98
    rounded rectangles, 99
    symbols, 145
reusable objects, 126
reuse objects, 138–139
Reverse Front to Back command, 219
Reverse Spline command, 219
RGB color, 210
    custom, 152
    name, 153
    save, 153
RGB Color command, 210
RGB color mode, 285
RGB color scheme, 25
RGB color spaces, 149
right-align text, 187
rotate
    flares, 137
    grouped objects, 110
    objects, 110, 130–131
    paths, 110
    spirals, 105
    symbols, 145
Rotate tool, 110
Roughen command, 202
Roughen effect, 202, 203
Rounded Corners effect, 300
Rounded Rectangle tool, 99
rounded rectangles, 98–99
rounded squares, 99
Rulers
    ⌘ + R keyboard shortcut, 28
    Ctrl + R keyboard shortcut, 28
rules, 28

S

Saturate command, 155
Saturate dialog box, 155
Saturate filter, 155
saturation, 155
save
    CMYK color, 151
    color swatches, 151
    colors, 172
    custom CMYK color, 151
    custom RGB color, 153
    documents, 14–15
    files in different formats, 15
    Illustrator files, 14
    RGB color, 153
Save As command, 14
Save for Web command, 296, 298, 304

Save for Web dialog box, 296–299, 304
Save for Web file-type dialog box, 297
Save Optimized As dialog box, 299, 305
scale
    bitmap images, 262
    bounding box, 113
    by dragging, 113
    non-uniform, 112
    with object properties, 112
    objects, 112–113, 130–131
Scale command, 112
Scale properties dialog box, 112
Scale tool, 60, 113, 115
Scallop effect, 135
scalloped edges around objects, 135
scatter brush, 162–163
scatter copies of artwork, 162–163
scatter graphs, 225
Scissors tool, 64–65, 122
screen elements, 8
Scribble & Tweak command, 203
Scribble & Tweak dialog box, 203
Search link, 18
search page, 19
segment paths, 64–65
segments, 46, 67
select
    by clicking object, 36, 38
    by dragging around object, 39
    by dragging object, 37
    parts of object or path, 38–39
    stray anchor points, 84
Selection tool, 36–37, 66–67, 74–75, 87, 111, 154, 193, 229, 265
Send Backward command, 119
separate colors, 274
Separation Setup dialog box, 289
Setup command, 23
shapes
    area type, 181
    overlapping, 90–91
shard-like objects, 135
sharpen blurry photographs, 211
Sharpen command, 211
Shear command, 114
shear objects, 114–115, 130–131
Shear properties dialog box, 114
Shear tool, 115
Show Grid command, 29
Show Pattern Swatches button, 170
Show Rulers command, 28
Simplify command, 82
Simplify dialog box, 82–83
"slalom" curves, 57
slice artwork, 293, 302–303
Slice Select Tool, 304
Slice Tool, 302
Smart Punctuation, 189
Smart Punctuation command, 189
Smart Punctuation dialog box, 189
smooth corner points, 47
smooth paths, 70–71
smooth points, 77
    convert curved corner point to, 79
    convert straight corner point to, 78
    convert to combination corner point, 76
    convert to curved corner point, 77
Smooth tool, 70–71
smoothness, 51
soften edges, 204–205
special effects, 7
spell checker, 190

INDEX

spell-check text, 190–191
spin object around points, 135
Spiral dialog box, 105
Spiral tool, 104–105
spirals, 104–105
spot color, 275
    choose from library, 278–279
    convert process color to, 277
    convert to process color, 279
    usage, 279
Spot Color icon, 277
squares, 98
stacked column graphs, 225
standard filter, 201
Star dialog box, 103
Star tool, 103
stars, 103
status bar, 8, 34–35
straight corner points, 47, 77
    convert curved corner point to, 80
    convert to curved corner point, 81
    convert to smooth point, 78
straight lines, 48–49, 54–55
    closed path, 62
    Knife tool, 123
straight quotes (' or "), 189
stray anchor points, 84–85
Stray Points command, 84
Streamline tool, 83
stroke, 156
    arrowheads, 205
    dashed, 157
    patterns as, 171
    thickness, 157
Stroke palette, 156
Stroke palette tab, 158–159
Stroke style, 215
Stroke units, 25
strokes
    color, 149
    customize, 157
Style Libraries command, 215
Style Options dialog box, 217
styles, 201
    apply, 214–215
    creation of, 216–217
    delete, 215
    drag and drop, 215
    edit, 213
    name, 217
    predefined, 215
    remove, 214
    shortcut for creation of, 217
Styles palette, 8, 201
    Default style, 214
    delete styles, 215
Styles palette tab, 214, 216
Stylize command, 204
sublayers, 246–250
    change layers to, 247
    clip mask, 259
    hidden or locked, 247
Swatch Libraries command, 155, 278
Swatch Options dialog box, 151, 153, 277
swatch set, 155
Swatches palette, 149, 279
    custom CMYK color, 150–151
    manage colors, 151
    New Swatch, 151, 153
    predefined gradients, 167, 169

Swatches palette tab, 156, 170
    List View, 276
    New Swatch button, 151
    Show Color Swatches button, 154
Switch View
    ⌘ + Y keyboard shortcut, 26
    Ctrl + Y keyboard shortcut, 26
switch between views, 26–27
Symbol Options dialog box, 139
Symbol Screener effect, 145
Symbol Scruncher effect, 145
Symbol Shifter effect, 145
Symbol Sizer effect, 145
Symbol Sizer tool, 145
Symbol Spinner effect, 145
Symbol Sprayer effect, 144–145
Symbol Sprayer tool, 144
Symbol Stainer effect, 145
Symbol Styler effect, 145
symbols, 126
    break links, 141–142
    colorize, 145
    creation of, 138–139
    delete, 141
    edit, 142
    effects, 144–145
    insert into artwork, 140
    move, 145
    multiple instances, 145
    as painted effect, 145
    pull apart or together, 145
    resize, 145
    rotate, 145
    as stand-alone objects, 141
    transparency, 145
    update, 143
    when to use, 126
Symbols command, 138
Symbols palette, 138
    Break Link button, 142
    Delete Symbol button, 141
    delete symbols, 141
    insert symbol from, 140
    New Symbol button, 139
    Place Symbol Instance button, 140
    views, 139
Symbols Palette (Shift + F11) keyboard shortcut, 138

T

tearoff toolbar, 52
template layers, 253
templates
    layers as, 240, 252–253
    revert layers from, 253
text, 7, 178
    above path, 182
    align paragraphs, 186–187
    along path, 182–183
    area type, 181
    below path, 183
    center-align, 186
    copy, 192
    left-align, 187
    link text blocks, 192–193
    objects in front of, 195
    paste, 192
    point type, 180
    right-align, 187
    share with other applications, 7
    spell-check, 190–191

vertically aligned, 183
warp, 132–133
wrap type around object, 194–195
text areas, text flow through, 193
text boxes, 192
text flow through text areas, 193
three-dimensional objects, 220–221
tips and news about Illustrator, 19
title bar, 8
Toolbox
    Direct Selection tool, 38–39, 58–59
    Fill and Stroke boxes, 172
    Fill button, 234
    Line Segment tool, 48
    Pen tool, 54, 56
    Pencil tool, 50
    Selection tool, 36, 37
    Zoom tool, 34, 35
tools
    keyboard activation, 9
    keyboard shortcuts, 24
    mouse activation, 9
    name for, 24
trace images, 266–267
Transform command, 111–112, 265
transform images, 265
transparency, 145, 174
Transparency palette, 283
Transparency palette tab, 174–175, 283
trap, 275
    amount necessary, 281
    colors, 280–281
TrueType fonts, 179
Twirl effect, 135
Twirl tool, 135
two dashes (—), 189
two-color gradients, 166–167
type, 178
    area type, 181
    change case, 188
    convert to outlines, 196–197
    outlines, 179
    point type, 180
    vertical, 183
    wrap around object, 194–195
Type & Auto Tracing command, 71, 266
type blocks, link, 192–193
Type command, 184, 186, 229, 231, 233, 235
type effects, 179
Type Path tool, 182
Type Text Below
    Alt + Shift + Down button keyboard shortcut, 183
    option + Shift + Down button keyboard shortcut, 183
Type tool, 180, 301
Type units, 25

U

undo
    commands, 42–43
    curve reshaping, 59
    image transformation, 265
    layer deletion, 242
    levels, 25
Undo command, 42, 59, 265
    ⌘ + Z keyboard shortcut, 42, 59
    Ctrl + Z keyboard shortcut, 42, 59
Undo Deletion command, 242
Undo Move command, 59

Ungroup command, 120
    ⌘ + Shift + G keyboard shortcut, 120
    Ctrl + Shift + G keyboard shortcut, 120
ungroup objects, 120
Units & Undo command, 25
Units & Undo option dialog box, 25
unpainted objects, 85
Unsharp Mask command, 211
Unsharp Mask dialog box, 211
Unsharp Mask filter, 211
update symbols, 143
uppercase text, 188

V

variable-width lines, 159
vector fonts, 179, 197
vector graphics, 6
vector-based artwork, 262
vector-based filters, 208
vector-based images, 262–263
Vertical Path Type tool, 183
vertical sheer, 114
vertical type, 183
Vertical Type tool, 183
views, switch between, 26–27
visible paths, 47

W

warp
    alignment, 128
    bend, 128–129
    images, 132–133
    localized, 135
    objects, 128–129, 132–133
    text, 132–133
Warp command, 128–129
Warp effect, 129, 135
Warp Options dialog box, 128–129, 132
Warp tool, 134
Web
    export sliced artwork, 304–305
    GIF (Graphics Interchange Format) file, 296–297
    JPEG (Joint Photographic Experts Group) file format, 298–299
    Pixel Preview Mode, 295
    PNG file-format, 297
    slice artwork, 302–303
Web art, 292
Web images, 292
Web page buttons, 300–301
Web Safe RGB, 149
Web-friendly images, 7
Web-safe colors, 152, 293–294
Windows
    close palettes, 9
    print artwork, 286–287
    start Illustrator, 11
work area, navigate, 8–9
Wrap command, 195
Wrinkle effect, 135
wrinkles, 135

Z

Zig Zag effect, 203
Zoom tool, 34–35
zoom images, 34–35

Read Less – Learn More™

Visual

with these full-color Visual™ guides

The Fast and Easy Way to Learn

Discover how to use what you learn with "Teach Yourself" tips

Title	ISBN	Price
Teach Yourself Access 97 VISUALLY™	0-7645-6026-3	$29.99
Teach Yourself FrontPage® 2000 VISUALLY™	0-7645-3451-3	$29.99
Teach Yourself HTML VISUALLY™	0-7645-3423-8	$29.99
Teach Yourself the Internet and World Wide Web VISUALLY™, 2nd Ed.	0-7645-3410-6	$29.99
Teach Yourself Microsoft® Access 2000 VISUALLY™	0-7645-6059-X	$29.99
Teach Yourself Microsoft® Excel 97 VISUALLY™	0-7645-6063-8	$29.99
Teach Yourself Microsoft® Excel 2000 VISUALLY™	0-7645-6056-5	$29.99
Teach Yourself Microsoft® Office 2000 VISUALLY™	0-7645-6051-4	$29.99
Teach Yourself Microsoft® PowerPoint® 2000 VISUALLY™	0-7645-6060-3	$29.99
Teach Yourself More Windows® 98 VISUALLY™	0-7645-6044-1	$29.99
Teach Yourself Office 97 VISUALLY™	0-7645-6018-2	$29.99
Teach Yourself Red Hat® Linux® VISUALLY™	0-7645-3430-0	$29.99
Teach Yourself VISUALLY™ Computers, 3rd Ed.	0-7645-3525-0	$29.99
Teach Yourself VISUALLY™ Digital Photography	0-7645-3565-X	$29.99
Teach Yourself VISUALLY™ Dreamweaver® 3	0-7645-3470-X	$29.99
Teach Yourself VISUALLY™ Fireworks® 4	0-7645-3566-8	$29.99
Teach Yourself VISUALLY™ Flash™ 5	0-7645-3540-4	$29.99
Teach Yourself VISUALLY™ FrontPage® 2002	0-7645-3590-0	$29.99
Teach Yourself VISUALLY™ iMac™	0-7645-3453-X	$29.99
Teach Yourself VISUALLY™ Investing Online	0-7645-3459-9	$29.99
Teach Yourself VISUALLY™ Networking, 2nd Ed.	0-7645-3534-X	$29.99
Teach Yourself VISUALLY™ Photoshop® 6	0-7645-3513-7	$29.99
Teach Yourself VISUALLY™ Quicken® 2001	0-7645-3526-9	$29.99
Teach Yourself VISUALLY™ Windows® 2000 Server	0-7645-3428-9	$29.99
Teach Yourself VISUALLY™ Windows® Me Millennium Edition	0-7645-3495-5	$29.99
Teach Yourself Windows® 95 VISUALLY™	0-7645-6001-8	$29.99
Teach Yourself Windows® 98 VISUALLY™	0-7645-6025-5	$29.99
Teach Yourself Windows® 2000 Professional VISUALLY™	0-7645-6040-9	$29.99
Teach Yourself Windows NT® 4 VISUALLY™	0-7645-6061-1	$29.99
Teach Yourself Word 97 VISUALLY™	0-7645-6032-8	$29.99

TRADE & INDIVIDUAL ORDERS

Phone: **(800) 762-2974**
or **(317) 572-3993**
(8 a.m.–6 p.m., CST, weekdays)
FAX: **(800) 550-2747**
or **(317) 572-4002**

EDUCATIONAL ORDERS & DISCOUNTS

Phone: **(800) 434-2086**
(8:30 a.m.–5:00 p.m., CST, weekdays)
FAX: **(317) 572-4005**

CORPORATE ORDERS FOR VISUAL™ SERIES

Phone: **(800) 469-6616**
(8 a.m.–5 p.m., EST, weekdays)
FAX: **(905) 890-9434**

Qty	ISBN	Title	Price	Total

Shipping & Handling Charges

	Description	First book	Each add'l. book	Total
Domestic	Normal	$4.50	$1.50	$
	Two Day Air	$8.50	$2.50	$
	Overnight	$18.00	$3.00	$
International	Surface	$8.00	$8.00	$
	Airmail	$16.00	$16.00	$
	DHL Air	$17.00	$17.00	$

Subtotal _____

CA residents add
applicable sales tax _____

IN, MA and MD
residents add
5% sales tax _____

IL residents add
6.25% sales tax _____

RI residents add
7% sales tax _____

TX residents add
8.25% sales tax _____

Shipping _____

Total _____

Ship to:

Name_____

Address_____

Company_____

City/State/Zip_____

Daytime Phone_____

Payment: □ Check to Hungry Minds (US Funds Only)
□ Visa   □ Mastercard   □ American Express

Card # _____ Exp. _____ Signature_____

Hungry Minds™

*maran*Graphics®